THE GLAMOUR CHASE

THE GLAMOUR CHASE
THE MAVERICK LIFE OF
BILLY MACKENZIE

TOM DOYLE

BLOOMSBURY

FOR MARJORY DOYLE

First published in Great Britain 1998

This paperback edition published 1999

Bloomsbury Publishing Plc, 38 Soho Square, London WIV 5DF

PICTURE SOURCES
Peter Anderson courtesy of S.I.N: pages 9 *top*, 12 *top*
Peter Ashworth: page 15 *bottom*
Christine Beveridge: pages 6 *top*, 14
Allan Campbell: page 8 *centre*
Peter Corio courtesy of S.I.N: page 5 *bottom*
Mark Guthrie: page 16
London Features: pages 5 *top*, 7 *centre left & bottom*
The MacKenzie Family: pages 1,2 *top*, 3 *top*, 6 *bottom*, 8 *bottom*,
11, 12 *centre*, 13 *top*, 15 *top*
Felix von Muralt courtesy of Peter Zumsteg: page 12 *bottom*
Alan Rankine pages 3 *bottom*, 4, 7 *top & centre right*, 8 *top*
Steve Reid: page 9 *bottom*
Tom Sheehan: pages 10, 13 *bottom*
D.C. Thomson & Co. Ltd: page 2 *bottom*

A CIP catalogue record for this book
is available from the British Library

ISBN 0 7475 4399 2

10 9 8 7 6 5 4 3 2 1

Typeset by Hewer Text Ltd, Edinburgh
Printed in Great Britain by Clays Ltd, St Ives Plc

CONTENTS

FOREWORD

The best aesthetes are working-class. Courage by contrast. Oscar Wilde on the buses, Versace down the chip shop, a falsetto voice on the terraces. Disco ball of nerves that he was, Billy MacKenzie was an aesthete. The Associates were a great group: we ripped them off. Billy was a great singer: I couldn't rip him off. He was Caruso on a balloon of oxygen. He was over the top of the top and reminded me of my mate and similarly persecuted cabaret volcano, Gavin Friday.

There was a gang of us that seemed to start school on the same day: Billy, Ian, Julian, Pete and myself. Similar, except we couldn't sing and Billy could. He had the opera . . . and when the world was brown or black or khaki and the raincoat was that year's duffle, Billy was ultra violet, ultra bright, ultra everything except ultra cool. As I say, he had the opera. Others were singing from a lesser, more protected place. Some had the stance, even the craft, but never the generosity. We wanted to break your heart; he let his heart be broken.

The last time I saw him he looked like a cross between a bus conductor and Marlon Brando in *On the Waterfront*, except instead of a lowrider he had a whippet that seemed to take him for a walk. He was a fairground attraction. I think he'd been taken for a few rides too. He seemed surprised that I was so happy to see him and so excited to hear his voice on tape. He thought the world had forgotten him. I hope it never does.

Bono
November 1997

INTRODUCTION

Mirroring and miniaturizing the dramatic beauty of the bridges of the River Forth fifty-seven miles to the south, the view upon entering Dundee by either its road or rail bridge over the famously silver-grey waters of the Tay – particularly at night with its lights sparkling all the way up to the foot of the towering Law hill that provides its centrepiece – can be a stirring sight for even the cynical, seen-it-all traveller. In many ways, however, it provides a deceptively languid picture.

From the tail-end of the 1950s through to the dawning of the 70s, Dundee slowly began to expand, eventually more than doubling in size, as low-cost council housing began to eat up the miles of rolling countryside surrounding it. The tenement slum-clearance system that had proved so successful in other Scottish cities was deployed to full effect, with the working class systematically decanted to the outer-lying acres of pebbledash obscurity or oppressive, prison-like scatterings of whitewashed prefab blocks blueprinted in Scandinavia. While there was nothing staggeringly unusual about this expansion – most other towns and cities in the UK were undergoing similarly ill-advised modernization – it ensured that Dundee would remain the fourth largest concentration of population north of the border.

But, somehow, it had become neither one thing nor the other. A walk down the extremes of its High Street would take even an unhampered pensioner a less than exhausting ten minutes, while the long and winding bus journey from east to west boundary might swallow up more than an hour. In essence, Dundee had become too sprawling to remain a town, too modest in size to consider itself a city.

With every revolution this city/town attempted to make, there would always seem to be one cog missing, and its tired machinery would once again lumber to a halt. Even after decades of the boatyards and jute mills lying disused, when the council announced a move into the Thatcher-led focus upon soft industries in the 80s by building a technology park, for years the site remained as green and undisturbed as every other park in the vicinity. There are often grim statistics bandied about concerning Dundee which seem to come and go and then are forgotten by those in power: 'HIV Capital of Scotland' (although this honour sometimes shifts to Edinburgh); 'Highest Number of Single Mothers Hooked on Heroin' (ditto); 'Second Only to Liverpool in Unemployment Figures' (believable); and, most telling and best of all, 'More Pubs Per Square Mile Than Anywhere in Europe' (easily believable).

In fact, the last two figures make for an interesting combination come Friday and Saturday night, when the buses from the housing estates ferry legions of their younger natives, armed with their week's wages or this fortnight's dole money or other, more dubious profits, into the small concentration of the town centre. Its weekend nightlife is spirited, to say the least, if a bit too handy with its fists, given the mouthy, have-a-go attitude of a huge number of the inhabitants, a moment of misplaced eye contact being considered an invitation for any manner of physical attack. In some choice bars, the timing of the table-chucking, knuckle and tumbler kick-offs were easily more dependable than a cheap digital watch for an indication of the time.

Perhaps understandably, the thin brochure produced by the luckless Dundee Tourist Board brushes over this notable aspect of the indigenous social habits. 'If after all this [savouring of Dundee's historical delights, the whaling museum etc., etc.], it's just a quiet pint you're after then you will be spoiled for choice,' it states. 'No matter where you go in Dundee you'll find pubs, some peaceful, some busy and some with live music, but whatever one you choose it's bound to be friendly.' Until you have the hard neck to steal a glance at the wrong bloke's pint, that is.

But that is to be overly dismissive of a city which has pockets of rough charm in an enviably picturesque setting. Seemingly every Dundonian generation has managed to spawn a thriving counter-culture of music and art, brimful of inspired nutters who somehow manage to pluck largely overlooked works and thoughts of wonder and ridiculousness out of the ether. Let us not forget that Dundee's most famous artistic son was the nineteenth-century poet William McGonagall, remembered more for his enthusiasm than his talent and for the unintentional hilarity of his rambling poems. Along with the garrulous spirit inherent in much of the population, there is a tangential, pinballing thought process evident in many, along with a characteristically cruel, often brutal sense of humour.

And although this place of extremes would continually repel him before slowly drawing him back to it again, Billy MacKenzie – with his black and white contrasts and headful of magnificent obsessions and contradictions – in some ways seemed to embody Dundee.

To be honest, despite the fact that I lived in Dundee and had been obsessed with records virtually since birth, I'd never heard of Billy MacKenzie until 1982, when he was already a pop star and I was still fifteen. So if you'll indulge me for a few pages while I write about Billy's impact on Dundee and that greasy-haired fifteen-year-old, it will help to lift my personal reminiscences straight out of the picture and hopefully go some way towards proving that this isn't a book written by a blinkered fan. That's not to say I was *never* a blinkered fan, though.

I'd heard his name once before. Since the age of about thirteen, burying my head in the music papers – usually *Sounds* – had become one of my few self-abusive youthful habits, and it helped me to daydream away the thirty-minute Saturday morning bus journey (top deck, back row, fag) into town for my weekly flip through the record racks. It was that strange and – to me – exciting period in between punk and the ensuing atrocities of New Romantic. Around then, I remember casting an eye over a piece about some 'new wave' band called the Associates. Reading on, I was quietly surprised to find their singer reminiscing about his childhood and demented, alcohol-saturated parties in Fintry – weirdly enough, the area that the bus was currently passing through. I just forgot all about it again. That's how it is when you're thirteen.

Nearly two years later, there he was on *Top Of The Pops*. The local paper was suddenly full of stories of the 'Dundee Man Makes It Big' variety. Now, to my knowledge, apart from some very lucky disco group a few years before, no one from Dundee had actually ever had a record in the charts, let alone one that sounded as if it was being beamed in from another remote, exotic planet. Everything about 'Party Fears Two' amazed me – the unnaturally wristy guitars, the classically tinged piano hook, and obviously, the voice, which sounded so otherworldly and original to my fairly naïve ears that it made my head swirl. This Billy MacKenzie from Fintry was snaking up and down what sounded like previously uncharted vocal scales, set to have musicologists scurrying off to rewrite the rule book. He didn't even sound as if he was actually *listening* to the music. He might as well have had his Walkman on. What's more, he was standing there on TV fronting this mutant musical offering with a huge, cheeky-bastard grin on his face – even watching himself on the monitors, just as other 'normal' people did if they ever got the chance to appear on the telly.

It turned out that back in Dundee he owned what in those days used to be called a 'boutique', on a hilly street that ran into the town, and so when I bought the Associates' third album, *Sulk*, on the day of release, I handed it straight into Plan 2 to get it signed (just the sleeve, though; not the precious vinyl). A few days later, I went to pick it up from his sister, who was working there. Yeah, he'd done it, she said, though the biro obviously hadn't been working at first, so it was a bit of an illegible scribble. But there it was: 'To Tam, Love, Billy MacKenzie.' Weirdly enough, although I've probably sold or lost hundreds of records over the years, I've still got it.

From then on, Billy's existence in the town became my magical two-way link between dreary old Dundee and the world that lay beyond the Tay Bridge. When he appeared on *Top Of The Pops* with '18 Carat Love Affair' a few months later, cosmetic scars decorating his cheeks and upper arms, my mum came home and told me she'd heard that some bloke had glassed him in a local pub the weekend before. As I later found out, this actually might have been true, since Billy was beginning to attract unwelcome interest in the town on his frequent visits back home. But still, it was make-up for the performance, and Billy was clearly ripping the piss, on national TV, for all the thugs to see, confusing the issue magnificently. Throughout the summer of 1982, in all of the good ways and, without doubt, all of the sickeningly violent ways, Billy MacKenzie made Dundee buzz.

At this stage my Saturday nights would involve drinking and puffing sessions held in the front room of whichever mate's parents had gone off down the social club (failing that, we'd find a derelict house and guzzle Super Lager like down-and-outs and smash all the remaining windows for a juvenile laugh), and then we'd make our way to Club Feet, Dundee's trendiest club at the time, which opened its doors from seven till ten for the under-agers. A night out at the Club Feet usually involved fly imbibing of smuggled-in vodka and Coke and then – hey – it was on to the floor for stupid, rubbery dancing to records by the likes of Joy Division and Echo and the Bunnymen. Then one week the DJ announced in his impressive mid-Atlantic accent that the Associates' Billy MacKenzie would be making a special appearance there the following week. The next week came. He didn't show. The week after that, though, he did – swaggering through the door in beret and trench coat, his brother-in-law in tow for moral support, around half an hour before closing.

I'm now sort of ashamed to say it, but I pretty much instantly began to pummel him with relentless questions about London and his lyrics and other groups and blah-de-blah and just wouldn't leave him alone to sign his autographs. The vodka fortifying my teenage cockiness, I even insisted upwards of a dozen times that I should definitely, no arguments, be the percussionist in the Associates. (I'd thought all this through and decided that the drum parts were too complicated.) He just laughed. And laughed. He was the first famous person I'd ever met, and although since then I've interviewed hundreds of them, many of them much more famous, the thrill is never the same. In my bladdered haze, I can even remember thinking he had Pop Star Teeth.

Then I grew up a bit, as you do. By the time I was seventeen or eighteen, Billy and I had a few mutual mates and I knew his brothers, so I'd often bump into him through one lot or the other. By then, the Associates Mark One had split up, Billy hadn't had a hit since, and the stories I was hearing were often bitter accounts of how he'd sometimes turn those manipulative powers that made him such an important character in the London music industry on folk back in Dundee. Mostly it was just bitching and bad blood on their part (or his), but I became a bit more wary of him, I suppose.

He'd begun rehearsing a new band in Dundee and I'd sometimes be invited there by a couple of pals who were in the line-up. Although I didn't exactly have a starry perception of Billy any more, it was still fascinating to watch him sing live (he hadn't done it publicly since the hits and rumours abounded that his voice was the result of studio trickery), or suddenly shout, 'Bring me my clarinets!' in moments of comic frustration with the guitarists. I intently studied the intricate little head games he'd play with the musicians to get them to do what he wanted. One night we were up at Billy's mum's house when he'd just received the test pressing of *Perhaps*, and I was riveted by the disregard he had for his own record, the way that he scratched it to fuck with a clapped-out needle on a cheap music centre as he picked out different tracks. I'd begun interviewing bands by then and I would often ask them how they treated their own records. Most said they had mint copies because they never played them.

Then came the blur that is your late teens, and while I still loved almost everything the Associates did, they weren't my main priority any more, although Billy's presence on the scene in Dundee still proved illuminating; particularly one night in a cavernous church converted into a bar, where he talked me down when I was in the throes of a speed-induced panic attack (a horror I didn't realize he'd had such first-hand experience of until I began researching this book). Another night he coolly introduced me to Matt Johnson of The The, whose records I loved, in the cocktail bar of the local club.

Every so often there would be wild parties at the MacKenzies' father's house in Bonnybank Road where people would dangle out of the windows and sit in the fish pond. Billy would stand in the packed living room and sing a cappella, while some watched on in hushed awe and others made derisory honking noises to try to put him off.

At the end of the 80s, I moved to London and ended up interviewing Billy for various magazines whenever he had a record coming out. But it was easy, even then, to see that he was growing less comfortable with his role.

On the release of his last proper Warners single, a lumpy reworking of Blondie's 'Heart Of Glass' that was clearly the result of some hare-brained record company ploy to get him back in the charts, he made excuses about the record, insisting, 'Oh, but it's still the electronic stuff I'm into though, Tam. You know that.' Then when he was subsequently dropped by the label, I interviewed him at length about the contractual palavers that had been involved. 'At one point,' he laughed, wearily, 'they were going to sign me over to another label – like me going from Celtic to Liverpool with the transfer fee paying off my debts.'

From then on, Billy was mostly back up in Scotland, so I didn't see much of him. Through a friend, I eventually learned that he'd moved down to London once more, and at an after-show party at a Sparks gig in '94, I suddenly heard him shout my name through the crowd at the bar. There he was, new page-boy haircut on show, resident twinkle in his eye. I asked him where he was living.

'Ach, Rotting Hill,' he grimaced.

'Love the hairdo, though, Billy,' I said.

'Aw, thanks,' he offered back, grinning and brushing down his fringe. 'It took ages to get it like this . . .'

We nattered away for a while and it was only after he'd gone that it dawned on me. Of course, Billy had always been receding badly, something that he was touchy about and blamed on a bad perm he'd once got in Edinburgh in his youth. The various hats had always concealed it. That night, he looked like some devilishly handsome indie pop star; Ian Brown's charismatic big brother. With a great wig on.

The last time I saw Billy was in November 1996 at a party at the basement flat he was sharing with his new musical partner, Steve Aungle, in Holland Road, west London. Although his mother had died only a couple of months before and, as it later turned out, he'd been slightly nervous about hosting such a full-on soirée, he'd just signed a new deal with Nude Records and so at least there seemed to be something to celebrate. He'd shaved his hair and dyed it blond, with Perspex shades perched on his cranium for the full effect. He appeared to me to be on fine form, the usual Billy: all charm and compliments one minute, playfully argumentative the next. At one point he cupped his hand and rested it on the top of my head, saying nothing, just to see what I'd do. So I did nothing.

We talked about his new stuff ('It's what Bryan Ferry *wishes* he was doing,' he bragged), about how it should do well since he was a bit of a music press darling ('Yeah, but it's no' just about *Q* and the *Melody Maker*, is it?' he baited me, knowing I'd been working for both). And then he quizzed me endlessly about the singer of a very well-known American band that I'd just interviewed, turning the tables on our first conversation when I was fifteen. I told him about how this rock star was incredibly affected in his every mannerism. When he walked in a room, he expected everyone to look at him.

'Poor boy,' Billy said, distractedly, gazing into space, standing in his own front room in a full-length fur coat.

At the end of the night, it was all hugs and see-you-soons, but that look has stayed with me ever since.

In the months of shock following Billy's death, whenever I met anyone who'd known him, even casually, the unavoidable pall of sadness would soon give way to one funny story or another concerning his legendarily mischievous carrying-on. Eventually I realized that these were stories that shouldn't be forgotten. Initially I was reluctant to write this book because it meant revisiting my own past as well as Billy's and that can often be a nightmare. But hopefully my understanding of his background, as well as my years of profiling hundreds of subjects other than Billy MacKenzie, gives me a unique and sympathetic perspective on his story.

In the countless hours of research and interviews that have gone into this book, I learned that even if Billy was keen to litter his past with the half-truths and red herrings that he frequently used to tease and taunt music journalists, the real story was actually far more remarkable than the embellished version. If anything sounded too far-fetched, it would transpire that it really happened.

Given his unique vocal gift, unarguably incredible life story and doggedly determined struggles with the 'oppressive' record industry – long before anyone else thought to challenge its autocracy in the 1990s – Billy MacKenzie certainly deserves far, far more than just a footnote in the pop history of the less than glorious 80s.

1

Vaulting the Fence

It could all have been very different. In fact, there might have been no significant story at all, apart from a tragic paragraph in the *Dundee Courier & Advertiser* reporting that an infant had been run over and killed in a misadventurous road accident the day before.

Bursting with hyperactivity and a nervous, kinetic energy, as a young child Billy MacKenzie had begun to develop an alarming habit of running out into the street and straight into the path of an oncoming vehicle. On the most serious occasion, after sprinting into the twin-lane Victoria Road where his grandparents had successfully turned a trade in linen, buttons and pins into a busy second-hand goods shop, the knee-high Billy had tumbled over in the road and ended up trapped under the chassis of a car, seconds after the driver had skidded to a near cardiac-inducing halt. It was 1961, the boy was four, and perhaps mercifully, the burgeoning trend for compact, lightweight vehicle design enabled his father, James MacKenzie, to lever the car up by hand and free the errant youngster.

The MacKenzies were Calvinistic travelling stock, part of a Romany tradition that hawked its wares throughout Tayside and Angus and as far north as Aberdeenshire. But when the brood of Agnes MacKenzie, Billy's grandmother, began to grow overwhelming, the family reluctantly decided to become what the north-eastern Scottish gypsies derisively nicknamed 'toonies': those who had forsaken the itinerant life to put down firmer roots.

There were six brothers – Davy, Willie, Sandy, Geordie, Jim, Ronnie – and one sister, Jean, who died as an infant, and as each grew to earning age, which in those postwar days often became a more appealing, or necessary, alternative to schooling even before a child had reached puberty, they were put to work in the shop. The MacKenzie sons were soon enjoying an unrivalled education in buying and selling that would earn them a lasting reputation as dealers in cheaply acquired used goods and furniture. Furthering their business efforts, the brothers began branching out into other premises. Headstrong and determined as the MacKenzie brothers were, a strong respect for blood bonding and a fierce sibling rivalry developed in their characters. Before long they were often in direct competition in their commercial exploits, and not above shaking one another down in their dealings. 'We'd rob each other,' Jim MacKenzie warmly remembers. 'We'd always be at it, pulling wee strokes on each other . . .'

Although over the following decades, Jim MacKenzie would go on to control a small empire of second-hand shops, while his brothers diversified their interests to incorporate carpet warehouses and other properties, in the mid-50s he was widely known locally as a young man with a tough, formidable reputation and more disposable income than most stashed away in their back pocket. Because of that very nature, he was never entirely short of female attention. But it was to be Lily Agnes O'Phee Abbott who would turn his head. According to local accounts, she and her sister Betty, born of an Irish lineage that had escaped to the west coast of Scotland during the potato famine of 1846, were two of the more stunning additions to any dancehall.

In keeping with the era's traditions of courtship and marrying young, the pair were soon wed in a Catholic ceremony in the town, Jim MacKenzie having embraced his wife's religion. Before long, they had a son, William MacArthur MacKenzie, born on 27 March 1957, in Dundee Royal Infirmary.

Blessed with an uncommon maturity, even in his formative years, the young Billy MacKenzie displayed something of a gift for assessing the world around him and seeing it for all its wonder and absurdity. His father was often amazed by his child's powers of playful manipulation. If Jim MacKenzie sent his son on an errand, he would later discover that Billy had somehow managed to coerce one of his other small friends into doing it, while he waited to collect the groceries, the change and the subsequent pat on the head for being such an obedient little lad. In tandem, he displayed extreme and unusual reactions, even in testing circumstances. Once, when he suffered a boyish accident that found him hobbling back to his parents with his big toenail hanging off, his father took him to a chiropodist to have the nail removed. Within the first seconds of the painful minor surgery, Billy began howling. But then Jim MacKenzie realized that his son wasn't crying; he was laughing, hysterically and uncontrollably.

Billy later remembered this period of his childhood as being largely undisciplined, except for random moments of recrimination. 'I had all the freedom in the world from the age of five onwards,' he said. 'I'd get up to all these terrible things and never get touched for it. Then I might just nick a biscuit or something and I'd get done in . . .'

Billy eagerly absorbed everything around him. He would sit for hours listening to his grandfather regaling him with tales of his travelling days, these romanticized yarns planting the seed of wanderlust in the attentive youngster's mind. In fact, Billy later recollected a certain sense of frustration and boredom with being a child: 'I was always dying to be an adult. I had ears like satellite dishes, picking up juicy titbits when they were around.'

Music, of course, was all around him. On his father's side, the passion was for the gypsy camp-fire tradition and the fiddles and accordions of Scottish country dance music, although in the 50s a couple of Jim's brothers had dabbled with guitar in country and western or rock 'n' roll groups. On his mother's side, jazz was the abiding love, and when allowed to stay up into the small hours at the frequent parties at home, Billy marvelled as his maternal grandmother, or his mother, held court with renditions of standards by Dinah Washington, Bessie Smith, Lena Horne and Billie Holiday. Remarkably, he would always claim that his granny could also blow a mean saxophone.

'There was always singing about the house,' Billy recalled. 'If it wasn't singing, it was fighting. If it wasn't a torch song, it was a torch argument.'

Inevitably, Billy became the centre of attention at these lively gatherings, indulged for his strangely adult behaviour and endearing mischievousness. At three years of age, he would peer up his Auntie Betty's skirt as she sang 'The Little Boy That Santa Claus Forgot'. Then, much to his childish reluctance, eventually he would be coaxed by his revelling relatives into doing a turn. It was in this way that Billy first discovered his natural singing voice.

By the time he was eight he was mimicking Tom Jones and showcasing what was increasingly becoming an explosive, effortless vocal range. Before long, Billy was being invited to perform the lusty Welsh pop star's songs, along with appropriately lewd pelvic grinds, for the old women who lived across the street, who would sit delicately dipping their biscuits into their tea as the young lad provided the entertainment. And although by nature a very unlikely cub scout, when Billy briefly joined the ranks of Lord Baden Powell's militaristic youth movement, he shone during one of their annual performances, where he performed 'Edelweiss' from *The Sound Of Music* to the rows of quietly impressed parents. Recognizing that he might be on to something profitable, Billy brought his wilier ways into play. To earn extra pocket money, he would often sing Nat King Cole numbers for his mother and her friends and then run off with pocketfuls of spare change.

Even while at his primary school, St Mary's Forebank, a strict Catholic establishment, Billy would duck and dodge the wrath of the nuns and priests and make amends for his seemingly untameable, boisterous behaviour by charming his tutors with his singing voice. Perhaps typically, however, once invited to join the school choir, he took advantage of having the loudest voice by attempting to throw the other choirboys off-key, since they were effectively following his lead. Having been taken under the wing of one teacher who recognized her pupil's talents and even harboured designs on having him recommended to stage school, Billy was singled out for individual attention and taught to sing obscure Latin hymns and strange Russian folk songs. For a time, he would fantasize about joining the Vienna Boys' Choir.

But it was the day-to-day transistor-radio reality of pop music that completely enraptured him, in that transitional period where the old-fashioned crooners and the young, relatively long-haired bands began to jockey for position in the hit parade. The first singles to make any real impact on Billy were the jittery rock of the Rolling Stones' '19th Nervous Breakdown' and Nancy and Frank Sinatra's cutesy, dumb romantic duet 'Somethin' Stupid'.

Pop stardom first struck him as a hugely attractive career option when he watched some long-forgotten 60s band performing on *Ready Steady Go* while dangling in mid-air on pantomime safety wires. Every aspect of pop culture seemed designed to fascinate him. In this area he even began to idolize his mother and loved to watch her singing to herself in the mirror as she put on her false eyelashes before a night out. To him, she looked like Dusty Springfield.

But he later claimed that his pop star ambitions also stemmed from another, less selfish motive – he imagined that when he became famous he would be able to buy his Auntie Betty a new carpet to replace her threadbare Indian rug. 'I just thought, Well, if you're a pop star – like the ones I saw on the TV – you're bound to be able to give things to people.'

With their potent mixture of Irish and gypsy blood, this generation of MacKenzies had now grown as expansive as the one that had gone before. Billy now had five younger brothers and sisters. First came his sister Lizzie, then his brother John, then sister Helen, followed by another two brothers, Alec and Jimmy. Growing up in Dundee could prove abrasive at times, and through their sheer numbers alone they learned how to handle themselves through their defence of one another, as well as developing a certain renown for unhinged exuberance. Before long, few dared to mess with the MacKenzie clan.

No less dramatically inclined than Billy, the brothers often played a game called 'Teatime Theatre' in which they would don headscarves and take turns wearing their father's spare set of false teeth, while they mugged at themselves in the mirror. Billy once tried to describe the high-spirited nature of his family by saying, 'Really we're not that wild – just alive. We all like dancing and doing somersaults. If there's a fence to climb, we'll vault it.'

Now attending St Michael's secondary school, Billy found his interests beginning to splinter into other, more athletic areas. Unbeknown to his parents, their son had become a decent footballer – although he would sometimes have to be sent off for joking around on the field – and an even better runner. One Saturday morning, Jim MacKenzie remembers, a teacher knocked on their front door to collect Billy, who was due to run for the Scottish Schoolboys sprinting team in a few hours, even though he had remained untypically quiet about the matter, perhaps as a result of being disquietened by the undue pressure. He triumphantly returned home later that evening with a bronze medal.

Since early childhood, Billy's other abiding passion was for natural history and wildlife programmes on television, and he often talked of his ambition to become a vet. As a tearaway five-year-old, he first encountered what would become his spirit animal, after falling into the local Stobswell ponds and resurfacing to find an inquisitive whippet staring at him. He was instantly attracted to this smaller, sleeker breed of greyhound, and convinced the dog's elderly owner to let him take it for walks after school. After she had agreed, Billy would devotedly trudge up to her small newsagents every evening, no matter how harsh the weather.

Billy's subsequent lifelong obsession with whippets may often have appeared bizarre to outsiders, but in many ways he shared key characteristics with his chosen breed: let loose in the outside world, whippets often mindlessly tear around in every direction; indoors, they are incredibly docile, contentedly lazing away the hours. In unpublished diaries covering his entire history of owning whippets, Billy wrote of these first experiences with the borrowed dog back in the early 60s: 'Armed with a Vimto and Bluebird toffee, we would head to the ponds, then over the playing fields where he would divebomb crows . . . it was the closest I'd get to watching a two-hundred metre final at the Olympics.'

Billy began slowly wearing his parents down with an unrelenting volley of requests for his own whippet. At first they dismissed it as a youthful fad, another example of a precociousness that would have him threatening to roll under a bus if his mother didn't buy him a Ben Sherman shirt. But when, at twelve years old, Billy remained as unshakeably determined, they finally gave in. At the time, he and his best friend Alan Torrs would earn additional spending money by sweeping up and polishing the furniture in his father's shops. When the pair were finishing up one June afternoon in 1969, Jim MacKenzie arrived and presented his visibly thrilled son with a pure-white, fawn-patched male dog that Billy decided to call Kim.

'I couldn't wait to get out into the country with him,' he wrote, adding cheekily, 'he hadn't chased rabbits before, but he soon got the hang of it.'

In the often frustratingly fleeting Scottish summertime, particularly in the north-east, it is berry-picking season. Painfully early in the morning, rickety buses from the local farms call at prearranged points around the Dundee estates, where groups of cash-strapped casual workers are picked up and spend their days in the fields, pricking and scarring their hands as they pluck at the raspberry bushes, filling punnets and buckets weighed at a designated point and exchanged for handfuls of coins. The craftier berry pickers develop a habit of relieving themselves in the bucket, so in essence, they are being paid a few extra pence for their own urine. In the summer months the MacKenzie family often went to 'the berries' for additional cash, in the drills surrounding the local village of Blairgowrie. It was back-breaking, mind-numbing work which Billy hated. As an alternative to suffering this grim communal activity, he and Kim spent one summer staying with his granny at her cottage on the rural flatlands outside Dundee, a time which proved inspirational for Billy as he imagined himself living on the vast emptiness of the American prairies, although in the end the isolation began to get to him.

As is often the case with the rush of hormones and mess of teenage emotions, certain aspects of his daily life suddenly became a source of mild embarrassment for Billy, the most acute being his developing vocal talent. At the same time, his relationship with his father was becoming increasingly strained, particularly when Jim MacKenzie returned home from the pub with a handful of lightly pickled mates and insisted that they should witness his son's remarkable singing voice. The sleeping fourteen-year-old Billy would be dragged from his bed – or when he got wiser to the situation, from a hiding position in a wardrobe – and reluctantly hauled downstairs for a wholly mortifying rendition of Nilsson's 1972 hit ballad 'Without You', which was enjoying an extended occupation of the upper reaches of the charts that winter.

Although always coy and somewhat cagey about this period until much, much further on in his life, during this time Billy began to develop an even wilder, parentally uncontrollable streak, and later he would teasingly hint that his post-puberty had involved a string of '*Cabaret*-esque relationships'. At school he and Torrs – who shared his enthusiasm for dogs and the more unusual fringes of music – took no small pride in becoming slightly awkward social misfits who paraded around the playground with Mantovani records tucked under their arms. 'We were the kind of cool ones,' Billy claimed, 'but we were singled out to be battered by the gangs from early on. I wasn't a wimp, but I would have to map a route home every Friday night to avoid trouble.'

There were others problems. Billy was increasingly being ticked off by teachers for focusing his attention during classes on the acres of potential dog-walking terrain that lay beyond the school windows. It was around this time that he realized the very real benefits of an unusual talent that he had discovered as a child: projectile vomiting at will.

'In class I'd say, "I'm feeling sick, sir,"' he remembered. 'They'd always say, "Shut up, MacKenzie", because I was a bit of a trouble-maker. Then I'd say, "I'm telling you . . . *yaaargh*" and throw up on my friend's jumper so he'd have to go home as well, and we would go up in the hills with the dogs.'

Saving up from the proceeds of the part-time work for his father, Billy had secretly placed an advert in the 'Wanted' column of the local paper, looking for a whippet bitch. When a call came through from Aberdeen, he was forced to confess all to his parents who, instead of hitting the roof, appeared mutely surprised by their son's organizational capabilities, however covert. Often Kim would make some daring, Colditz-like escape from the MacKenzies' home and trail Billy to school. Now, Honey, the gold fawn bitch would follow, and the two of them would hare around the school playing fields, much to the distraction of his classmates and the fury of the headmaster. Eventually a solution was found. Billy stopped going to school.

The first time Billy MacKenzie heard the sci-fi rock 'n' roll of Roxy Music's 'Virginia Plain', it nailed him to the wall. On opening one of the weekly music papers and finding the group's saxophonist Andy MacKay pictured with a whippet, he became a slavish devotee of their music, joining their fan club. The first Roxy Music album, along with the stacked-heel stomp of the glam David Bowie and the frenzied vocal histrionics of Sparks, would become the soundtrack to this period of his life. The radio was his only relief from the relentless tedium of work in the first months after he left school. At fifteen years of age he began a four-year apprenticeship with Scott's Electricians in Dundee, an opening arranged as a favour to his father. Since Billy was generally to be found sorely lacking where manual labour or domestic chores were concerned, his tenure was fated to be short-lived from the beginning; it lasted just under twelve weeks.

However, around this time Billy was cajoled by his father into entering a talent night held at his local pub, with a first prize of £50. Although still well below the legal drinking age, he competed alongside a string of semi-professional club singers, his short repertoire consisting of bar-friendly interpretations of the Kinks' 'Sunny Afternoon' and the Band's 'The Night They Drove Old Dixie Down'. To his own amazement, he won. 'And that was the last I saw of Billy with the fifty quid that night,' Jim MacKenzie states. 'It was like, "See you later, Pop", and he was gone.'

For the most part, Billy frittered away his days working with his father on the furniture-collecting van round, breeding his dogs – a first litter of six puppies were born at the foot of his bed as he slept – and attending whippet racing trials in nearby Forfar. But it was fast becoming clear that Billy's life was lacking any real direction or future. What's more, becoming increasingly individualistic, he had taken to dressing in 50s-style retro American clothing, while his peers were in tank tops and Oxford bags, and these exhibitionistic tendencies seemed to warrant unnecessary attention in Dundee in the early 70s. One night when Billy and Alan Torrs were walking through the town at night, the sixteen-year-olds were jumped by a gang and Alan's cheek was slashed with a blade. If Billy had been toying with thoughts of escape before, this horrific incident seemed to strengthen his resolve. He was leaving Dundee.

'I used to get ill at the thought of being trapped there,' he once admitted. 'Being in Scotland at that time was very claustrophobic and damaging. There was a very aggressive and oppressive attitude towards people like myself. I was getting beaten up too many times. When my best friend was cut up and carved and disfigured for life, I knew that I was next on the slab . . .'

2

International Loner

In an incident that would soon seep into American folklore, one winter night in 1967 Melvin Dummar, a plant worker from the small Nevada town of Gabbs, was driving the long distance home through the cold blackness of the desert, after an unsuccessful search for better-paid work in further-flung towns. Making a momentary pit-stop to take a leak, he heard the groans of what he initially assumed to be a down-and-out lying in the sand by the roadside. On realizing that the man was clearly injured as the result of a serious motorcycle crash, Dummar helped the injured wino into the passenger seat of his truck and offered to drive him to Las Vegas to seek medical attention. Initially the grey-bearded bum was reluctant, although realizing he had no other alternative but to accept the truck driver's aid, he finally agreed.

During the long overnight journey that followed, Dummar made several attempts to engage the untalkative vagrant in some form of conversation. When enquiring as to his background and the circumstances leading up to his accident in the desert, the man made a passing claim to be the billionaire Howard Hughes. Dummar – not being familiar with the spectacularly eccentric history of the legendary Hollywood producer and aviation tycoon turned troubled recluse, and having some reasonable vision of billionaires being slightly more groomed than his unkempt passenger – dismissed the claim in his own mind as merely the delusions of an injured man.

Having effectively saved the old man's life, early the next morning Dummar followed his passenger's instructions and dropped him off behind the Sands Hotel on the Las Vegas Strip, at that time owned by Hughes. Handing the man what spare change he had in his pocket, no more than a handful of nickels and quarters, he drove off, giving the incident no further thought.

While the validity of this now-fabled tale has never been proven, it was to have no real effect on Melvin Dummar's life until nearly ten years later. Not long after the incident in the desert, the terminally luckless Dummar split with his wife Veronica, in the wake of persistent money difficulties that had forced them to live in a trailer in Gabbs with their young daughter and become the serial victims of the repo men. Following a brief reconciliation only months later when Veronica announced that she was pregnant with the couple's second child, the pair relocated to California, where Dummar found work as a milkman. But it was to be an ill-fated affair, and in the mid-70s the couple suffered an irreparable split. Within a year, however, Dummar's fortunes would take a dramatic turn, earning him a lasting notoriety.

In April 1976 it was widely reported that Howard Hughes had died in Mexico at the age of seventy. At the time, Dummar was running a gas station in a back road of Willard, Utah, with his second wife, Bonnie, and this became the scene of a second, no less fantastical incident, later derided as the wild claims of an ambitious fraudster. A stranger, the account went, arrived at the gas station one spring afternoon and as Dummar was attending to his car, left an envelope on the desk in his office. The documents contained within, Dummar later claimed, appeared to be the handwritten last will and testament of Howard Hughes, listing the garage worker as the benefactor of one-sixteenth of the billionaire's fortune, a sum calculated to be around $156 million.

Following the details of mysterious instructions attached to the will, Dummar surreptitiously dumped the documents into an in-tray at the reception of the offices of the Church of Jesus Christ of Latter-Day Saints in Mormon Square, Salt Lake City, with a scribbled note declaring that the will had been found near the home of the founder of the Mormons, Joseph Smith, and that it should be brought to the attention of the president of the church. Examination of the document revealed that the document might feasibly be the work of Howard Hughes, and the will was filed in a

Las Vegas county court. In a remarkable twist, it seemed that the pump attendant was now set to become a multimillionaire.

More bizarrely, however, for a brief period in the mid-70s, Billy MacKenzie's life was to become interlinked with that of Melvin Dummar when, following a fateful chain of events, he became his brother-in-law.

In 1973, at the age of sixteen, Billy was torn between latent thoughts of studying to become a veterinary surgeon, a nagging instinct to somehow pursue the promise he'd shown as a sprinter and, of course, his growing unease with his environment and urge to desert it. Since the first option would inevitably involve him being forced to go back to St Michael's to complete the Higher exams he'd skipped out on, this was instantly dismissed. Athletics, it seemed, was just as unlikely or impossible a career path as pop music. With no other reasonable alternative presenting itself, Billy began to search for potential escape routes, turning once more to his family, and in particular, the network of MacKenzie relatives dotted around the globe.

In the summer of that year, having sensibly weighed up his closest option as being the most appealing, Billy first experienced the scenic six-hour train journey that winds its way down Britain's east coast from Dundee, through Edinburgh, Newcastle and York, to London's King's Cross station, and that was subsequently to become a well-worn track for him. At the time, his Auntie Betty – Lily MacKenzie's sister – had moved down to the south London suburb of Clapham and ended up living in the same terrace as her brother Davey, who had agreed to share the responsibility of looking after their wandering nephew.

Clearly viewing this less as a holiday and more as a welcome opportunity of a permanent move to England, Billy used his unbridled energy and confidence to land himself a job as a junior sales assistant at the Scotch House – that corner of Regent Street that is for ever Caledonia – where he spent the summer months selling kilts, expensive single-malt whisky and tartan travel blankets to mainly Japanese and American tourists. Keen to continue steering in the general direction of this new beacon on the horizon of his fortunes – no matter how dreary the daily reality of his work would prove at times – Billy would often be forced to bite his lip to avoid confrontations with the more difficult customers, but the blunt frankness and surface emotions of his upbringing were often difficult to suppress.

One day in the shop Billy was politely bantering with a Scottish expatriate, when the customer enquired after the geographical source of Billy's accent and then made a glib comment that Dundee was 'not exactly Scotland'. As Billy colourfully recalled later, 'I honestly felt like stotting it right on him.' Not long after, he quit the job, and suddenly experiencing the first pangs of home-sickness, returned to Dundee.

Once he was back on that familiar terrain, however, his feelings of restlessness returned. A couple of years before, the MacKenzies had moved to a spacious house in the quiet, residential Bonnybank Road, near the centre of Dundee, becoming neighbours with their equally large mob of cousins on their Uncle Sandy's side, and the two families had begun plotting a mass emigration to New Zealand. Only weeks before the planned departure, with the whole family having already gone through the painful vaccination programme that was a condi-tion of their entry into the country, Jim MacKenzie suddenly changed his mind and backed out, leaving his relations to travel alone.

Having kept in contact with his cousins through occasional letters and phone calls, Billy soon found himself attracted to their enthusiastic descriptions of dramatic landscapes, exotic wildlife and bubbling hot springs. On the premise of it being an explora-tory trip, Billy managed to coax from his father the price of a return plane ticket to New Zealand.

Armed with a photo album of family snapshots to offer some comfort in any pining moments, Billy was given a typically emo-tional send-off at the railway station by the MacKenzies. Despite his distinct lack of experience of the alien machinations of airports, and worse, discovering himself to be a white-knuckled flyer, thirty-six hours later he landed at Auckland airport, on the North Island. There he was met by his relatives and driven to the town of Ngaruawahia, where they had settled.

After finding work in Hamilton, some thirty miles to the south, Billy began to ease into his new life. The locals initially teased him about his strong accent and unusual appearance – the unfashionable 50s quiff not being common among young New Zealand farming stock in the 70s – although they soon learned that the boyish Scot himself possessed a savage tongue, and he came to earn their respect. More importantly, Billy was happy once again to be living closer to nature, the soul-stirring mountainscapes and rolling green countryside reminding him of Scotland, albeit with a more appealing climate.

Soon tiring of the exhausting routine that required rising in the early hours to catch the bus to Hamilton, Billy found a job in a local quarry. His daily working routine involved waiting at the quarry's summit for the delivery lorries to dump their load of boulders into a huge mechanical vice, where he would pull the device's starting handle. It was mindless, back-breaking work, often carried out in torrential rain, and not without danger. If the rocks refused to break up, Billy would be forced to clamber up to the top of the vice to rearrange the contents and run the risk of falling in. Then, one day, the foreman asked him to ferry the broken loads back down to the foot of the quarry in a truck. Billy had neglected to inform his employers that he didn't own a driver's licence – in fact, he had never even taken a lesson – and so, unsurprisingly, his first attempt to manoeuvre the truck very nearly killed him.

'Driving on a steep slope at the quarry edge,' he later wrote, 'my foot slipped on the clutch and I was careering towards a four hundred foot drop. How he did it, I will never know, but the foreman sprinted towards me and managed to pull me off and away from the edge.'

'Vehicles,' he decided, with a mixture of fear and determination that would endure throughout most of his life, 'are definitely not for me.'

These adventurous endeavours proved short-lived, and within eight weeks Billy was back in Dundee, although once again it would prove only a temporary measure while he plotted his next move. His spirits were undampened by his recent experiences, and a developing passion for the string-drenched soul records emanating from Philadelphia stirred an interest within him to visit America, where he had family connections in both New Orleans and Los Angeles. Once more he charmed his increasingly bewildered father, who further indulged his son's seemingly tireless wanderlust by booking him a return air ticket to New York.

In the summer of 1974 Billy arrived alone at John F. Kennedy Airport. He hadn't yet decided whether to travel south to Alabama – to soak up the black music traditions, and, nurturing a youthful fantasy that would mark his first real decision to develop his vocal talent, to join a gospel choir – or to venture west to California. In the end the widescreen romantic lure of Hollywood proved stronger, and Billy made the coast-to-coast trek by Greyhound bus, eventually arriving at the Long Beach home of his once-removed cousin Veronica, who at the time was married to one Melvin Dummar.

By day Billy would make forays into West Hollywood to search for some form of employment, and to marvel at the decayed glamour of Sunset Boulevard, where he was quietly amazed by the sight of transvestites parading up and down the sidewalks, a decadent vision wholly at odds with the conservative values of Dundee. Drifting through a succession of menial jobs, he sprayed sports-car bumpers at a garage, served behind the counter of a Red Cross store, and, in his longest engagement, peeled and chopped onions in a hamburger joint.

Lacking any other friends in California, Billy would spend his free days hanging around the beaches, a time he later described as being 'kind of wild . . . cars and hot nights and hilarity'. Somewhere in the middle of all this, he began to enjoy a summer romance with Dummar's younger sister, Chloe, a big-boned, twenty-two-year-old recently divorced from her second husband. Essentially the relationship remained a one-sided affair, with the Utah-born girl slowly becoming besotted with 'my little Scotsman'.

Before long, however, the Californian immigration authorities were alerted to the fact that Billy was working illegally. Suddenly backed into a corner and threatened with deportation, he managed to strike a deal that seemed to suit all parties involved. Marrying Chloe Dummar and making an alarmingly paltry $200 payment to her would enable him to stay on in the States and begin to carve out some manner of career in music, perhaps by becoming a club singer. Since Billy was still a couple of months short of his eighteenth birthday, it was decided that the two should travel across the desert to Las Vegas, where they could obtain a special licence from the state of Nevada.

In a ceremony held in early 1975, the exact date of which has been lost along with the wedding certificate, Billy MacKenzie and Chloe Dummar took their vows in the Wee Kirk on the Heather, a Scottish-themed Las Vegas chapel. Billy later recalled it as a surreal experience: 'The Pastor or whatever you call him, he had nail varnish on and kept giving me the eye. Some other wigged creature was playing Liberace sort of stuff in the corner. Then they asked, "Would you like a tape of the ceremony?" It was a bit like that. But you do these things when you're seventeen and you're bored.'

Within five months, displaying whimsical, childlike qualities that belied his state of young adulthood, Billy was growing bored of married life and what he viewed as the suffocating attentions of his new wife. The ink on his wedding certificate barely dry – and despite his spouse's protestations, for whom the whole affair had obviously become much more than a simple business transaction – Billy telephoned his father in Dundee, who had only recently learned of this important new development in his son's life.

'I didn't know anything about him getting married,' Jim MacKenzie explained, 'and when I did hear about it, I wasn't very happy. But the next thing I got this phone call that he'd decided to come home.'

'It was just teenage frivolity,' Billy dismissively said of the marriage years later, 'just frolicking nonsense.'

From April to December 1976, Melvin Dummar became the subject of intense media attention. His endearing naïvety and backwoods ways helped to clear him of any suspicious involvement in this seemingly fanciful story, which understandably attracted a series of worldwide TV news reports and reams of speculative newspaper copy. In October of that year, following up a possibly exclusive angle on the story focusing on the comments of Dummar's relatives, a reporter from the *Sunday People* managed to contact Billy at his father's home in Dundee, more than twelve months after he had returned to Scotland.

In fact, the short article subsequently printed concentrated on the runaway husband's unwillingness to return to his American wife, a decision whereby he renounced his share of the Dummar family's new-found wealth. Under the headline banner 'Divorcing A Fortune', Billy was quoted as saying, 'I never really loved the girl. Getting married seemed the thing to do. It was going to solve my problems, or so I thought. When I realized her brother was getting a fortune, it made no difference. I didn't want to sponge off anyone. Now I want a divorce.

'I certainly will not be sorry,' he continued, adding, with barely concealed venom, 'and she is used to it. Although she's only 23, I was her third husband. It was an education though. Some people's marriages only last three days.'

Speaking from her new home in Utah, the spurned Chloe retaliated by saying, 'Billy never really loved me. He only married me to be able to stay on in America to carry on with his career. I admit I loved my Scotsman. It's a pity he didn't give marriage a chance. He even flew home without giving America a real chance.'

In June 1978 the case of what had become known as 'The Mormon Will' was thrown out of court in Nevada, the document having been exposed as a crude fake. The final blow to the authenticity of the will was delivered with the alleged discovery of Melvin Dummar's finger-print on a book in the Webster State College library entitled *Hoax* that examined previous forgeries of Howard Hughes's handwriting and showed genuine examples of the tycoon's hand. Melvin Dummar has always maintained his innocence in this matter, blaming a conspiracy by Hughes's estate to discredit him. For years he has stood by his account of the events in the Nevada desert in 1967.

Two years later, by which time he was once again in London, Billy wrote a letter to friends back home in Dundee. Whether through dramatic affectation or a spirit of playfulness, it was scribbled on the back of the original copy of his divorce papers. These showed that Chloe Dummar had moved to become legally separated from him on the grounds of 'mental cruelty'.

3

Mental Torture

The year before punk succeeded in tearing apart the very fabric of the commercial music industry, forcing mid-career crises in every long-haired, prog-derived rock act – whether globally successful or still dragging themselves around the pub circuit – Billy MacKenzie was waging his own unique war against the hippie contingent of Dundee. Part 60s soul boy, part devotee of 50s Americana and the rock 'n' roll fashions that were elsewhere serving to spawn the official King's Road punk, in 1976 Billy cut a peculiar figure in stark contrast with the patchouli-oiled, Afghan-coated brigades in his home town, parading around in his James Dean bomber jackets, straight-legged jeans and winkle-pickers.

Any sense of alienation from his peer group that Billy might have been experiencing – or wilfully attracting – soon diminished around the time he struck up a new friendship with Angela Forbes and Patricia Wilson. The two local girls shared his interest in more oblique fashion values, his passionate love of Sparks' adrenalized rock and Kraftwerk's cold, precise electronics, and his equally passionate hatred for what he viewed as the humourless indulgences of Genesis and Led Zeppelin. Together, the trio would spend their idle time foraging around in second-hand markets for tailored suits from the 40s and hatching a plot to form a group – which may or may not have for a time been called Billy Trag and the Mysterons – fronted by all three and attempting to bridge the unexplored gap between Tamla soul and Sparks.

Comprising a makeshift line-up of older, time-served musicians from Dundee working men's club bands, the outfit was destined to fulfil only two engagements, one locally and one in a village near the Isle of Skye, off the west coast of Scotland; neither gig was of any great success or significance. With the girls dressed provocatively and flanking Billy at the front of the stage, the group performed a selection of soul classics such as Smokey Robinson's 'Tears Of A Clown' and the Isley Brothers' 'This Old Heart Of Mine' to largely uninterested pub crowds better pleased by covers of Bay City Rollers songs. Unimpressed by the poor earning potential of this unlikely troupe, the backing band began to look elsewhere for work and the act soon petered out.

Yet, in a cabaret profession littered with failed talent-show contestants and vocal chancers, these first steps into the local band scene helped to earn Billy a wider reputation as a fledgeling singer with an uncommon talent. Through the grapevine, another local group caught wind of this young soul singer and invited him to audition. Stan and Deliver was their feebly punning name, and they were to become the basis of Billy MacKenzie's first real musical efforts.

In the wake of the Scottish outfit the Average White Band's Top Ten success with their single 'Pick Up The Pieces' in March 1975, a trend for white funk had begun developing among the pub and club bands of Dundee. While Stan and Deliver were among its chief exponents, they often slipped Tamla or Stax numbers into their set (much to the delight of their new lead singer) and were not too proud to bang through the odd crowd-pacifying rendition of a Queen hit. Witnesses to a 1976 performance by the group at the Dundee pub Laing's recall Billy fronting this competent, if unspectacular outfit, resplendent in a suitably showbiz white jump suit and, in the breaks between their sets, standing at the opposite end of the bar from the other band members, whom he was beginning to find 'cynical and pompous'.

Nevertheless, the situation provided a suitable platform for Billy to develop his vocal style, equally influenced by the blues and jazz singers his mother had first brought to his attention, the more erratic moments of the Berlin-dwelling Bowie's *Station To Station* period and, most indelibly, the octave-scaling phrasing of Russell Mael of Sparks.

The band began to attract bookings from further afield and one night, when they supported a touring black funk quartet named the Fantastics at Tiffany's Ballroom in Stockbridge, Edinburgh, a young Linlithgow musician called Alan Rankine was in the audience. 'I saw this guy singing,' he recalls of the first time he ever heard Billy MacKenzie, 'and I heard his voice and I thought, Bloody hell. I'd never heard anything like it. The band was cod funk, not very good, but this voice was just shining through.'

At the time, the eighteen-year-old Rankine was engaged in a similarly unfulfilling musical apprenticeship as the guitarist in an Edinburgh cabaret band, Caspian, who had a residency at a city-centre hotel. Caspian's soon-to-be agent Ian Sclater recalls a similar reaction on first witnessing Rankine's skills as a musician. When he walked into the hotel bar one evening to find the house band's youthful guitarist playing a note-faithful rendition of Santana's 'Samba Pa Ti', he says, 'my jaw just dropped'.

Born on 17 May 1958 in the village of Bridge of Allan near Stirling, the son of a primary school headmaster and medical secretary, Alan Rankine had been forced to spend most of his childhood moving from town to town throughout Scotland as his family repeatedly upped sticks to follow his father's postings after a subsequent promotion to schools inspector.

Rankine first picked up a guitar at the age of eleven, following the lead of a classmate who could play 'The Skye Boat Song' on a cheap, jumbo acoustic and always seemed to be surrounded by attentive girls. Deciding to go one better, Alan learned to play the far groovier 'Delilah' by Tom Jones – coincidentally, one of the key numbers in the young Billy MacKenzie's repertoire. From then on he became inseparable from his first guitar, teaching himself to play, since his only previous experience of academic music lessons had ended in a physical tussle when his piano teacher made inappropriately affectionate advances.

At this age Rankine was attracted to the more artful fringes of pop music: 'You'd get Herman's Hermits, but then some of the records in the charts felt different . . . stuff like Paul and Barry Ryan. The records that really started to get me going were "Everlasting Love" and "Rainbow Valley" by the Love Affair. I'd listen to the sounds and think, Wow. I suppose that was the beginnings of me picking out the bits in these records that were filmic and cinematic.'

Elsewhere, Alan Rankine's teenage energies were channelled into tennis, a sport for which he displayed a natural skill that earned him a place in the finals of Junior Wimbledon ('I didn't get to go because I used to wet the bed and I was too embarrassed'). On moving to Glasgow with his parents at the age of fifteen, the young guitarist would find it difficult to build friendships with other musicians, since the second guitarist in many groups he rehearsed with viewed his prodigious talents as something of a threat. 'When I'd play,' he once said of the discovery of his relatively enhanced musicality, 'they'd just stand agape.'

Now on the books of an Edinburgh-based agency, Sclater/Mayer Management, Caspian found themselves looking for a singer. Co-director Ian Sclater remembers the day that he filled out classified 'Vocalist Wanted' ads for the three major music papers of the time – *Sounds, NME* and *Melody Maker*. The envelopes were lying in the office's out-tray when Rankine arrived to say that the ads wouldn't be necessary: they'd discovered the name of that impressive singer from Dundee, he'd already auditioned, swallowing his hatred of hippies to offer up a nape-tingling a cappella take on Clare Torry's near-transcendental vocal solo in Pink Floyd's 'Great Gig In The Sky' – and effortlessly bagged the job.

'The Billie Holiday thing was definitely there in his voice at that time,' Rankine recalls, 'but Bill could sing anything. You'd say, sing "Bohemian Rhapsody", and he could do it. And then he would go into a Sparks song. The octave-leaping thing was there from the start.'

'I met Alan through a friend of a friend who said I was a great singer but a pain in the arse,' Billy said, years later. 'Someone mentioned that there was an all right little soul boy singing up in Dundee – I used to sing Motown and Smokey Robinson things to all these vicious Bob Seger lovers.'

'He hated musos,' Rankine explains, 'and if someone was a muso, he just couldn't talk to them. I think there was a lot of that with Bill and the musicians in Dundee. They couldn't see where he was coming from and he couldn't relate to them. So a lot of the time he was probably looking for an outlet, but never finding it.' Within two days of the audition Billy had taken up semi-permanent residence on the couch in the front room of the flat Rankine shared with his girlfriend in Linlithgow.

There followed six months of trawling around working men's and miner's social clubs or the glitterballed dancehalls of local hotels. For tax reasons, at one stage the group were operating under at least four different names. One night they would deliver a pop set as Hideaway, the next they would be the balladeering Mike Lawrence Quintet. The loungey nature of the latter musical set-up appealed greatly to Billy. In neat, round-collared shirts and ungainly clogs, the easy listening combo would perform Burt Bacharach and Perry Como standards and even a tongue-in-cheek version of the Beatles' 'The Fool On The Hill' set to a bossa-nova beat. Their deceptively clean image had a special appeal among the middle-aged female members of the audience, with whom the singer and guitarist would, of course, flirt outrageously.

Soon Billy and Alan, still only nineteen and eighteen respectively, were both taking home around £100 per week, an enviable pay packet for the average late-teenager in 1976. Whatever was left after the lavish and prolonged drinking sprees that would inevitably mark the close of any gigging night was shrewdly ploughed back into new equipment.

'It was quite a mature view, considering how young they were,' Ian Sclater reasons. 'Most bands just don't really think it out.'

Increasingly displaying more of the entrepreneurial spirit of his upbringing, Billy had talked his father into setting him up in the lucrative business of the high-fashion 70s boutique – by no means an enterprise that would experience much stiff competition in the Dundee of the time. Situated in a prime location on the gradual winding slope of Princes Street, which leads down into the town centre, The Crypt soon became the centre of fashionable activity for the Dundee hipster. Bearing a mock obsession with all things grisly or macabre and featuring both a stuffed snake and a mongoose, the shop took up an entire three floors, with the changing rooms – coffin-shaped – in the basement.

The idea had first occurred to Billy when, after placing a small ad in the local paper looking specifically for menswear from the 1920s, he had been surprised by the level of response for what had essentially been an exercise in adding to his personal ward-robe of antique clothing. Much of the initial stock for the shop was accumulated in this way, with the emphasis on Italian casual wear of the 50s. 'It was all 50s suits and trousers,' Billy said. 'There was a big market for them in a place like Dundee because there were a lot of soul-boy types who would be really into all those cuts. We used to be able to get £20 or £30 for a pair of trousers back in 1976.'

In time, through his understanding of his customers' tastes, and possibly imagining a marked increase in profits, Billy began sketching his own designs, employing a sweatshop in Leeds to produce the garments. On frequent trips down to Yorkshire to collect this more exclusive stock, often followed by intensive buying sessions in London's West End, Jim MacKenzie marvelled at the canny ways in which his son would convince him to fork out for more stock than they'd originally intended to bring back home. 'I'd say, "Right, we're only spending so much money." But he'd get you to dig deeper. He could always get around you with a wee smile. As soon as you heard, "Hey, Dad, what d'you think? . . ." it was like, Oh here we go. And it was never just a pound or two, it was always thousands he talked about.'

One regular customer to The Crypt during this period was a student teacher, Christine Beveridge, who was to form a lifelong, if periodically volatile, friendship with Billy. 'The shop really was like nothing that I'd ever seen at the time,' she says. 'Me and my pals used to go in there as often as possible and it was just really to see him. I'd remembered noticing him before – in those days people didn't dress like him or look like him in Dundee. I couldn't wait to get my grant, so I could get back in that shop to spend all my money. Once I spent my whole grant in that shop and had to work in pubs for the rest of the term to eat.'

On one occasion when Beveridge and her friend Patsy were trying on clothes, Billy sauntered down to the basement to ask them out for a drink with his friend that night. The pair were secretly thrilled, although there would be a certain drama involved in the evening's events.

Arriving home after their night out, Beveridge remembers: 'I couldn't find my keys. My flatmate had arrived home earlier and so she let me in. I looked everywhere for the keys and still couldn't find them, so I decided that this whole night had really been a ruse to get this revolting cheap furniture that all the student flats were furnished with in those days, and what was going to happen was that he was going to come with a van when we weren't in and clear the house out. So I phoned the police.

'I sat there and waited, then there was a knock on the door. It was Billy, and he just said, "You forgot your keys." I'd left them in the pub. I had to confess what had happened. So when the police arrived, Billy answered the door and said, "Hi, I'm the burglar." I think Billy just thought that it was so outrageous, we were mates from then on.'

Later that night, as Billy sat on the edge of one of the girls' twin beds in their tenement flat, he serenaded them with the Billie Holiday standard 'God Bless The Child'. 'Then one day, he just turned up with his suitcase,' Beveridge recounts, 'and neither me or my friend commented on it – we just let him move in.'

His time spent living at 39 Lyon Street would provide an important step in Billy MacKenzie's social and musical development. At themed parties thrown at his suggestion, this proto-punk crowd would imbibe cheap amphetamine pills and listen to the kitsch 50s and 60s recordings of Matt Monro, Peggy Lee and Jeannie C. Riley. Alan Rankine often travelled to Dundee to attend these gatherings, but admits that he never felt truly comfortable at them. 'There was definitely a part of me that didn't connect with that. I always felt like I was a bit of a curiosity to them. I think they sensed that I didn't feel at ease. I didn't want to be in Dundee, I wanted to be in London or wherever working with Bill.'

If anything, the more scathing, merciless side of Billy's nature led him to take advantage of Rankine's feelings of isolation in Dundee. Future Associate Steve Knight remembers Billy first pointing the guitarist out to him in a local pub as if he was a stranger: 'Rankine was standing in the corner and Billy said, "Look at that cunt. Isn't he the ugliest bastard you've ever seen in your life?" And he was too, I had to agree. Rankine had sort of long hair and he had this Afghan coat on and he was just a mess basically.'

One night at Lyon Street, Rankine suffered an enforced make-over at the hands of the three flatmates. 'My pal Patsy happened to be a hairdresser,' Beveridge says, 'so the hair was cut and the Afghan coat had been torn apart and burned with lighter fuel and chucked out the window. Billy vomited on it to make sure Alan wouldn't go out and rescue it. But he scrubbed up quite well. He was a very good-looking guy, Rankine. He had a very Valentino-ish look.'

As punk rock slowly began to infiltrate the provinces, the frustrated working-class youth, taking their cue from music-press reports, served to reshape the movement with a tougher, more committed edge. According to his friends from that time, Billy, while clearly identifying with the insanity of the whole affair, was never entirely comfortable with the fashions and philosophies of punk rock. In Dundee, as in most cities and small towns, it spawned a glut of frenetic new bands determined to stir up the local pub-rock scene.

One of these local groups, Bread Poultice and the Running Sores, fronted by a minor comic genius named Steve Falconer, would arrive on stage with a twisted, off-key version of Shirley Bassey's 'Big Spender', providing the suitably skewed accompaniment to the imminent arrival of their enigmatic singer. Falconer, parcel-taped into two black plastic bin liners, would be carried on by two of the band's roadies and dumped on the stage. Then, slashing through the plastic with a knife, he would emerge in front of the microphone with a full pint of lager in his hand, much to the rowdy appreciation of the crowd. Another of his gimmicks was to announce that in the next song he would play guitar with his teeth, in the style of Jimi Hendrix, before taking out his two false front teeth and using them as a plectrum.

Billy was regularly in the audience at these gigs, and one night at a jam session in a local arts centre where the Running Sores were to be the backing band, Falconer failed to show, having dropped acid and somehow ended up on a bus heading to the nearby town of Forfar. That night Billy first met the band's guitarist, Steve Reid, who, having earlier heard someone describe MacKenzie as having 'the greatest voice he'd ever heard in his life', invited him to become their replacement singer for the night. By all accounts, it was a shambolic affair, in which Billy was coerced into performing Fleetwood Mac's 'Black Magic Woman' and offered a band-less rendition of his first-ever, jazz-flecked composition 'Blue Soap', concerned with the un-likely topic of bath-time paranoia. By the end of the night, with the band quickly running out of material, the gig collapsed into an endless bluesy dirge with Billy improvising scat lyrics over the top.

Steve Reid was something of a character on the punk scene in Dundee, renowned for taking his tangential flights of imaginative fancy to more ridiculous, physical levels than anyone else dared. Around this time, with nothing better to do, he and his pack of unruly, lager-refreshed mates would go on what they liked to call Roy Orbison Marches, boisterously sauntering around the town shouting the words to 'Pretty Woman' and waving banners declaring 'The Big O Lives'. Of course, at the time, Roy Orbison was very much alive and well and living in Nashville, Texas, with his second wife Barbara. 'We thought he was dead,' Reid deadpans, 'but he wasn't. He just hadn't had a record out for a while.'

Through their sharing of this oblique sense of humour, Billy and Steve became friends, each egging the other on to new mischievous highs. When Stan and Deliver, now adopting a more punk-friendly stance, performed at Dundee's Duncan of Jordanstone Art College, the pair made a drunken attempt to sabotage their gig by switching the stage power off mid-set. Reid remembers: 'We said, Right, we'll pull their plugs out and then just run onstage. Billy ran out first, but the keyboard player jumped on him and they started rolling about on the stage. I ran on and tried to close the curtains and the drummer jumped on me. Eventually they got us off, turned the power back on and restarted their gig.'

At numerous house parties around the time, Billy began to develop a habit of using his voice to become the centre of attention, often standing up unannounced and belting out a 60s hit in the middle of the room. As a break from the alcohol-fuelled chaos and relentless pounding of Clash records in Steve's flat, Billy would take up a position on the sofa-turned-stage and sing a blues or jazz standard for the small mob of punks who would waste their days lying around the front room. Following a quick round of applause, the intense strains of Joe Strummer would fill the living room again.

Billy's relationship with his parents – who had suffered a brief split and reconciliation three years before – now found him increasingly intimidated by his larger-than-life father and growing devoted to his mother. According to Billy, Lily MacKenzie had once harboured desires to become a model or work in the fashion world, long forgotten once her children began to appear, and so she clearly admired the wild, creative streak in her son, who in turn would always try to include her in all areas of his social life. On one occasion when Edinburgh's 60s-sci-fi-fixated new-wave group the Rezillos played in Dundee, Billy persuaded his mother to come along with him and later proudly recalled her 'at the back of the hall pinching glasses of snakebite'.

Having begun writing songs together very soon after their initial meeting, Billy and Alan Rankine had developed a regular working routine which involved Billy closing The Crypt at five o'clock on a Saturday evening, jumping on the train to Edinburgh, catching a connection to Linlithgow and arriving around seven to begin a full night's drinking with his musical partner. Hung-over, they would spend every Sunday intensively writing songs. Rankine claims there was an instant musical bond between the two.

'I'd never had it with anyone else. You'd be listening to a record and something would happen in the music and we would look at each other and we understood each other. It could be a chord change, it could be a sound, it could be a trick that someone had used and you'd just connect and catalogue it away and know you're going to tap into that later on. We seemed to find the same things funny. The same things musically turned us on and the same things musically turned us off. We'd spend hours listening to things like Black Sabbath just to slag them off.'

Perhaps strangely, part of their inspiration lay in a nine-album box set that Rankine owned of easy-listening cover versions produced as a promotion for *Reader's Digest*. Featuring instrumental reworkings of film themes and popular hits, including orchestral takes on Bob Dylan songs and what Billy described as 'vibrant and bright early cartoon music', it turned them on to the possibilities of dramatic chord changes being matched with what they viewed as an askew humour. The first song they co-wrote was an unrecorded soul track, 'Johnny Come Home', which cribbed its title from the 1965 TV drama about a runaway teenager, *Cathy Come Home*, although their writing together would quickly veer off on a decidedly less commer- cial tangent that fused punk with Bacharachesque melodrama.

Backed by an assortment of Edinburgh session musicians, in late 1977 MacKenzie and Rankine booked into Craighall Studios in Edinburgh for session time paid for by Billy's father and recorded six wildly named songs – 'The Shadow Of Your Lung' (which lifted its middle eight from the crooner staple, 'The Shadow Of Your Smile'), 'The Luncheon Pack Of Rottenham', '2000 Years Of Mental Torture', 'Do The Call Girl', 'Schmaltz' and the succinctly titled 'You Better Mortice Lock The Door Before He Slips Out In The Night, Baby'. The tracks, mostly performed at an impossibly breakneck pace, document the beginnings of Rankine's frenetic, finger-sapping guitar style and the edgy, operatic vocal that would become Billy MacKenzie's trademark.

While for many years Billy would claim that this outfit was called the Abscorbic Ones – indeed most rock encyclopaedias list it as being the name of the duo's first incarnation – Rankine insists that this was purely an invention: 'The Abscorbic Ones was a fantasy band that Bill and I dreamt up to give ourselves a past.' Instead, for some time the duo traded under the more biographically embarrassing name of Mental Torture.

While these early demos revealed a talent for a vibrant punk pop, Ian Sclater, now managing his cabaret musicians' more ambitious efforts, admits that he felt a certain frustration with the results. 'I was pleased in that musically it was very good, but it didn't meet the objective, which was to come out with two or three singles. At the time, if you didn't have a single, you weren't getting signed. So Billy and Alan went in there and proceeded to disappear up their backsides.'

In tandem, Billy's working relationship with the other members of the cabaret band was becoming increasingly strained. At one gig, suddenly overwhelmed with hatred at the sight of the band's 'greasy-faced' bass player thrusting his pelvis in time to the music, Billy ran over to him, bit his leg and then exited the stage. In the van travelling back from gigs, Billy would play his cassette of Kraftwerk's *Autobahn* album, suffering the derisory comments of the other band members, who, he noted, were 'behaving like baboons'. In a memorable incident, one heated argument erupted into a full-on fight. 'I ended up pulling this guy's face out of the van,' Billy admitted, 'and smashing it in.'

From then on, effectively, Billy MacKenzie and Alan Rankine's cabaret days were over.

In March 1978 Billy turned twenty-one, the event celebrated with a function held at the Ballinard Hotel in Broughty Ferry, an upmarket waterfront suburb of Dundee. Encouraged to sing even at his own birthday party, Billy and Alan Rankine agreed to perform a cabaret set in support of the hired headlining act, a female singer colourfully named Little Miss Dynamite whose act the guitarist recalls largely consisted of her 'shaking her arse around'. On the night, Billy suffered his first serious attack of the pre-gig stage fright that would remain a recurring problem throughout his performing life. After fortifying himself with generous measures of Pernod and blackcurrant, minutes before the pair were due onstage he vomited over the edge of the spiral staircase that led to the attic dressing room, providing an unsavoury decoration for the cigarette machine that lay below.

During this period, Rankine admits, he felt increasingly un-settled during the time he spent in his collaborator's home town. 'Dundee at that time seemed more violent than even Glasgow,' he explains. 'There was just this thing where you didn't make eye contact with people. I had a colouring – all I know is that I'm an eighth Danish and it must be a throwback from something – so people always thought I was Italian or Spanish. I always felt that if anyone was gonna get picked on in Dundee, it was gonna be me. So I never made eye contact with anyone.'

Billy's attitude towards violence at this stage reveals one of the many contradictions within him. While flighty and camp in his mannerisms when around those he felt comfortable with, he would never shy away from confrontations and could easily adopt a tougher exterior. 'Bill was totally street-wise then,' Rankine says. 'He knew what he could and what he couldn't do. At the time I'd go to parties in Dundee with him where there'd be a fight and Bill would end up lashing out all over the bloody place . . . but only in a restraining way. He seemed to know what was necessary, but he always said he couldn't stand it.

'I can remember one time in The Crypt when a couple of guys came in and they were obviously there to see what they could nick or whether they could hold up the till or something. I was shitting myself, but he faced them up. I think Bill knew that if anything started, I wasn't gonna do anything. But Bill was ready for it. He just faced these guys up and they backed off. It was just that half-threatening "What're you wanting, boys?" There was no argy-bargy, but it was very very tense.'

Billy once admitted: 'I can't stand in the same room as violent people without them riling me. But I couldn't do what other boys from our area would do – crush a bottle in your victim's face, and then go away without the slightest pang of guilt about it.'

In the early spring of 1978 Ian Sclater travelled to London to tout the Mental Torture demos around the capital's record companies. Largely the response was the one the manager had predicted: no one could hear a hit record. During one meeting with Chris Parry, a former Polydor Records A&R man who had signed both Siouxsie and the Banshees and the Jam, leading to the company funding his semi-independent offshoot label Fiction, Sclater felt he was at breaking point: 'I remember it was just me and him in his office. He was reading his copy of *Music Week* while the demo was playing, like they all do. I felt like just ripping it out of his hands and saying, "Listen you bastard, this is good stuff."'

But, despite his apparent lack of interest, Chris Parry was encouraged in particular by the guitars and vocals on the demo. The record boss played the cassette to Adrian Thrills, a journalist working for *NME*, on his car stereo as they drove back from a gig in Redhill, just south of London, after seeing the Cure, another band that the A&R man was becoming keen to sign to Fiction: 'I remember playing it to Adrian and saying, "This is a band I'm really interested in." He said, "Oh God, it *sounds* like bloody mental torture." To me it sounded exciting actually. I thought, Woah, a bit operatic. But it was also very searing and very different . . . and a mess of mad lyrics as well, and I tend to be a sucker for things that are a bit different. So I kept this tape as something very interesting. I had a sense that maybe I could develop something of it, but not for the immediate time. I just felt, let's see what happens. It was very early days.'

Nevertheless, Parry was sufficiently intrigued to pay for the group to return to Craighall Studios in Edinburgh, where, at his insistence, they reworked the potentially commercial new-wave stomp of 'Do The Call Girl' as well as recording a new power-pop number, 'Jukebox Bucharest', along with the manic fervour of 'Double Hipness' and frantic operatic rush of 'Logan Time'. The hugely stylized results were unlike much of the punk or new-wave music around at that point.

'We were too musical just to thrash around in the same way as all those other bands,' Rankine reckons, 'so all these influences were coming through. We would get this punky riff going and right in the middle of it, Bill would go off on a cabaret tangent . . . This was us finding our feet.'

Ian Sclater clearly remembers being more encouraged by this second batch of recordings: 'They'd learned their lesson from the first time round, and they came out with a batch of songs that were three minutes long with some single material in there.'

At a late 1978 showcase in Laing's, the same Dundee bar where Billy had performed with Stan and Deliver two years before, Mental Torture were publicly unveiled at a gig intended to be a showcase for record companies. Although they delivered a blistering performance in which Billy reportedly blew three microphones in succession through the sheer energy of his untrained vocal, Parry – really the only interested party – failed to show.

Their days were spent rehearsing in a corner of the vast carpet warehouse owned by Billy's uncle, and the group – now augmented by Steve Knight on bass and Euan Parry on drums – often benefited from the financial input of Billy's father. Still, they were plainly amazed one afternoon when a spirited Jim MacKenzie arrived back from the pub and insisted that he take them down to Largs, the largest musical equipment shop in Dundee at the time, where they were to pick out a whole new backline of guitars, drums and amps at his expense. Steve Knight recalls the following morning when the new equipment was delivered: 'We were all going mental using all this new gear, and then this guy came in and said [to Billy], "Ah your dad's changed his mind – he was pissed . . . it's all got to go back." So we were back to the old shitey gear again.'

If the musicians had allowed Billy to follow every one of his musical whims back then, there would more than likely have been no equipment left working at all. A recurring notion of the singer's at the time involved filling the drums with water to achieve a uniquely sploshy effect.

'We'd hired this really groovy drum kit,' Knight notes, 'and he suddenly came through with a big hosepipe and said, "I don't like the sound of the drums, I want to fill them up with water." Of course, we just said, "Are you fucking mad?" See, Billy was hard to work with then because he had absolutely no musical knowledge at all. If he was trying to get you to do something in particular on the bass, he'd try to describe it by saying something like, "Give me a brassière from Marks & Spencer." It's funny because the longer you worked with him, the more you got to know what he meant.'

Having missed the Laing's gig, Chris Parry travelled up to Dundee to watch Mental Torture play for him in the carpet warehouse, Billy having hired in an enormous, ear-shredding concert PA especially for this key rehearsal. Parry recalls that Billy's father adopted a protective stance as they watched the group nervously perform their short set: 'I remember him saying to me, "You gonna look after them then?" I said . . ."Yeah I'll look after them, do what I can, but being a recording artist is one of those careers where there's nothing certain at the end of the day." I thought they were a couple of interesting characters, though. Alan was quite a swarthy, handsome guy and Billy was completely . . . mental, really . . . all over the place. It was fantastic.'

Although impressed, Parry suggested that MacKenzie and Rankine should ditch the rhythm section. Naïve and over-keen, they agreed. Steve Knight recalls the moment that the duo sheepishly announced that they were sacking both himself and the drummer from the band: 'That was very tearful. I remember being in Billy's kitchen in Bonnybank Road and they were saying, "Ah well, man, it's showbiz." I just said, "OK, fair enough."'

Shortly afterwards, worried about his own future and growing impatient with the sluggish progress, Sclater resigned as the band's manager. 'I suppose I jumped before I was pushed,' he reasons, pointedly adding, 'they weren't above using people.'

Attracted by Parry's offer of free recording time in Morgan Studios in London's Willesden, the duo decamped south to Billy's relatives in Clapham. Although broke and frequently unhappy during this time – Christine Beveridge recalls that Billy would often 'get drunk and cry on the phone basically . . . he never liked being away from home' – it was to be a creatively productive time. Bandless and without the means to hire session musicians, the pair would experiment with hitting plastic chairs and bags to build up drum beats, slowly working through a variety of songs they'd begun stockpiling back in Scotland. It was here that one day, as both were chatting over a urinal in the toilets at the studio, that Billy suggested the Associates as an alternative name for their outfit, having been inspired by his own enquiry as to what Parry's publishing company APB Music – Association of Parry (and partner, Monty) Babson – actually stood for.

While Parry could see that this outfit now calling themselves the Associates were developing rapidly, the label boss doubted their commercial potential. Much to the urgent young duo's frustration, Parry admits he was reluctant to sign them to either his label or publishing company and kept them hanging on: 'Yes, I did to an extent . . . I was deliberately keeping them on a bit of a line . . . not giving them what they wanted. They wanted to be signed with salaries, and I was saying, "Look . . . be cautious, give it a bit of time." To be honest, I had difficulty trying to figure out what to do with them. I had times where I thought they were crash-hot and times of despair where I wasn't sure about it at all. It was just a bit different to everything else, and I didn't know whether I could get this thing going.

'Billy was just so intense – he wanted everything right there and then, and I was a bit worried that I couldn't deliver all that. I tried to get him to understand that this wasn't going to happen overnight. He tried to get to me to understand that it was the only way it *was* going to happen. He was sort of very butterfly-like, it was difficult to pin him down, but he wanted fame badly, he wanted success *now*.'

The Associates, for their part, were growing weary of arranging meetings the Fiction boss would be too busy to attend.

'Parry used to exasperate us,' states Rankine, 'because it was all so blasé. But we were desperate to make a record. We could feel it boiling up inside us and we had to get an outlet . . .'

4

Plan 2

As agitation turned to quiet despair, in 1979 the Associates found themselves hatching what appeared to be a hare-brained plot to somehow attract attention to their efforts. In May of that year, with the first single culled from *Lodger* – the final instalment in what was subsequently known as his Berlin trilogy of albums – David Bowie released the insistent art-rock pulse of 'Boys Keep Swinging', which effectively ended a commercially barren period for him when it peaked at number seven in the British charts. Before the single had even begun its descent from the Top Ten, though, the Associates had already decided to cover the song and release it as their first, self-financed single, with one arch twist – they wouldn't bother seeking the approval of the rock star's music publishers.

Having returned, deflated and disillusioned, to Edinburgh, where they rented a communal flat in Elgin Terrace following their brief time spent – as they viewed it – dangling on the whims of Chris Parry in London, Billy MacKenzie and Alan Rankine had been humbly forced to re-employ the services of the rhythm section the label boss had advised them to sack. Once again dipping into the resources of Billy's father, the Associates returned to the studio, originally with designs on releasing a rendition of Barry Ryan's gothic 60s hit 'Eloise'.

According to bassist Steve Knight, the idea of the Bowie cover first came from Billy, and struck the rest of the band as slightly ludicrous: 'He said, "Why don't we cover that and not get permission for it? Then maybe somebody'll get in touch with us and like it.'' I thought it was crazy, so did Rankine, but Billy got his dad to pay for the whole thing.'

In keeping with the spirit of cottage-industry punk, 'Boys Keep Swinging' was issued on the Associates' own independent imprint Double Hip in June 1979 with a pressing of 500 seven-inch singles, and distributed by the band on foot around the trendier record shops in the Scottish capital at the time, including Bruce's (owned by Simple Minds' manager Bruce Findlay) and Ripping Records. Through the former's standing as a sales return shop for the sketchily compiled independent charts of the time, the Associates – on the strength of having sold only one copy of the single, as local folklore would have it – made a début showing at number fifteen in *Record Mirror*'s Scottish chart in the week of this modest release.

Ronnie Gurr, then living in Edinburgh and working as a free-lance live reviewer for *Record Mirror*, was confounded by the single. 'Why they did "Boys Keep Swinging" was beyond me,' he states. 'I hadn't heard their version because nobody was playing it, but I thought, What a bizarre thing to do. I just thought they were a pub covers band, which was in keeping with what I knew of Alan's past. It was so close to Bowie's release to be almost pointless, unless this band were a chicken-in-the-basket thing. But it probably flagged up the perversity of what they were about at a very early stage.'

Although sorely lacking in decent production values, with wafer-thin drum beat, rattling bass and tinny guitar sound, 'Boys Keep Swinging' reveals itself to be a pacier, if slightly flowery-chorded reworking. But Billy's voice – so high up in the mix that it dwarfs the gentle musical patter surrounding it – is as rich in vibrato and resonance as any of his subsequent recordings, sweeping from baritone to falsetto in the space of one short line, and leading Bowie's original interpretation on a merry dance in both its unaffected lunacy and unstudied technical precision.

In support of the release, the Associates played their first gig under this new trading name at the Aquarius Club in Edinburgh's Grindlay Street, with much of the Scottish 'indiescenti' in atten-dance. Reports suggest that this was the first public airing of the fleetingly manic live persona of Billy MacKenzie, an act that involved him throwing himself around the stage and violently shaking as if in the throes of some severe epileptic fit, while the rest of the band stood stock-still around him. Paul Haig, who had recently formed the influential Postcard Records band Josef K, was in the crowd that night. 'We went along to see them and thought they were amazing,' he recalls. 'They all had red shirts on and Billy was dead physical, the guitar was a wall-of-sound and the tracks were different from anyone else. They didn't really adhere to any other musical movement at the time.'

Ronnie Gurr remembers: 'When they walked out, I said, "Where do I know that guitarist from?" Somebody said, "He was in Caspian", and I was like, "Oh for fuck's sake." I'd seen Alan in the appalling Caspian and what was so remarkable was his reinvention. I wasn't expecting much, but then they dug in and they were extraordinary. For me it was an absolute revelation. They weren't the tightest of bands, but they threw themselves at you.'

Within weeks Billy's seemingly ridiculous plan was miraculously beginning to work. On hearing 'Boys Keep Swinging' aired on John Peel's late-night Radio One show, a publisher with a part interest in the Bowie song, Hal Shaper of the Sparta Florida Music Group, managed to contact the Associates. Billy later recounted the substance of this phone call with no little bravado: 'Bowie's publisher phoned up and said, "You're causing me a lot of trouble" and I said, "So what?"' Nevertheless, interested in 'Mona Property Girl', the Associates-penned B-side of the single, Shaper invited the band to London for a meeting in which he enquired whether they had any other songs. MacKenzie and Rankine, eager to have any real contact with the music industry, naïvely proceeded to assign twenty-six song titles – none of which the latter claims they ever provided tapes for – to Sparta Florida. The duo hadn't even considered asking for a publishing advance.

Through Sparta Florida, however, 'Boys Keep Swinging' was licensed by the American-founded record company MCA, providing the Associates with their first major label British release, albeit in the slight form of 500 water-testing promotional seven-inches, destined to become even more obscure than the Double Hip pressing. An unfussy photo session was arranged with the four members posing in the back of a London cab and the mail-out of the single was accompanied by a shoddy, hastily written MCA press release, revealing only the most essential details of the outfit's history and displaying their reluctance even at this stage to divulge too much of their recent musical past:

'A sparse New Pop version of Bowie's "Boys Keeps Swinging" recorded by a Scottish quartet who started out performing Billie Holiday standards in Edinburgh Chicken In The Basket And A Bottle Of Corrida joints? Yup, and here's why:

'"We did it to get into trouble without getting too heavy. Shock tactics," pleads Associates vocalist Bill MacKenzie (22). And the Thin White Duke may well be pleasantly surprised by the version of his recent hit . . . Bill MacKenzie and guitarist Alan Rankine (21) have been writing songs together "for years". They are both self-taught musicians and were forced into the cabaret circuit by that wonderful euphemism, financial embarrassment. The duo met Stephen Knight (22) 18 months ago and only found their current drummer, 16 year old John Sweeney, a mere 4 months ago.

'With tongues placed deftly in cheeks, [they] number their influences as Gary Glitter, Billie Holiday, Simon Dupree, Jeannie C. Riley, Mantovani, Jack Jones and Sixties film music (especially *Room At The Top*) . . . They'll only go as far as saying, "We love melodies" when asked to define their music, but a wee dram elicits the descriptions "animalistic" from Bill and "very sexual" from Alan.'

Back home in Scotland, where the news of the record deal was magnified and glamorized in the perceptions of their peer group, the Associates were now considered to be on the verge of an imminent success. Shortly after Rankine had buckled under the weight of parental pressure and enrolled for college, the *Linlithgow Gazette* ran an article with a photograph of the four seated around a pub table – Billy pulling a dimpled, impish face – and a typically sweeping headline: 'Alan And Associates On The Road To Stardom'. 'This deal is a great break which could lead to better things,' Rankine is quoted as saying in the feature, 'but we've no idea what the future prospects will be.'

In their first experience of the promotional rigmarole that eats up much of the average recording artist's working schedule, a day of regional press interviews held at the Albany Hotel in Glasgow was swiftly organized by MCA. Rankine remembers their publicist fawning over the American rocker John Hiatt, who was staying at the hotel and generally ignoring the Associates: 'You didn't feel that these people cared about you at all.' Instead MacKenzie and Rankine managed to manoeuvre their way into the company of Billy Connolly in the hotel bar and ended up getting uproariously drunk with him on Black Russian cocktails.

When Chris Parry learned of the Associates' sudden involvement with both MCA and Sparta Florida, he was apparently furious. By testing the level of interest he had shown in MacKenzie and Rankine, he now realizes that the pair in effect forced his hand: 'Did they bloody ever!' Perhaps then, it is an indication of Parry's powerful standing in the London music industry of the late 70s – and the weakness of the contracts MacKenzie and Rankine had signed – that within weeks both deals had been terminated, although Sparta Florida would retain the rights to the songs they had acquired. Fiction Records offered the Associates a five-album term that included a weekly retainer of £25 for each of the group's two songwriters and a publishing contract with a token advance of £100. Still, for the duo – and in particular Billy, who had led this conniving attack – there was a certain feeling of vindication: 'We went to Chris Parry and said, "Look, you've got to get us out of this, get off your arse." We used Bowie's publisher to kick Parry up the bum and that's how we got on Fiction.'

The relationship, however, got off to a decidedly shaky start. Undergoing the toughening-up process that most pre-début album acts are forced to endure, following a warm-up support date in Hull with Siouxsie and the Banshees, Parry sent the Associates out on the road as part of a Fiction package that included the Cure and the Passions, who would enjoy a lone hit two years later with 'I'm In Love With A German Film Star'. The tour, as it transpired, was a disaster. Parry's analysis of the problem again pointed to the Associates' rhythm section, and in the fallout from the band being taken off the tour after only fourteen dates, bassist Knight blamed the lack of drumming experience of the sixteen-year-old John Sweeney: 'He'd start things really fast and at the end of it, he'd be really slow. The band was falling to pieces.'

In addition, both Billy and Steve Knight had begun an emotional tug-of-war over the attentions of the former's ex-bandmate Angela Forbes, now taking care of The Crypt while the shop's owner devoted his time to music. According to the bass player, this growing mood of conflict and unease erupted in a fist-fight between the two one night in Bradford: 'It was a *ménage à trois* that wasn't going to work out. I'd fallen totally in love with Angie to the point where I wasn't caring about the band as much as I should've, and that's what eventually led to me parting company with the Associates. It was really the worst mistake.'

Parry, for his part, had decided that perhaps the Associates' strengths lay in other areas. 'It became obvious to me as we went along that this was a band of a searing creativity,' he admits, adding, 'but they were never that great touring.'

'The venues were really seedy and we were playing with terrible equipment,' Billy later said, in dismissing this first concentration of live work. 'It was like playing your favourite single with a clapped-out needle.'

The bedtime routine involved a single bed and a fur coat, and the two musicians would take turns – one getting the mattress, the other stuck with the coat and the bed's hard base. In the long, cold winter that heralded the dawning of the 1980s, MacKenzie and Rankine, reduced once more to a musical duo, were broke and sharing – according to the latter – the 'fucking freezing' spare room of Chris Parry's father-in-law's house in Victoria, following a lodging stint at the label boss's home in Watford, where, since Parry was often away from home on tour or in the studio with the Cure, it was often left to the Fiction head's then wife to keep a watchful eye over her husband's new investment. While most of their days were spent at Morgan Studios working on exploratory demos, the pair were often forced to walk miles across London to the Willesden recording facility since neither could raise the tube fare.

At this stage they hooked up with Michael Dempsey, the former bassist with the Cure, who had quit the group the year before on the brink of their success, due to increasing friction with his former schoolmate Robert Smith. To the two working-class Scots, the middle-class Dempsey proved something of a curiosity with his roundly vowelled tones and relative air of sophistication. For his part, the bassist admits that becoming caught up in the creative whirlwind of the MacKenzie/Rankine partnership served as something of a crash course for him in the experimental possibilities of music, as opposed to the relatively straight guitar pop of his previous band.

'Billy could play instruments in a strange way,' he explains. 'He would just put his hands down on the piano and something would come out of it. Whether he could repeat was another matter. Alan was the opposite – he was a well-honed mature musician right from day one. I was very much in awe of what he could do, but looking back on it, he would just devise a system, a way of handling any instrument. He was a very complete musician without being too forced.'

As arrangements were being made for the Associates to begin recording their début album for Fiction, however, it was mutually agreed that Dempsey was perhaps not yet ready for the task, and that the duo would make the record alone, with Rankine playing all instruments ('Winging it all the way,' he says) except drums, which were to be provided by a session player. Preliminary sessions began in the first week of April and a certain obsessional intensity in the pair's working methods became apparent even in the initial days. Their creative synergy seemed to work on counter-balance; Billy presenting a relentless torrent of off-kilter and often unworkable ideas, like a firework ricocheting around the walls; Rankine acting as the foil to dissect and interpret these, meld them to his own and then tear around from guitar to bass to piano to marimba.

Employing the unusual system of recording everything to a cheap club organ-styled beatbox with the drums to be added later, the pair began to multi-layer heavily effected instruments and playful sonic trickery to create the tracks that formed *The Affectionate Punch*. The tape might be slowed down to record marimba parts that, when played back at normal speed, would sound almost humanly impossible to play. The beat could be the sound of Rankine kicking his guitar amplifier to rattle the reverb spring inside. When the session trumpet player turned up pissed, it was agreed that he might offer a more unusual performance in his inebriated state.

At this stage, Billy and Alan still considering drugs to be a criminally hippie distraction, these sessions were fuelled on adrenalin alone, although the pair – staying in the vacant flat of a Fiction secretary – would knock themselves out every night with a shared bottle of the potent whisky liqueur Drambuie. Although the Associates were clearly revelling in at last being given the run of the studio, co-producer Mike Hedges, who had recently cut his teeth at the production helm of the Cure's début, *Three Imaginary Boys*, sometimes attempted to rein them in. 'I don't think Mike knew quite what to make of us,' Rankine says. 'We were very very Scottish. Mike was just coming onstream and this was very different for him because the Cure had probably only used about nine tracks. It was very simple, whereas it was everything but the kitchen sink with us right from the word go. There was a couple of times where Mike said, "No, I'm not doing that." We just stood our ground and he backed down.'

In one memorable experiment, the duo enlisted the services of a session-fixer to find them a bagpipe player to play on the brooding ballad 'Logan Time'. Rankine laughs as he recalls, 'This guy turns up in a fucking kilt! And he says to us, "What key's the song in?" I told him it was G and this guy says, "Well, I can only do it in B flat or E flat." So we tried slowing the tape down and it was like, "Oh, for fuck sake, he's never gonna get this, he's just playing bollocks." So we got an amalgamation of what he did and stuck it at normal speed and then said to him, "Just play anything." Then we mashed it up with echo and buried it in the drone of the song.'

At Billy's suggestion the pair endured a torturous night-time photo session on the running track in the grounds of Wormwood Scrubs prison for the cover of the album. According to Rankine, Billy's sleeve concept had simply been 'Let's be wet and let's be running', and so, decked in white Adidas vests and shorts, the pair were constantly showered with cold water to create the desired perspiratory look. The cover of *The Affectionate Punch* depicts Rankine crouched in the starting-block position with Billy standing to his left, his expression intently concentrated on the command of some imaginary whistle. As a visual metaphor – the beginning of a race that both seem fiercely determined to win – it offers a striking image for a début album, as well as providing the intended undertones, since MacKenzie would often reveal a certain pride in his and Rankine's athletic backgrounds, of striving for the Olympian ideal. But it was to prove the crux of their first major disagreement with Fiction: the Associates insisted that the sleeve be in colour; the label claimed the budget would only stretch to black and white.

Released in August 1980, *The Affectionate Punch* created only a mild ripple of interest among record-buyers, with sales eventually creeping to around 10,000, although it would prove an admired and influential album among the Associates' new-wave contemporaries. While it suffers slightly from the over-compressed, boxy production standards of the time, the ten tracks that make up *The Affectionate Punch*, while aping early Roxy Music in the title track or offering the straightahead rock of 'A Matter Of Gender', are consistently knocked off the more predictable course by a pioneering musical twist or the edgy, elastic, excitable vocals of MacKenzie, shrieking in falsetto one minute, seductively crooning the next. Rankine's guitar work was minimal and semi-detached in its execution, from the intricate mesh of simple notes in 'Paper House' (a style that subsequently surfaces as a recurrent feature in the playing of U2 guitarist the Edge) to the sharp, staccato runs of 'Deeply Concerned' and the epic wash of reverb that ghosts the guitar in 'Logan Time'.

Lyrically, MacKenzie was developing an interest in exercising with words in a free-associated style, which resulted in couplets that were largely impenetrable, even to his partner ('I have to say that sometimes I didn't know what the hell Bill was singing about') and revealed much character in terms of the singer's obtuse imagination, but actually very little of himself. In the alphabet-contorting, breakneck chant of 'A', there are hints of abstract sexual playfulness ('I've known Zeds who've only taken Bs to bed') and in 'A Matter Of Gender' a theme of Catholic guilt and an affair with the fictitious Marguaritte, a married woman ('Thou shalt not commit the seventh commandment/Don't let slip my name while you're making love'). The character in 'Logan Time' – the title was inspired by *Logan's Run*, the 1976 sci-fi film of a Utopian society where the inhabitants are ritually slaughtered at thirty – whose 'voice deep with age talks in tongues of younger days' is weary and aching with the distance of time, while 'Transport To Central' even dangerously toys with Aryan imagery ('His jawline's not perfect, but that can be altered').

For the most part, however, the lyrical accent is on the angular or eccentric, throwing up references to surgeons and naval fleets, manors and brown-peppered mattresses, nervous coughs and levitation.

In their preparation to tour in support of *The Affectionate Punch*, MacKenzie and Rankine assembled a new Associates line-up around Michael Dempsey and drummer John Murphy, an Australian who had arrived in London that summer and taken up residence in a squat in Maida Vale. Generally described as a 'scrawny, Pigpen-type character' by those who knew Murphy at that time, the drummer would mooch around Morgan Studios in a dirty old raincoat with a Burroughs paperback poking out of the pocket. As a result of the influence of his jazz-drumming father and his friendship with Nick Cave's gothic punk outfit the Birthday Party – who had also recently decamped to London – his drumming style was skippy and erratic and perfectly suited the Associates. Still, Murphy's hard-line punk friends ribbed him for playing in what they viewed as a pop-rooted band and the musician was often slightly embarrassed by his presence in the Associates.

But Rankine remembers that the group adopted Murphy, almost in the nurturing sense of the word: 'He had a great style about him, but we said to him, "John, this stuff's gonna take a lot of stamina and we think you're a bit skinny, you need to build yourself up." We'd take him up to Morgan and we'd get this great big platter in front of him – steak, chips, salad. We did that for a couple of weeks, and we noticed that he still wasn't putting on any weight. Then we found out that if we saw him every three days, that was the only meal he was having.'

Throughout the summer this new line-up went through a process of bonding and solidifying their identity, driving around London in Dempsey's Vauxhall Chevette, resplendent in matching fur coats. However, when they were returning from a party in Croydon one night, their drunken antics turned dangerous, very nearly causing their premature demise. Each had been taking a turn at the wheel, giggling like schoolboys, when Billy insisted on driving. Dempsey remembers: 'For some strange reason it didn't strike me as odd, so we just went slowly down the road, started turning around the corner, and then it dawned on me – Billy can't drive. We started to get up faster and faster and he hit the kerb and just did a big circle, and I could see this large picket fence coming towards us. I was thinking, That's all right, it's made of wood. But typical of him, he found a section that had concrete bunkers behind it. So the car crashed into them and turned over. He hit his chest on the steering wheel. I went through the windscreen.

'I had to have twenty-one stitches in my face and Billy was so upset and apologetic and also, of course, in pain. We told the police I'd been driving and swerved to avoid a cat in the road. But we had these two policeman – one was very junior, the other was senior and it must've been the junior's opportunity to look after the incident himself. Fortunately, Billy managed to charm him and we got away with it.'

In the wake of this accident, the Associates moved up to Edinburgh, where they took a flat in Bellevue Avenue, blueprinting the communal arrangement that seemed to best suit Billy: the others could have their pick of the rooms, he was going to bed down on the sofa. 'In all the time I knew Bill,' Rankine says, 'he never had a bedroom in any of the flats we shared. It never occurred to us to get a flat with three bedrooms – it was always me in one, Demps in another and Bill on the couch. He just seemed to like it that way. He was definitely not a morning person, and although everything else was going on around him, he'd stay under his quilt until two in the afternoon, just as long as he had a good supply of tea. He used to drink about twenty-five cups of tea a day, to the point of it being manic. He just lay there with the telly or the music on.'

Michael Dempsey has his own view on Billy's contentment with this unorthodox flat-sharing set-up: 'I think it might have been so that he felt he was never stuck there, becoming too domesticated. Maybe it was also so that he could keep an eye on us from a central position and see all the comings and goings.'

Since neither the drummer or the bassist was receiving a retainer from Fiction, the latter's abiding memory of this period was of general poverty and permanent hunger. Rankine, luckily, had the option of making the journey to his parents' home in Linlithgow to supplement his diet. The Associates began rehearsing, following an unsuccessful search for a keyboard player – none that they auditioned could play even the most basic parts and as Dempsey notes, 'With Bill's sharply developed sense of aesthetics, a lot of people were out straight away just because of the way they looked or acted'. The outfit soon began touring around the alternative circuit of pub and club venues around Scotland, performing a repertoire that omitted the more ambitious cuts from *The Affectionate Punch* and included certain songs ('No', 'Nude Spoons', 'It's Better This Way') that wouldn't surface on record until two years later.

In Glasgow, however, where any vaguely alternative band were still considered to be anarchistic punk rockers, there were no venues to play. Following a gig by the Stranglers at the City Hall in 1978 where a stage invasion by the audience at the close of the set had been construed as a mini-riot by the authorities, punk was effectively banned from the Glasgow area. To compound this, the local licensing laws at that time prohibited pub landlords from charging admission if a band were booked to play their lounge – meaning there was no money to pay the acts – and stipulated that a seat be supplied for every member of the audience, making for a less than punk-friendly atmosphere. Instead, nearby Paisley became punk central and in the semi-legendary Bungalow Bar, Glasgow-based journalist and broadcaster Billy Sloan first witnessed the Associates live: 'What made them different was this guy's amazing voice. Up to that point, Scotland was full of very traditional rock singers – people like Alex Harvey or Frankie Miller – but he was nothing like that, he was more sort of . . . if anything, European.'

Dempsey recalls this period in the development of the Associates as markedly lacking in glamour: 'We played in some really appalling pubs and the music was very wild. It had a tremendous energy, really fast and frenetic, these complicated melodic songs. The reaction was varied: in some places it was terrible and in some places they went mad. At this time Billy was very much into performing, there was no kind of reluctance – although I do remember at the first gig, there was no sign of him and he turned up as we started playing the first song, making this very dramatic last-minute entrance on stage, much to Alan's chagrin. It was probably the only time in his life that Billy toured with any rigour and that was possibly because he felt comfortable that it was on home ground. He didn't really see it as touring, I think; he just saw it as driving around the Scottish countryside.'

In one incident that left a lasting impression on Rankine of the MacKenzies' reputation in Dundee and how it would occasionally ease potentially difficult situations for Billy, the Associates' van was pulled over by the police on the outskirts of Dundee in the early hours following a gig in Aberdeen. 'I think they were going to breathalyze us or search the van for drugs. They began asking for names and Bill said his and the policeman said, "Is that the MacKenzies from Bonnybank Road?" Billy said, "Yeah", and the policeman said, "Drive on."'

Having moved to a new location in a recently built shopping centre in Dundee, The Crypt was struggling to stay open under the pressure of a crippling weekly rent of £500. When Billy realized that the business was finally going under, he decided to go out in style, throwing a champagne closing-down party for his staff and the neighbouring shopkeepers.

Around this time, his younger brother John, who had been forced to spend the past eighteen months in a List D school in Glasgow following persistent truanting in Dundee, joined the Associates on tour, after Billy had convinced the school's head that he would gainfully employ his tearaway sibling as a roadie. 'I was like one of his whippets, a bit of security for him,' John MacKenzie reasons. 'He was a wee bit wild and if I was around, that safeguarded him from being too extreme. He would never get pissed because he thought that it would go back to our mum. I was his borderline that he couldn't cross.' As an indication of the brothers' playful relationship, on the night of John's seventeenth birthday, the Associates performed in Manchester and Billy corralled the audience into singing 'Happy Birthday': 'He started saying, "Where are you, John?" I'm standing there thinking, Fuck off . . . My face was totally beetroot.'

Touring life for the Associates naturally had its ups and downs. Four songs in at their first gig at London's prestigious ICA, Rankine, who had been suffering from food poisoning all day, was forced to dramatically leave the stage following a bowel-related emergency. At a ball-gown bash at St George's Hospital School of Medicine, in south London, where the Associates had secured a lucrative booking, Billy Sloan watched the band play to a swiftly dispersing audience, following an opening instrumental, 'Arrogance Gave Him Up', in which MacKenzie played a one-stringed guitar with a fork: 'Without exaggeration, if there was four hundred people there, about three hundred and seventy five of them left, totally freaked out, and the band ended up playing to literally twenty-five, thirty people.'

But in other areas the Associates were far better received, particularly during a month-long Sunday-night residency at London's Marquee club. Rankine recalls that at these shows, however, the band initially experienced a similarly muted response: 'It was unnerving because they wouldn't clap. They'd watch the set, gape the whole way through, and then they'd just go absolutely bananas at the end.'

At one support slot with Siouxsie and the Banshees at Hammersmith Palais, Billy managed to turn the audience's reaction around by facing up to them in a typically lurid and spectacular fashion. Midway through the set, furious that pockets of the crowd had been showing their lack of appreciation for the Associates by attempting to drown them in spit, Billy exited the stage, downed four Pernod and blackcurrants, came back on and projectile-vomited over the front rows. 'There was this shocked silence, they were totally stunned,' Rankine says, 'and then they started cheering. It was like, "Enough respect . . . this guy can really spew."'

The live reviews of Associates gigs that appeared in the music press at this time proved warmly favourable, if not ecstatic. 'A performance bleaker and more tense than the LP due to the absence of keyboards,' Clive Farrell wrote of a second appearance at the ICA in *Sounds*, 'the intricate guitar work formed a fine mesh over which the vocals popped, squeaked and soared. An impressive set which should improve when they learn to relax a little.' In *NME*, after attending a performance at the Rock Garden, Paul Du Noyer wrote: 'Mixing equal parts ham and genuine passion, Billy MacKenzie's amazing voice soars and swoops from a wobbly falsetto to a deeply effective boom capable of penetrating every corner . . . his voice is used more as an instrument, so you're better just standing back and enjoying the spectacle. Much of this stems from MacKenzie himself, who matches his gushing golden flow with exaggerated mannerisms reminiscent of an extrovert drunk playing at being Tom Jones on Saturday night.'

At times, Billy could be seen physically doubling up onstage through the sheer pain caused by the exertion of his singing style. 'That's because I have no wind left,' he admitted. 'It feels as if my heart's going to burst. The blood is just draining away from me.'

More and more, however, the Associates were beginning to feel that their efforts were in vain, with sales of *The Affectionate Punch* proving sluggish and the title track, released as a single, failing to even chart. On the band's arrival in any given city on tour, there would be no fly posters advertising their show to be seen. They had already been unhappy with the cut of the album, which to their ears sounded muddy when compared to the studio playback, and now this lack of success and promotional commitment from Fiction Records' parent label, Polydor, began to fuel their determination to make a break. Somehow, they decided, they would have to free themselves of their contract and find another deal.

Accordingly, overnight the Associates became stubbornly uncooperative when it came to any of Chris Parry's suggestions, causing the label boss to amusingly brand them 'multi-talented megalomaniacs'. Chris Carr, soon to become their publicist, also suggests that the Associates' rivalry with the Cure was partly to blame for MacKenzie and Rankine's subsequent split with Fiction in December 1980: 'Robert Smith *is* Fiction and as soon as the Associates in any shape or form started to compete, a certain line was toed by Parry. It was definitely Robert Smith that went in and said, We're not having it. I think Chris knew which side his bread was buttered on at the time, and had to kow-tow to that.'

Parry, for his part, claims that Fiction was underfunded and under-supported by Polydor at this point and experiencing financial turmoil: 'I felt that this band might be one too many and what I needed to do was to concentrate more on the recording career of the Cure, but keep a relationship with the Associates as a publisher. Billy and Alan came and said they wanted to get off the label and do their own thing – they thought they'd put out a really good album and that it should've done better. I just thought that if they really wanted to get off the label and we had such a fundamental difference about how this thing was going to pan out in the future, then it was probably for the best. I realized that it would've been a complete fucking nightmare trying to hang on to them anyway.'

Parry let the Associates go, and so, skint and label-less once again, they made a permanent decision not to go back on the road until – as Billy put it, highlighting his hatred of long-haired tour technicians and roadies – they could 'de-hippiefy' the organization.

5

Tell Me Elephants
Have Giraffe Necks

For Billy MacKenzie, being forced to live off his wits alone was never really a problem. Buying, selling, bargaining and scheming were instinctive, and so, following his lead, the duo slowly began to deal with the music industry on their own, wily terms. The first step in this markedly shrewder approach had prompted them to ask Fiction Records to pay six months' advance rent on a not inexpensive two-bedroom flat in Carlton Hill, St John's Wood, shortly before they split with the label. Deciding that the landlord of this nature of residential address would possibly be horrified by the notion of letting out one of his luxury apartments to a band – probably scabby punk rockers in his broadsheet-reading assessment – it was arranged as a company let by Fiction to house a few of their 'record producers'.

Variously described as 'ridiculously chi-chi' and 'a bachelor pad par excellence', it would be the first real indication of the Associates' developing penchant for expensive tastes, the prime feature in the lounge being a pearl-white grand piano. Of course, this existence was a vacuous sham and they were often forced to get up early in the morning to steal bottles of milk from doorsteps or nick a few rolls from the bread delivery left lying outside the local grocery. 'We were like something out of a Siberian camp,' was Billy's description of the Associates at this time. 'We'd roughed it for so long we were like lizards.'

A frequent visitor to Carlton Hill, Sunie Fletcher, then working as a journalist for *Record Mirror*, bears witness to how broke the

Associates were at this time: 'They were living on rice sandwiches. I used to buy them groceries sometimes because I was working, so we just became as thick as thieves and I used to as good as live round there. Alan had one room and Derek [Reid, roadie] and Billy shared the other bedroom, which, because they weren't pulling at the time, was nicknamed "The Room of No Desire".

'It was very seductive to me, all that camaraderie and to be part of a club. I remember Alan was lazy, indolent and because of his very very dark features, he was nicknamed Captain Dark or Mole. Michael Dempsey was lampooned as being frightfully English all the time and he really played up to that. John Murphy would be caught at parties eating leftovers out of people's old saucepans in the kitchen and Billy was . . . mad, very very happy a lot of the time, oblique in his approach to things. He'd kind of go off at tangents in conversation and come out with unexpected things. Real *joie de vivre.*'

Having been taken under the wing of publicist Chris Carr, who was at that time running one of the trendier PR firms for pop and alternative bands in London (with an enviable roster that included Siouxsie and the Banshees, Depeche Mode and UB40), the Associates, having nothing better to do, would hang out at his office on Kilburn High Road during the afternoons. In many ways the publicist was their only real lifeline to the music industry by then. 'Alan and Billy did have a rep for being scallies,' offers Carr. 'They weren't *entirely* unmanageable, but they already knew how to scam the industry to a certain extent, and I suppose they viewed me as someone who could help them do that. So it became loosely a business relationship, but like anything that you did with the two of them, they schemed . . . Billy was an arch schemer. Then it kind of turned from business and friendship into what I termed "The Grocery-Buying Years" because they were constantly skint and if they couldn't touch Parry up for publishing money, they came to me.'

A plot soon began to develop. Since most of the A&R personnel of the major record companies were aware of the fact that the Associates were no longer under contract to Fiction, there was some interest in the band, although initially it would stretch only to the labels footing the bill for studio demos of new MacKenzie/Rankine compositions. However, Peter Kent of the Beggars Banquet-funded independent Situation 2 had expressed an interest in doing one-off singles deals with the Associates, the terms of each release involving an advance of £3750 to cover recording costs. Weighing up their options, Carr and the Associates concocted an arch plan: they would use the demo time paid for by the majors to record the singles and deliver older, previously recorded songs to them; they would then give the new tapes to Situation 2, and pocket the entire advance. If the scam dried up, they could put the squeeze on Chris Parry as their publisher for studio time and the records would still be costing them nothing to make.

Twelve-hour recording stints at Morgan Studio Two, running through from Sunday night to Monday morning, became the pattern. Perhaps as a result of this environment, the Associates' music began to take on a denser, darker feel, with Billy's voice growing edgier and more skewedly operatic, haunted by paranoia at certain points, unnaturally ecstatic at others. In the first of these labour-intensive sessions, the pair produced the noir electronic march of 'Tell Me Easter's On Friday', a tense, strident pulse of treated guitars and staccato synthesizers that in April 1981 became their first release on Situation 2.

Although making for heavy, distinctly uncommercial listening, 'Tell Me Easter's On Friday' garnered some plaudits in the singles columns of the music press. 'The Associates suffer from sounding a little too much like a certain Factory Records group [Joy Division],' the NME reviewer decided, 'however their endeavour is worth a mention for the mini-hearted bass pumping a constant heady beat, guitars and synthesizer embellishing without smothering too much of the melody.' The irreverent fortnightly pop magazine Smash Hits, perhaps listening to some other single than the Associates' most hard-line, left-field release to date, noted, 'The singer still gets a bit too close to Bowie's slightly crazed falsetto for comfort but the Associates have at least abandoned that harsh military backbeat in favour of a hazier, more spacious approach.'

In the first instance of the press being alerted to the fact that Billy MacKenzie was effortlessly capable of providing reams of entertaining, if teasingly evasive quotes, the Associates' singer said of the single in *NME*: 'It sounds like *Spartacus* to me . . . it wasn't anything to do with religion, it was just, "Tell me elephants have giraffe necks."' He later told *Melody Maker* that when recording the track, 'I was listening to the combination between Rankine's guitar and my voice and I had an orgasm . . . it just shows how much music can get me in a froth.'

Two months later, in June, the even darker 'Q Quarters' appeared, a mournful electronic track replete with acoustic guitar plucked from a Morricone soundtrack, synthesizer effects that emulated the eerie bleeps of a submarine deck and even phlegm-throated coughs providing the backing vocals. Over the top, in a cold baritone croon, MacKenzie delivered his blackest lyric yet, culminating in the vivid couplet: 'Washing down bodies seems to me a dead end chore/Floors me completely, beauty drips from every pore' – a reference to the gruesome task his grand-mother was forced to perform during the Second World War, although Billy would later claim that 'Q Quarters' was more specifically about 'egotistical politicians and corruption in Dun-dee'.

The music press began to warm to this rich, dark seam that the Associates were continuing to mine. 'Here's another of the Associ-ates' desolately beautiful records,' ran the *NME* review, 'a quietly moving account of the scene of some military disaster delivered in hushed tones to haunt the memory.' *Record Mirror*, in the lumpen mixed-metaphor writing fashion of the time, stated that 'Q Quar-ters' was 'a lucidly measured weave of delicacy and poise, Billy MacKenzie's seductive voice floating along the surface of a bottle-dark pool that spells mystery and unease.'

The engineer-turned-producer, Flood, whose credit roll in-cludes key work with U2, Smashing Pumpkins and PJ Harvey, was a nineteen-year-old studio teaboy during the recording of *The Affectionate Punch* and a first-time co-producer on the Situation 2 singles that came out of these Sunday-night sessions at Morgan. 'There was an element of chaos about those recordings,' he states.

'There'd always be half a dozen people there. The pair of them were full on, just hyper-creative and a good laugh. With Billy, of course, I just thought, Wow, what a voice, but I remember he would spoof-vomit . . . just as a big laugh, outside the door of the session. They were pretty fuelled and go-faster on the sessions and a lot of ridiculous things went on.'

The contradictory musical emotions expressed within these tracks, from speedy euphoria to gloomy introspection, might have revealed that drugs – in particular the serotonin rush of cocaine – had entered the picture by this stage. 'By the nature of the time of night, these sessions weren't all that clean,' Rankine admits. 'You'd get to three or four in the morning and you'd basically need it. Having said that, we were so green. One night we got a quarter of a gram of cocaine, and thought, Oh, that was quite nice. The next Sunday we got half a gram . . . The next Sunday, of course, we got a gram.'

Dempsey, 'not an instinctive drug taker' by his own description, says he disapproved of these dabblings with cocaine: 'I felt that it was massively predictable and we were getting tiny amounts of money, so spending it all in one night on drugs would be the reason we wouldn't eat for the next week. I was beginning to feel that we weren't doing what we should be doing to get ahead. We were working all night in the studio, which was fine, but the next day we'd spend in bed recovering from a whacking great hang-over and it was from nine o'clock to six o'clock that the decisions were made by the record company. We weren't picking up the phone until five-thirty when we were all coming to and their day was done. At the time I think Billy liked me being disapproving of it . . . Alan was just adventurous. But I was fairly pragmatic in thinking this was not going to get us very far.'

One night, in the absence of cocaine, MacKenzie and Rankine purchased two grams of speed to fuel the session. Normally this far cheaper and more potent drug, generally cut with other, more suspect chemicals, is difficult to ingest in large qualities, due to its potency and rougher, gut-rot quality. The Associates had never taken powdered speed before, and perhaps unluckily, they had managed to buy it in a purer form than normal. The nasal burn was negligible and they could take it as regularly as coke, unaware of the considerable difference in strength. By nine o'clock on the Monday morning, when Billy was still frantically attempting to record vocals and the celebrated keyboard wizard Rick Wakeman was knocking on the studio door to begin his daytime shift, the Associates were wired to the teeth.

Having also drank, in Rankine's estimation, around eight dozen cans of Fosters between them, the duo repaired to St John's Wood, scrabbling together the price of another case of lager *en route*. At home, when one of them returned from the bathroom to inform the other of his alarming discovery that a chief physical side-effect of speed is a shrivelling of the male genitalia, both freaked and began hyperventilating to the point of panic attack. Rankine then remembers Billy imposing an authoritative air of coolness and calm on these anxious proceedings, snorting the last eighth of a gram of speed in order to focus his thoughts, and shakily padding upstairs to a neighbour's flat to call an ambulance. When the hospital staff arrived, realizing this to be a recreational drug-related emergency, they informed the duo that if they could walk to the ambulance unaided, the police wouldn't be alerted. If not, they would. Naturally, the pair managed to walk those few short steps and were taken – if not exactly rushed – to nearby St Mary's Hospital.

'We thought we were gonna die,' Rankine says, grimly recalling this palpitating moment. 'We were shitting ourselves by this time, really in a bad way. The people look at you as if you do this every weekend and obviously, we didn't. The doctor gives you a lucidity test to find out how out of your tree you are. He says, ''What's your name?'' ''Alan Rankine.'' ''Where do you live?'' ''Fifty-two Carlton Hill, St John's Wood, London NW8''. ''Who's the Prime Minister?'' ''Uh . . . no fucking idea.'''

And so, over the next three days, the pair became in-patients at St Mary's, their heart rates constantly monitored.

''We can each see each other's heart machines,' Rankine continues, 'so you're lying there and every time someone else's heart rate goes up, you get nervous and *your* heart starts going. We had to endure this with no Valium – they wouldn't give us anything to calm us down. You haven't slept for at least forty-eight hours, you can hardly drink anything because your body's rejecting everything and you're hallucinating.

'Bill's lying there going, "Oh Holy Mary, mother of God, get me an oxygen tent, get me out of here." He's flipping. He's going, "I cannae breathe" and the doctor's saying, "Well, how come you're shouting at the top of your voice then?" The nurses would come in and give you a bed bath when your cock's tiny and say, "Good morning, hot rod."'

'We were just about dead,' Billy later said to *Melody Maker*. 'It was the first time I'd taken speed and I didn't know anything about it. We just . . . seriously overdosed. I just thought, This is OK, and then the next minute . . . I was a virgin, pharmaceutically. They never gave us anything. Freakin' out, man! For three days . . .'

As if attempting to capture this chaotic mood and sense of lost control on vinyl, the Associates' next single, 'Kitchen Person', released in August 1981, was their most demented recording yet. A manic, breakneck blending of jittery marimba, psychotic organ and molar-grinding guitar, the rhythm provided by the juddering of an electric typewriter at the end of its line and the vocal sung by Billy through the tube of a vacuum cleaner, it earned the duo their first *Melody Maker* Single of the Week (' . . . a vicious surge of a song . . . turns much of today's music inside out'). Aside from the heart-fluttering crisis, many of his friends and collaborators recall this as an idyllic time for Billy, with the simplicity of the transactions with Situation 2, the recognition the Associates were beginning to attract from the press and the quick-burn turnover of the releases amounting to a peak of creative satisfaction.

'That was the one time when he could do what he wanted to do,' Dempsey states. 'If you're used to the dignity-of-labour approach to making money – for him he had his shop in Dundee . . . he'd make the clothes, sell the clothes and move on to the next thing – the music industry normally doesn't work like that. But we'd be up all night, do an A- and B-side and then the next morning we'd take the masters to Beggars Banquet, they'd give us the money and we'd go and have some breakfast. Those singles were almost like magazine publishing in that respect – he wanted a bi-monthly edition, which is not a bad idea, but of course it exhausts the public.'

Working outside of the corporate umbrella, MacKenzie and Rankine found themselves in complete control of their output – Situation 2 never tried to interfere with their musical direction in the manner that most major-label recording artists are forced to endure, and the wider operation was very much run on a hands-on basis. Chris Carr says that Billy even developed a light-fingered way of controlling the group's approval over their promotional photographs: 'They would come in, and a couple of days later we'd go to the photo file if we were doing a press release or something. We'd think that everything was there – fifty of this, fifty of that – and the file would be empty. Billy had decided that he didn't like the shots after okaying them, and even though there were always four or five people in the office at any given time, somehow he'd manage to steal them.'

The promotion activity in support of these releases was sporadic, but never less than enthusiastically fulfilled. Appearing as guests on *The Music Week*, Radio Clyde's live record review slot anchored by Billy Sloan, MacKenzie erupted in mock anger when Rankine began to talk about guitar chords, making him promise that he would never inflict muso-speak on the listeners again, and managed to confound the host with his appraisals of the featured single releases.

'I can't remember which record we were playing at the time,' Sloan begins, 'but MacKenzie said, "You know that feeling you get when you eat twelve Cadbury's Creme Eggs one after the other? Well, that's how I feel having heard that record." Then later on in the same programme he said about another record, "You know when your mother takes you to the fairground and you're queuing up to go on the Ghost Train and you hear a record playing on the Waltzers? Well, that's what that record sounds like to me." As a live-radio host, there's not really an awful lot you can say to that . . .'

Throughout the summer of 1981 Billy was becoming a regular face on the London gig and club scene, the Associates' growing status always assuring him a place on the guest list. Often his cohorts in these after-dark shenanigans were his old punk-rock friends from Dundee, Steve Reid and Christine Beveridge, now a couple and living in a London squat, the latter teaching business studies at a secondary school. Around this time, the doily-on-the-head fashion excesses that would spawn the much-ridiculed New Romantic movement were springing up around London at themed club nights such as Le Kilt, Club for Heroes and Le Beat Route.

The trio's club nights would usually begin with them attending a gig, although on occasion Billy – an enthusiastic drinker, albeit one who could rarely handle its effects – would be virtually comatose by closing time, once falling asleep on top of a bus shelter in the Strand following an Echo and the Bunnymen gig. He was eventually rescued by Reid, who clambered up to wake him. At a performance by King Crimson guitarist Robert Fripp's avant-garde instrumentalists the League of Gentlemen, Billy, standing in the middle of the crowd, suddenly took it upon himself to begin wildly improvising vocals to accompany the music – harmonies loudly provided by Reid and Beveridge – his powerful voice undoubtedly acknowledged by the musicians onstage. 'Steve, Billy and I . . . there was a really powerful vibe between the three of us,' says Beveridge. 'That night was one of those moments where we all felt like we were immortal.' Around this time, MacKenzie even touted Reid and Beveridge's musical outfit Orbidöig to Peter Kent at Situation 2, resulting in a one-off release, 'Nocturnal Operations', on which Billy was credited for playing tubular bells. 'He really championed us,' Beveridge adds, 'but I used to find it embarrassing.'

The Associates, meanwhile, had moved on to the next phase of what was fast becoming a not entirely immodest master plan, generally thrashed out in afternoon-long meetings at the offices of Chris Carr. Having stockpiled songs from their productive early period of first writing together in the late 70s, MacKenzie and Rankine had now picked out two as potentially chart-friendly singles. One, 'Club Country', was designed to be a shimmering rush of a dance record, although it was rougher and more urgent in the demo form the duo recorded that summer. The other, 'Party Fears Two' had originally been written in 1979 around a sparkling piano riff that the pair imagined could almost be a jingle used to advertise soap powder on television. They instantly dismissed it as too commercial to use at the time. 'This was the tail-end of punk and it was too tuneful, too pretty,' Rankine explains. 'It wasn't hip at that time. But we knew, absolutely, without question that it could be a hit record.' Having gone through the working titles 'I Never Will' and 'Don't Make Me Do What The Atheists Do', 'Party Fears Two' found its name in a phrase coined by John MacKenzie after he witnessed two girls violently attempt to gatecrash a party in Dundee by hurling their stilettos through a window.

The demos of these two songs were creating serious interest within the music industry and the meetings with Carr would generally involve the Associates fantasizing about how they planned to deal with what they reckoned to be an imminent bestowing of money and power upon their shoulders. 'These brain-storming meetings would always start sensibly and then end up a bit of riot when Billy became bored,' the publicist remembers. 'They would degenerate as they got beyond the realms of possibility. Billy had grand designs – he would sit and talk about how much they were going to ask for and the cars they were going to be driving – and Alan would go along with him, and Dempsey would try to be the voice of reason. It's kind of commonplace now, but Billy wanted an Associates label and their own studio. He was talking about taking things to a level that very few other people at that time would've even considered.'

As their spokesman, if not their appointed manager, Carr trekked around the record labels with the four Associates in tow, and the appointments began to develop something of a ritualistic pattern of events. Possibly through nerves, Billy was often forced to run to the nearest toilet cubicle to throw up (legend has it that he was once caught short, splattering the shoes of the financial director of RSO Records), and then, when the group had settled down in the A&R man's office, mildly intimidatory tactics would ensue. 'We would sit opposite the record company bloke in a little semicircle,' Carr continues. 'Alan would then hand over the tape, sit cross-legged and go into this meditative trance thing, while Billy was sussing out the label guy full-on . . . getting up, wandering around the room, and every now and again, doing this excited little dance, saying, "What do you think? It's brilliant, eh?"'

This period was not without its pressures, however. Around this time, the Associates were evicted from their chintzy St John's Wood flat. Although still broke, Billy, in a typically whimsical move, had one day arrived home with a water bag full of exotic tropical fish, claiming he had bought them because he was pining for the fish pond in the garden of his father's house in Dundee. Since there was, of course, no tank to house the fish, the ever-sensible Dempsey drove Billy to the King's Road, where the pair bought a plastic base for a fish pond which was then installed on the balcony of the Carlton Hill flat. When it leaked, Dempsey bought an old bath-proportioned tank from a friend and this too was left on the balcony. Perhaps inevitably, on a weekend when the Associates were gigging outside London, the tank split, ruining the flat's expensive carpets and flooding the luxury apartment below. On their return, the Associates found a note from their landlord that simply read: 'Gentlemen, words fail me.'

Perhaps mercifully then, in a complicated deal that involved them signing to Beggars Banquet Records with funding and marketing to be provided by WEA (more commonly known as Warner Brothers), their records to be released under an Associates imprint, the group were given an advance of £60,000, including recording costs. In an unparalleled moment of sensibility, half of this was paid to Mike Hedges for a three-month block-booking of his recently built studio facility Playground, in Camden Town. (When not working themselves, they would sublet their time at the studio to other groups, including the Cure, Siouxsie and the Banshees and Bauhaus.) The Associates got straight down to work – although notably not for their Warner Brothers paymasters – by continuing work on singles for Situation 2.

A swift succession of releases followed – Fiction lifted 'A' from *The Affectionate Punch* in the light of the band's recent successes, and from the preliminary sessions at Playground, the Associates issued the murky, angsty funk of 'Message Oblique Speech' in October and the epic, atmospheric electronica of 'White Car In Germany', their sixth single of the year (containing the possibly classic MacKenzie couplet: 'Lisp your way through Zurich/Walk on eggs in Munich') the following month. For the recording of 'The

Associate', the largely instrumental B-side of the latter, Billy – displaying the prankster traits that would become a constant of their time at Playground – insisted that for the screaming effects that feature throughout, the group gaffer-tape teacups to their heads for the performance. John MacKenzie, visiting this session, remembers: 'With Billy, it had to be the most extreme, mad vibe. After they'd done it, they came back into the control room, and he made them smash their cups like they were at a Greek wedding. The only cup that wouldn't smash was Mike Dempsey's and he was getting quite angry. I would just watch all this and giggle myself to sleep at night.'

To mark the end of their period with Situation 2, in October the best of the Associates' singles work of 1981 was compiled and released on the eight-track *Fourth Drawer Down*, their second album. The origins of this seemingly mysterious title were simple enough: the fourth drawer down in the chest at Carlton Hill was where the Associates kept their supplies of over-the-counter herbal relaxant tablets that when taken by the handful, rather than the recommended dosage, would act as a sleeping aid as well as producing a pleasant bedtime buzz.

The cover of *Fourth Drawer Down* was shot in the swimming pool at the Manor residential recording studio in Oxfordshire. Having insisted that they should appear even wetter on this album cover than they had for *The Affectionate Punch*, Billy – who was always terrified of water – swallowed his fear and jumped in, not realizing that the pool was still covered with a protective sheet of transparent bubblewrap. 'Fucking deadly,' Rankine notes. 'That stuff can swallow you . . . it just sucks you up. Both of us got into a bit of difficulty.'

At the close of a hugely productive year, one more single appeared bearing MacKenzie and Rankine's names. Exercising a clause in the Associates' contract with WEA that allowed them to record for other labels if Billy didn't sing lead vocals on the A-side of any release (in effect, nullifying the company's exclusivity), the duo, along with Christine Beveridge, released a version of Simon Dupree & the Big Sound's wistful 1967 hit, 'Kites', on RSO Records under the name 39 Lyon Street. 'Him and I fought all the way through it,' Beveridge admits. 'We hated each other by the end of it. They always wanted me to sing in that girly way, but I was always dead nervous and I couldn't perform. He used to get really mad at me because he knew what I could do, and that only made me worse. Billy got pissed, just to deal with me basically, cause I was calling him a tyrant. He sang the chorus to that song lying flat on his back in a pile of bass bins or something, with me holding the mic to him. He couldn't stand up.'

Later on in the sessions, the trio gathered in the studio's live room to record group backing vocals. Billy by this stage was suffering from a particularly severe bout of hiccups, and after endless takes it was decided that the situation was unlikely to improve, so the luckless Flood set about the cheerless task of editing each individual hiccup from the take. When he soloed the track, however, behind the vocals there was the faint sound of tinkling water . . . Billy, mid-take, pissing on the studio floor.

6

Orchestrated Chaos

Whether simply distracted by the urgency of their temporary homelessness or just plainly naïve, when the Associates had gathered up their possessions from their ruined St John's Wood flat and found themselves standing at the reception desk of the Swiss Cottage Holiday Inn at the beginning of what was likely to be a lengthy stay, it failed to occur to them to negotiate a long-term rate. As the first symptom of the wanton frittering of the £30,000 they had left over from the Warners deal, five days into their residence at the hotel the extras bill alone stood at just over £1000.

Once again, however, they were living a deceptively glamorous lifestyle. In reality, three of them – MacKenzie, Rankine and Dempsey – were sharing one twin room, with a fold-down cot bed to supplement the cramped sleeping configuration. Before long they weren't the only ones jostling for any square foot of comfortable space in the already overcrowded room. Billy's two recently acquired whippet puppies, Tonto and Vanda, were a constant presence and one that – according to most accounts – frequently narked Rankine. 'Most of the time, I liked the whippets fine,' the guitarist protests. 'They were intelligent dogs and they weren't nasty. But you'd wake up and there'd be shit all over the floor and, of course, you'd step in it.'

There was nothing else for it, Billy decided. The whippets would have a neighbouring room entirely to themselves, charged to a Warner Brothers account. Perhaps through their mild desperation, the others consented. When the expenditure was eventually queried by the record company, Billy innocently insisted that the room had a necessary outlay for Joey, his 'pal'. More wildly extravagant still, the dogs were usually fed on room-service meals. 'Every week that went by, they'd give us our bill at the desk and this fucking computer would spew out page after page,' Rankine recalls, with mild incredulity. 'There'd be sixteen pages of printout of cocoas and brandies for us and smoked salmon and hard-boiled eggs for the whippets. Bill used to phone up and get six helpings at a time and say, "But give me the shells too", because the albumen is apparently good for their bones.'

In their financial dealings at the time, the Associates' money was generally dispersed in the manner of a sawn-off shotgun gang dealing out piles of notes in the aftermath of an armed robbery. Cheques were instantly transferred to cash, and whoever was present at the time would sit around a table (notably, John Murphy would often be absent on these pay-days and was therefore dealt a rawer deal) to decide who would get what. A lump sum was usually creamed off the top for Dempsey and the remainder split between MacKenzie and Rankine. 'Where money was concerned,' the bassist remembers, 'Billy had no eye for tomorrow, which in a way is admirable. They were always generous to me. I wasn't given a third because I wasn't part of their partnership and that worked for all three of us. They were never mean and Billy, in particular, was far too generous. Alan probably knew that he couldn't stop Billy being what he was and so he just went along with it, and I suppose I started to reconcile myself with that as well – the whippets getting their own room or the huge cab bills he was running up. Billy was never worried about keeping the cab waiting for a couple of hours.'

Even if was bound to be for a limited period only, the Associates lavishly indulged themselves and were soon caught up in a bohemian whirlwind of cocaine, champagne and cashmere. 'We all went daft,' Billy admitted. 'I've got this cashmere fetish . . . I bought about sixteen cashmere jumpers and put them on the bed and rolled on them. I think it's great we didn't hang on to the money like freaky little introverts. I mean, at twenty-four you're meant to spend. You'd be some kind of bedroom weirdo if you hung on to the money.'

Squandering in the fashion of an excited pools winner hurtling headlong into bankruptcy, when his share of the advanced money inevitably began to drizzle out, Billy simply charged more items and services to the various Warners accounts set up by a huge list of companies around London, or attempted – with a certain persuasive charm – to wheedle more money out of the Associates' hapless A&R boss at Warners, Tarquin Gotch. A dentistry bill for £80, for instance, would suddenly land on Gotch's desk, accredited to a Mr MacKenzie for having had his teeth polished. Clothing budgets provided by the record company were spent on expensive designer outfits that MacKenzie's friends or siblings were seen wearing just as Billy – who rarely had a reasonable excuse for the disappearance of the cash – was putting his hand out for more money for clothes that still had to be bought *somehow*.

Once, when he and his Auntie Betty were at Heathrow Airport waiting for a flight to Scotland that had been delayed for two hours, Billy suggested that they catch the next flight to Eire for an impromptu shopping trip. On arriving in Dublin, they had a quick scout around the airport's duty-free area and caught the next flight back home, with an armload of gifts, including – the bass player remembers – an expensive, badger-hair shaving brush for Dempsey.

As the funds were swiftly depleting, Dempsey suggested that to cut down on their considerable cab bills, the Associates should buy a band car, with a loan of £5000 arranged through the bassist's bank, to be paid off with their next influx of cash: 'Having no knowledge of the Associates, my bank manager said, "I can't see any reason why you shouldn't have a company car . . . very sensible . . . What is it?" We said, "It's a 1963 convertible Mercedes", and he said, "Well, I suppose we can stretch a point . . ."' Shortly afterwards the Associates actually found themselves in possession of a modest fleet of luxury vehicles, following the cheap purchase of a funereal Ford Dorchester from Billy's father, driven by Dempsey while the others sniggered behind the interior glass panelling in the back. 'Terrible vast, vast car,' the appointed chauffeur remembers. 'Impossible to find anywhere to park it. We ran up hundreds, probably thousands, of pounds in parking tickets.'

Offsetting these capricious financial shenanigans, both Rankine and MacKenzie took great pleasure in offering proof to their families of this new-found solvency by giving their fathers money. Billy went some way to repaying the investments his dad had made in the early days of the Associates; Alan simply left £2000 in his father's sock drawer.

Chris Carr confirms Billy's peculiar rationale where money was concerned: 'He would go shopping for shoes and take someone along and if he was getting a pair, they would get a pair. But then I've seen him be the opposite, unnaturally tight, and he would have a reason for it that he wouldn't explain. In a funny way, those that he was closest to were those that didn't reap the necessary benefits. You'd have John Murphy living in a squat and Billy could've certainly sorted something out there and he didn't. But then it wouldn't be past Billy to meet up with John and take him out for a meal and lavish a different side of life on him. I think Billy had his own agenda, he intended to build some sort of self-sufficiency. He would confound record company people. They would term it as him being unreasonable, but he was one of the most instinctive people I've ever met – if Billy's instinct told him to do something or not to do something, he would act on it.'

In effect, the Associates blew their first year's advance within twelve weeks of signing to Warners. Within a mere six months they were forced to eat into the funds allocated to the second term of the contract in order to pay off a VAT bill. In Dempsey's comparatively ordered mind, alarm bells were beginning to ring: 'I was desperately thinking, Hang on, this is ludicrous. I imagined that one year's advance should last for one year . . . which was rather rash of me. Billy would just say [to Warners], "I need £2000," and they'd say, "What do you need it for?" and he'd say, "I just need it." I was thinking, Oh, this is so Chuck Berry. I knew we were being cornered. The Associates were straight away on that hamster run of chasing money that had been advanced to us. As for Billy, it sort of demonstrated that it was never really going to be possible to turn him into an organized machine – he was much too much of a free spirit.'

Soon even the management of the Swiss Cottage Holiday Inn were beginning to tire of this free-spirited resident, particularly since Billy was increasingly taking advantage of the hotel's specialist dog-sitting facility, normally a service provided to rich wives whose poodles needed looking after for an afternoon while they flexed their husband's gold credit card around town. Often, if Billy promised the dog-sitter that he would be back no later than midnight, he wouldn't roll in until around ten the following morning, by which time the sitter had long since been reluctantly forced to give up and the whippets had begun decorating the carpet in their room and gnawing an escape tunnel.

Perhaps unreasonably viewing the unwelcome grief he was now receiving from the hotel management as yet another infuriating link in the chain of authoritarianism that had stretched from teachers to A&R men, Billy decided to deliver a one-fingered salute in their direction. Christine Beveridge, now coincidentally living in a council flat across the road from the hotel, often joined the Associates for a Buck's Fizz breakfast in the mornings before Billy ordered a VIP car on the Warners account to ferry her to work. One night Billy chanced upon a notion to how best rile the hotel management and asked to borrow Beveridge's clothes. For the remainder of the evening the pair sat in the hotel bar, Billy in full drag, fur coat and stiletto heels, straight-faced and legs daintily crossed. 'The way he was built, he could get away with it quite well,' his accomplice notes. 'But he didn't go all the way – he still had the stubble at the same time. It wasn't a real attempt, it was just a carry-on.'

Time was clearly running out in the Associates' relationship with the Holiday Inn. When Dempsey made a comment – intended to sober his band mates – that for the ridiculous weekly rate the group were shelling out on their stay at the hotel, they might as well be renting a flat in South Kensington, this became the new plan of action and the bassist was entrusted to scan the Flats to Let columns of the *Evening Standard* to find a suitable property in this upmarket enclave for anything up to £350 a week. The trio looked at several houses in the area, many of which were instantly rejected by the aesthetically minded MacKenzie, one in particular on the grounds that it was decorated with peacock wallpaper and – of course – he considered the kaleidoscopically hued birds to be unlucky.

Eventually the group viewed a horrifically garish, tigerskin-rugged flat in Bury Walk, on the Chelsea side of the Fulham Road, of the kind normally let out on three-month contracts as a holiday home for wealthy visitors to London. Apparently Yul Brynner was also interested in the apartment, but the bald star of *The King And I* had a dog and the block had a no-pets policy. Billy had already realized that this could pose a problem and had temporarily shipped his dogs back to his family in Dundee.

And so the Associates – who could now claim that they owned not so much as a small, teething whippet or floundering tropical fish between them – moved in.

Throughout the latter half of 1981, of course, it didn't really make much difference whether the Associates were residing in a suite at the Hilton or dossing in a skip in Kentish Town, since most of their time was spent recording at Playground with Mike Hedges. Situated on Bayham Street in Camden Town, one of the main routes for traffic heading from north London into the West End, Playground took up a substantial corner of an industrial warehouse that was partly devoted to storage space – rented by faceless individuals – of the more shady variety, with entire store rooms full of car stereos and other assorted consumer desirables surrounding it. Visitors to the studio remember it as having a half-built, ramshackle charm that perfectly suited the orchestrated chaos of the sessions for the key album in the Associates' history, *Sulk.*

MacKenzie and Rankine by this point were on a creative roll, and if the culmination date of the *Sulk* sessions remains largely elusive in the minds of its participants, then its beginnings are even less clear, since the recording of the group's last singles for Situation 2 blurred straight into the start of the work on their next project. All of the material that the duo began recording had in fact been in their 1980 live set in support of *The Affectionate Punch*, and with no songwriting worries to cloud the horizon, the sessions began to soar to new heights of fried intensity, a constant stream of brilliant, if characteristically unhinged ideas sparking between the two. 'We knew that we were just really on it and this album was going to really be something,' Rankine explains. 'It just felt unstoppable. We knew that what we were making was what we'd been leading up to for the last five years.''

Billy, for his part, seemed to be revelling in the hell-bent creativity and even the confusion of the *Sulk* sessions. 'The best moments are the moments that click,' he told *Melody Maker*, 'when Alan and myself get extremely excited about something. That's a certain magical bit, when you get this amazing feeling out of a number and you just go, "Weeeeeee". It's the only time that really works for us. So maybe that's why we run around in circles, chasing our tails because we're looking for that magical feeling. But maybe we'll just tie ourselves up in knots, and can't see the trees for the forest. Maybe we throw all these things in our path to kind of distract ourselves.'

Dempsey remembers that at this time Billy was first showing signs of an overdeveloped sense of perfectionism that manifested itself as irrepressible speediness: 'He was obsessive, always on top of every detail. It was even down to whether you were wearing the right shoes because that was part of the composition and the production to him. But they were both like that in different ways. To my mind at least, Brian Wilson at his peak was probably like Billy MacKenzie and Alan Rankine rolled into one.'

Nocturnal by choice rather than through the cheap-rate necessity of their recent past, the Associates employed an extremely open-ended attitude to musical experimentation. Assembling the backing tracks as before, by layering instrumental passes and 'found sounds' over basic drum machine patterns, the duo, with Mike Hedges as their ever-encouraging ringleader, took advantage of the warehouse space by rolling anything vaguely circular down the long, empty corridors, recording vocals in the natural echo of an industrial toilet, shaking sheets of thin metal through swathes of reverb to thunderous effect, and smashing pretty much anything they could get their hands on.

Aside from all this playfulness in the childlike sense of the word (making the studio name seem all the more fitting), the Associates had decided that their music could be enhanced by a female vocal foil for Billy. At first he asked Christine Beveridge to join the group and she declined: 'I said no because I didn't want to play second-fiddle to him. Can you imagine trying to be a singer and having Billy MacKenzie figure big in your life? What would be the point of opening your mouth?' Instead, at the suggestion of Warners, Billy called up Martha Ladly, a pretty blonde Toronto-born Canadian living in London after the break-up of Martha and the Muffins, the group she had moved to Britain with as keyboard player, following their sole number-ten hit, 'Echo Beach', in March 1980. Ladly had since released a couple of unsuccessful solo singles on the Virgin-funded subsidiary label Dindisc and was consequently on the lookout for other musical outlets. Her initial visit to Playground, she remembers, left a striking impression upon her: 'As I suppose everyone did, I just thought that Billy had an amazing voice and that Alan complemented him through being a brilliant musician. There was just a fantastic energy . . . ideas firing off all the time.'

Ever the flirt, Billy insisted that all their vocal parts be recorded live with both of them performing in the booth at the same time. 'We had fun singing together,' Ladly says. 'Luckily I had a loud enough voice to compete with him. Half the time he'd be showing me what to do and yet he'd be able to sing higher than me, so I'd be singing in full voice but imitating this mad falsetto stuff that he was doing. He wanted me to sing in a sexy girly voice to offset the big, round, operatic sound he was making. So it was either kittenish stuff or screaming, which was a great release. I think the only time I let him down was when he wanted me to do some whistling and I wasn't very good.'

Inevitably, considering the grand musical gestures being committed to tape, these sessions were fuelled by increasing quantities of cocaine and for a time the Associates, wearing their abuse on their sleeves, became slightly notorious for their intake. In fact, the duo became so bored of chopping out lines, they began to carve their initials in it, just for the novelty value. 'I can remember racing from either end of the desk to the middle with one giant line,' Rankine admits. 'It was like, "See you at Channel 24." Other bands were doing a lot more drugs than us, but they seemed to have a mechanism through their PR or their manager that kept it in check as far as journalists went. Whereas we just didn't. You'd see these bands and you could tell they were out of their tree in a big way . . . We were novices compared to them.'

Martha Ladly remembers: 'There some pretty mad drug-induced experiences. There was one incident where this drug was produced – I'd never seen it before but I think it was some sort of large animal sedative. The sensation it managed to induce was complete bodily drunkenness but a clear mind. We went to this club and we all looked like we were out of brains, but we were mentally clear. I tended to steer clear of the worst excesses of that just because I was more interested in drinking than taking drugs and I never had any problem finding a companion in Billy on that score.'

While admitting that there was certainly an artificially stimulated edge to the *Sulk* recordings, Dempsey is keen to stress that drugs never dented the Associates' creativity: 'There were drug dealers coming and going, but even though there may have been some of that, it wasn't wayward in that respect. It was very concentrated energy, a lot of work was getting done. It was focused and any madness was energy that could actually be channelled into the record. Nothing the Associates ever did stands out in my mind as being obsessive because it wasn't out of character and it was never out of place.'

Aside from the financial pressures of having the Associates on their label, Warners – for whom the group were an attractively hip addition to a roster of toothy pop acts like Dollar and Modern Romance – were hugely encouraged by the first work-in-progress results of the album sessions. In Tarquin Gotch, the Associates had been fortunate enough to find an A&R man that they liked a great deal and who refrained from any attempts to pour water over his artists' creative fire. In fact, he would be an active participant in the general mayhem, even if he now admits to a certain frustration with Billy's eternal search for what he viewed as vocal perfection.

'We were just trying to get the tracks finished,' Gotch explains, 'and you'd have this eccentric guy who would say, "Oh, no, I don't like it." You'd go, "Well, what's wrong with it?" and he'd say, "I just don't like it, I can sing it better." As an A&R man and a business guy, you don't know how heavy to be. You've signed these people because they *are* mad and they *are* creative, but when they then behave in a mad and creative way, it frustrates you. So you're always trying to walk that line – you're trying to be liked but you're trying to move it on. It was exciting to go down because you always were hearing great stuff, but it was a little out there . . . There were drugs about, and I'd be quite happy, if there was blow there, to have a bit. It was all that early-80s fast living.'

Around this time there was an enduring rumour that the Associates had played a potentially lethal trick on Gotch by chopping out a line of the scouring agent Vim for him. 'Yes, it is true,' the former A&R man admits. 'Fortunately . . . get my nose near anything like that, I'd suss it, and I didn't actually snort it. If I had, they'd have been off the label . . . or who knows? I knew they were taking the piss because when somebody's playing a practical joke, there's just something not right.'

Growing increasingly aware that the internal machinations of the record industry are little more than an elaborate power play for status, the Associates would rarely afford Warners an inch. Priding themselves on their punctuality, the group once arrived at the company's offices in Broadwick Street, Soho, and were left waiting for five minutes in the reception area – a common ploy, of course, in one-upmanship. As soon as the Associates were asked to take a seat, however, their shared internal clock was ticking and when the five minutes had elapsed, they got up, left and a Warners minion was sent scurrying down the street to retrieve them. Following a huddled discussion, the Associates decided that there was no way they would go back after this slight and informed the employee that another meeting would have to be arranged.

At other times the group would exhaust the record company's staff with their devious ways. In one instance, Billy insisted that they would only be photographed by a friend of his from Scotland. After much reluctance, Warners agreed, and he reportedly replied: 'Great . . . ah, the thing is that he's no' got a camera at the moment.'

Somewhere along the line Billy cajoled Mike Hedges into ordering a five-foot industrial canister of helium to be delivered to the studio, and for a few days the Associates set about filling the control room with balloons and blown-up condoms with tiny lights ingeniously flickering inside. Once this newsworthy story had leaked to the press, however, Billy was dogged by industry murmurings that he actually needed the gas to achieve the high-pitched falsetto vocal effects on Associates records. Although untrue, this damaging disinformation infuriated him. Another erroneous report stated that the Associates, in a surrealistic pact, would arrive at Playground to begin recording with fresh fish pinned to their lapels. Still, these rumours were not entirely wide of the mark.

With the necessary budget at his disposal, Billy had at last fulfilled his experimental ambition to fill an entire drum kit with water. Unfortunately it sounded terrible and by the next day the shells of the expensive hired kit had turned to mush. Similarly, when Rankine noted that a hired top-range acoustic guitar sounded 'pish' in spite of its value, Billy proceeded, for comic effect, to piss in the hole of the guitar. It was later emptied out and the lavatorially scented guitar returned to the hire company. 'It was just stupid things to override the boredom,' Billy insisted. 'Like, I'd drink maybe three bottles of Bailey's Irish Cream, one after the other, then puke it all up. Daft schoolboy things like that. Mike Hedges was totally mad and encouraged every sort of stupid whim.'

If anything, it seems, Hedges was more capably equipped to handle MacKenzie than probably any other producer the singer had yet encountered. When recording the dramatic, show-stopping vocal for 'No', *Sulk*'s widescreen John Barry-echoing ballad, at the height of the song Billy blew the diaphragm on the microphone and the take had to be terminated. The mic duly repaired, Hedges asked Billy to take a step back to avoid blowing the new diaphragm, and he refused. Hedges then informed him that if he bust it, he would have to pay for it. Billy cheekily enquired whether the producer had any cheaper mics. After being told that, yes, they did have a slightly cheaper model, Billy retorted, 'Well, put that one up then – I'll save myself fifty quid.'

But it was not all fun and head games. Having overheard John Murphy – whom the group were partly responsible for excluding from the clique – deriding the Associates while on the studio phone to a friend in Australia, Billy in no uncertain terms told the drummer to take a walk. To compound the pressure, *Sulk* was now wildly over-budget and long overdue, with the Associates' funds from the time sublet to other groups now being used to increase their stay. When that eventually ran out, they began to put pressure on Warners to extend the studio time.

'What *Sulk* cost in reality, I don't think anybody would really know, partly because of the games,' Chris Carr says. 'I got quoted things like £150,000 before they'd even begun mixing. When you think of how much that was worth in those days, it sounds to a certain extent ludicrous, but Billy and Alan had gone for broke as far as I was concerned. They believed in it so much. Again it was this status game where they thought that the more they got Warners to spend on the recording, the more they were going to need to spend on the marketing to recoup and the more valuable the Associates would become. This was one of the areas that I tried to get them to understand – that we needed to get in a money man. One of the saddest things for me is that I never got them a decent financial controller who would've been able to explain to Billy that there are limits to what you can do.'

Whatever the financial risks, *Sulk* turned out to be nothing short of a masterpiece, albeit a flawed one. Cabin fever had gripped the Associates during the final stages of the album, with their pursuit of perfection – and needless to say their cocaine intake – having given way to paranoia. As a consequence the tracks were worked, reworked, overworked and often mixed up to ten times. While the dawning of the digital age was elsewhere making for increasingly bright, pristine record productions, *Sulk* sounded as if parts of it had been recorded underwater, with even its more sparkling moments bearing an audible tarnish. But then *Sulk* was a truly individual record. Apart from the electronic thud of the Simmons kit – ubiquitous in 1981 – it displays none of the common production values of its time and is almost Spectoresque in its use of layering and reverb. Like Prince's most important and hugely influential work to follow later in the decade, it even managed to inject no little amount of character into the often soulless sound of the 80s. At the time it actually sounded like a bit of a mess. Now it sounds strangely timeless.

Book-ended by two instrumentals – the closer being 'nothing-insomethingparticular', a vocal-less remix of the future single '18 Carat Love Affair', which had been considered too poppy for inclusion on the album – it begins with the Associates' old live-set opener, 'Arrogance Gave Him Up', showcasing the inimitable skittery drumming of John Murphy, playing a kit that the duo had constructed entirely from snare drums. In a sense the track betrays MacKenzie and Rankine's roots in that, with its air of showbiz glitter and audience expectancy, it has the feel of a cabaret big-band opener, at the end of which the star performer will enter stage right to a storm of applause as he steps up to the mic.

In this case, however, the first song the singer delivers is the most desolately moody number in his repertoire. Driven by a slow, electronic pulse and classically chiselled piano phrase, 'No' is Billy MacKenzie as the anxiety-racked crooner, his voice treated in such a way that it sounds as if it's echoing through a series of ghostly rooms. The lyric, although largely impenetrable, appears as a series of scattered, worried thoughts. Perhaps typically, since he was always less than keen to describe any possible meanings behind his tangential word games, Billy flippantly told a journalist that 'No' was about sitting at the dinner table at his parents' house and failing to balance peas on the back of his fork. A psychoanalyst might have argued that the lines 'Tore my hair out from the roots/ Planted them in someone's garden/Then I waited for the shoots' possibly concerned a fear of receding, but then Billy might likely have argued back. Rankine admits he can shed little light on most of MacKenzie's lyrics: 'Is "No" a song about inadequacy? I don't know.'

Since it was idiosyncratic in the extreme, Billy's voice throughout this period was often accused of sounding grating to some ears, and perhaps the breaking point of aural torture is reached with two particular hard-line tracks, 'Bap De La Bap' and 'Nude Spoons'. Over the dislocated beat and siren-like synth riff of the former, Billy's voice is, by turns, menacing and terrified; the latter features the most elastic, melody-dismissing vocal of his entire catalogue over bonehead bass and drums. While both songs are enduring favourites among Associates devotees, it has to be noted that for the US release of *Sulk*, these were the two tracks that were omitted.

At the opposite end of the spectrum, however, the Associates' minimalistic funk take on their singer's Billie Holiday favourite, 'Gloomy Sunday', proved that MacKenzie was far more than an easily excitable, avant-garde operatic singer, as he offers a more introspective, emotive performance that breaks up with distortion in the emotional peaks. 'His voice would move to such wild extremes in the dynamic spectrum,' Dempsey explains. 'He would often say, "That's the take, leave it", and he wouldn't worry about the distortion.' In 'Skipping', the Associates had achieved something close to perfection in their own minds amid the flamenco guitars, rubbery bass line and filmic washes. Here Billy offered his most obtuse line ever ('Breathless beauxillous griffin once removed seemed dwarfed') and slipped into a respectable impersonation of what can be determined as either Humphrey Bogart or Sean Connery, before tailing off with the hint of a laugh. 'I can remember Billy playing "Skipping" over and over again,' Dempsey recalls, 'saying that we'd finally got the essence of what we were trying to do.'

It is, however, *Sulk*'s two singles that provide the real high points of the album. With 'Club Country', the Associates accidentally stumbled on house music five years before its invention in Chicago, although here it is augmented by guitars that sound like balalaikas, impossibly slippery bass and an energetic chorus that turned the couplet 'A drive from nowhere leaves you in the cold/Refrigeration keeps you young I'm told' into what sounded like a possibly radio-friendly chant.

But it was with 'Party Fears Two' that the Associates knew they had struck gold. If the blueprint for the classic pop record is that it should be addictive, adventurous, alluring and slightly dangerous, then 'Party Fears Two' is surely a classic pop record. As the celestial introduction and brightly hammered piano motif give way to Billy's opening gambit, 'I'll have a shower and then phone my brother up/Within the hour I'll smash another cup', the listener is instantly hooked. Although the lyric gives the impression of a diary entry that has been ripped to tiny pieces and then randomly sellotaped together again, there is a twin meaning to be found in the line 'The alcohol loves you while turning you blue' (blue as sadness, blue as first sign of overdose) and even a certain emotional depth wrung out of as oblique a line as 'Even a slight remark makes nonsense and turns to shark'. In the song's outro, Billy's voice achieves vertical take-off into the ether, possibly reaching a pitch that only his whippets could register. At its close, he repeats the opening lines to himself a cappella, drenched in reverb, as if walking through an empty nightclub in the small hours as the cleaners are sweeping up. The last sounds are the smashing of three cups in quick succession and the singer spitting out his chewing gum.

The eventual completion of *Sulk* was a hugely emotional moment for the Associates. 'When we got to the end of it,' Rankine admits, 'I just burst into tears through sheer stress and the release of tension.'

7

Winding Up, Winding Down

The wet patch had started off as a tiny damp dot, but alarmingly, it was spreading fast. Alan Rankine made a mental note: take a bit more care in the toilet when you're wearing silk trousers – particularly if it's only minutes before you appear on live, national television for the first time. The Associates, in the first step of the promotion for *Sulk*, had been booked to perform 'Party Fears Two' and 'Skipping' on BBC2's midnight-straddling arts programme *Friday Night, Saturday Morning*, hosted by the Scottish broadcaster and dabbling novelty-record pop star B.A. Robertson. Rankine, resplendent in yellow cashmere jumper and red chiffon scarf, was quietly relieved to have an acoustic guitar to balance in front of his crotch. Meanwhile, Billy – cutting a dash in a pilot suit hired from a theatrical costumier – was nervously chewing gum throughout the camera rehearsals, as the director gesticulated wildly in a failed effort him to make him spit it out.

The performance, as it turned out, was a memorable televisual début and the first airing of MacKenzie's mercurial onscreen charisma. Perched on tall stools, the duo performed the songs with the studio lights glinting off the brim of Billy's pilot cap as he sang and nervously wriggled and smiled, keen to stare any-where, it seems, apart from directly into the camera's lens. In the short interview that followed, Billy name-checked his favourite singers as being Paul Haig and Christine Beveridge. Both had tuned in that night and were equally shocked, although their reactions differed greatly: 'I was amazed because Billy was already known as one of the best singers about and all I do is sing in a monotone voice,' the former states; 'I was mortified,' the latter bluntly recalls.

Just before the release of 'Party Fears Two' on 6 March 1982, Billy spoke to *Melody Maker* of his frustration that none of the Situation 2 releases had succeeded in skimming even the lower reaches of the charts. 'At the beginning of last year I thought it was going to be the year of singles,' he said. 'And it was. The thing with our singles was that they got peeled off the turntable halfway through! We want to keep our singles on the turntable this year . . .' As it was soon to pan out, this very much became a fulfilled statement of intent. Since it was both strikingly unusual and enormously catchy, promotional copies of 'Party Fears Two' became almost instantly glued to the turntables at Radio One, the number of plays increasing directly in relation to the record's ascent of the charts: the first week, the single reached 57, the next 46. Then, when it entered the Top 40 at number 23, the Associates were invited to appear on *Top Of The Pops*.

While the viewing figures for BBC1's robustly indestructible chart programme may have withered over the years, it has, of course, remained a worthwhile and entertaining platform for the extremes of pop music – the banal, the wonderful and the toe-curlingly bad – and in their own small way the Associates' handful of appearances on *Top Of The Pops* would provide a footnote in the history of this pop institution. Even now, their performances are still spoken about, by many of those who witnessed them, in tones of riotous amusement and inspired awe. If anything, the Associates served to remind a significant cross-section of the record-buying public that pop music should be both thrilling and ludicrous in equal measure.

But in fact, their first appearance on *Top Of The Pops* very nearly didn't happen. The Associates – rootless again following the lapse of their Bury Walk tenancy – were staying in the Columbia Hotel in Bayswater, an establishment widely renowned for its rock-star clientele and its tolerance of its guests' more extreme, intoxicated behaviour. On the Wednesday morning of the show's recording, Dempsey received a call from Billy calmly informing him that he was backing out of the appearance because he'd just had a haircut that he was too embarrassed to unveil in the street, never mind on nationwide television. 'I said he was crazy and went to see him,' the bassist remembers of this worrying moment. 'Then, of course, I had to convince him that it didn't look *that* bad.'

Since, in 1982, VCRs were still something of a middle-to-upper-class luxury item, the only domestic tapes that remain of these performances are grainy, colour-distorted, fifth-generation 'porn' copies, although the Associates' *Top Of The Pops* appearances remain as riveting and entertaining as memory serves. In the end, with offensive haircut concealed under black beret, Billy donned a fawn raincoat for this first performance, accidentally patenting what would become his most enduring image in the minds of the public. Surrounded by 'futuristic' aluminium-foil piping and knee-deep in clouds of dry ice, Dempsey appears in French sailor fringe and pony-tail, wrestling with an oversized semi-acoustic bass. Ladly, in expensive black cocktail dress and blonde bouffant, trips through the piano part with elegantly gloved fingers. Rankine, heavily made up, stands poker-faced at the back in a white fencing suit, chopsticks in his hair, playing a banjo, while in front of him Billy fidgets his way through 'Party Fears Two', his eyes once again darting everywhere except in the direction of the camera crew. Spying a bespectacled geek in a rainbow-coloured knitted jumper who is staring at himself in the TV monitors to the left of the stage, Billy allows his face to spread into a huge, dimpled smile and he also turns to watch himself in the monitors. Then, for the remainder of the song, he rarely glances at the audience again, instead laughing and watching himself on TV, as he performs on TV, as if posing in his bedroom mirror.

As the song draws to its close, Ladly can barely conceal her amusement at the singer's comically insular delivery. On reflection, she now realizes that this was perhaps as much a playful gimmick on MacKenzie's part as it was a bolt-hole through which Billy could shake off his stage fright: 'I do remember Billy being really self-conscious and looking in the monitor the whole time. I couldn't quite figure out why he was doing that because he'd done lots of performing before and he was an incredibly charismatic front man.' Dempsey adds: 'I never realized that he was a nervous performer because he was so full of confidence. The thing was, he would never have admitted it.'

Two weeks later 'Party Fears Two' had leapfrogged to number nine and the group were invited back for a return visit, sandwiched between Depeche Mode performing their third hit, 'See You', and the horrendous loincloth- and bikini-wearing trio Tight Fit at number one with 'The Lion Sleeps Tonight'. Growing ever more confident, Billy in black mod suit, pencil-thin tie and pork pie hat, mimes the words through a grin the width of the Tay. Still, this appearance had less impact than their début, and the single, nearing the end of its commercial life, began to slip back down the chart.

Although he was slowly acclimatizing to the pop-star life, Billy was often flippantly dismissive of *Top Of The Pops*, informing a journalist from glossy style monthly *The Face*, 'I'd much rather be on *Pebble Mill At One* or playing at Batley Variety Club.' Nevertheless, this new-found mainstream fame greatly thrilled the bosses at Warner Brothers, who threw a celebratory party for the Associates at a Fulham brasserie on the night of this second show. And celebrate the Associates certainly did, ordering crateloads of Calvados apple brandy until four in the morning, in the process somehow losing track of Dempsey, who had collapsed in a toilet cubicle and was roused by the cleaners long after everyone else had left.

But these, after all, were abusive times. Chris Carr remembers one night in the bar of the Columbia when he and Rankine drained a bottle of Glenfiddich, followed by a bottle of Courvoisier, and had to be helped to their rooms by a hotel employee 'because we were incapable of doing much else . . . this was also to kind of cock a snook at the industry because it was done in public.' Meanwhile Billy and Martha were running riot upstairs, perilously teetering around the banister on the top level of the hotel's high staircase and climbing up an exterior fire escape on to the roof. 'When I look back on that stuff,' Ladly muses, 'I think to myself, How did I actually get out of that in one piece? We were definitely partners in crime, Billy and I. Alan used to get really scared and Michael Dempsey used to just think, They're two maniacs, I'll just leave them to their own devices. We used to spur each other on . . . and Billy was always willing to go that bit further than me.'

In April the fruits of Billy's first extracurricular efforts were released on the British Electric Foundation album *Music Of Quality And Distinction Volume 1*. An offshoot of Sheffield-born electronic funk outfit Heaven 17, the album had been the ambitious brain-child of the group's two producer/musicians, Martyn Ware and Ian Craig Marsh, and featured orchestral and synthesized cover versions of cooler pop tracks and easy-listening standards, per-formed by a variety of vocalists including Tina Turner, Sandie Shaw and Gary Glitter. Billy shone with his two tracks – Roy Orbison's heart-wrenching 'It's Over' and 'The Secret Life Of Arabia', the funk workout closer of David Bowie's 1977 album *Heroes*. The latter track in particular greatly appealed to Billy – his voice had always been likened to Bowie at his most operatic, and it wasn't exactly a comparison that the younger singer found unflattering. Recording 'The Secret Life Of Arabia' only served to strengthen their link. As if to cement the growing recognition of Billy MacKenzie in this first half of 1982, the majority of the album's reviews raved about his contributions.

'He was the star of the album really,' Ware says. 'We regarded ourselves as being very lucky to have him on it. At the time, having a singer with a nuclear-powered voice doing an old Roy Orbison number with an orchestra . . . it was a genuine risk. The sessions [at the Garden in Shoreditch] were completely nuts. I'd try to explain to him in plain English what we were trying to do and he'd go, "Och, Martyn, it's really exciting, it's like angels flying on rainbows, I can't wait to sing on this" . . . he'd just go off on one. I've never been in the studio with somebody who enjoyed being creative more than him. He'd actually come up and physically hug you a lot of the time in the middle of doing something that demanded quite a lot of concentration.'

When Billy talked to *Record Mirror* about the BEF sessions, he admitted to having been shocked by the strenuous demands the producers had put upon him: 'Ian and Martyn were saying to me, "Do this, do that." We did forty takes of "It's Over" and I was so drained. Now, that was discipline, but I enjoyed it. Then they asked me to do "Arabia". Well, I thought, if it gets out that I refused to do a Bowie song and stand that comparison, it'll look worse. At least I can do a fair job of it and say, "Look, I had the courage to get up and do it."'

For his part, Ware's lingering memories of the recordings are of being intrigued by Billy's frequent disappearing acts: 'He'd be really excited and intensely working on a vocal and then he'd say, "This is fantastic . . . anyway, I must go now . . ." He always had a driver and a car waiting. He was a man of mystery right from the word go. Nobody really knew where he was going and what he was doing.'

By spring, MacKenzie and Rankine had both drifted back home to Scotland. Since the Associates no longer had a permanent London base and were spending their time flitting from hotel to hotel, it seemed a logical move. Coyly, the pair also admitted in the press that this northerly move was also intended as relief from their relentless hedonism.

Back at his family's home in Dundee, Billy was afforded no pop-star graces and would even jump in his dad's van to help with the furniture-collecting round. But, according to John MacKenzie, Billy's mess of mixed emotions concerning his home town had grown only more complex: 'He hated the village mentality of Dundee, but there were loads of people there he adored. He couldn't handle the thought oppression of Dundee because he was so flippant with his thought.'

Worse, there were further reminders of the violence that had forced Billy to leave Dundee as a teenager. At the end of one night at a local club, when the house lights were on and the staff were clearing the tables, Billy and his friends were straggling behind and leisurely finishing their drinks when an argument broke out between himself and a particularly persistent bouncer. As MacKenzie lifted his glass to take the last sip of his drink, the bouncer forcefully pushed it into his face and it shattered. The broken shards, by rights, should have lacerated his face, but remarkably, they didn't.

'I get quite a lot of flak from people,' he nervously admitted a month after the incident. 'I've been the object of four physical attacks. I got a tumbler in my face just 'cause it was me. And then I had a fight with these gamekeeping lads, pointing their guns at me and everything. I was out exercising and one of them clocked me: "There's that fucking little pop star." A week before that I got spat on. People are always trying to impress themselves. But that tumbler in my face a few weeks ago should've cut my face open . . . it just left a little mark.'

Sulk was released on 15 May, in the week that 'Club Country' – issued seven days before – entered the charts at number 35 and began a now familiar, slow upwards crawl. The multi-hued cover of the album had been shot in a conservatory of a Surrey mansion by the fashionable photographer Peter Ashworth, who gel-lit the background of tropical ferns and yuccas to create an effect as exotic as much of the music contained – in those pre-CD days – within the sleeve.

Rankine and MacKenzie sit in the forefront on park benches underlit in aqua blue and green. The singer is in black – suit, peaked cap and jackboots – with a slightly quizzical expression. The instrumentalist is also in black, with a red cashmere shawl draped around his shoulders, his eyes half closed, as if blinking from the flash. Although this looks like a photographic accident, Rankine maintains that his possessed look on the cover of *Sulk* was wholly intentional: 'That's how I wanted it. Peter Ashworth took about seven hundred photos and I'm in the same position with the same look on my face in every single one and Bill's all over the place.'

Although MacKenzie's unbalanced, operatic vocal style had undeniably been an influence on the long, drawn-out notes that Tony Hadley, singer with the sartorially painful Spandau Ballet, had imitated on the kilt-wearing group's early hits in 1980–81, at this stage the Associates were keen to distance themselves from the New Romantic trends, particularly with the cover of *Sulk*. 'I wanted to look mental,' Rankine firmly states. 'I didn't want to look like some New Romantic, because we were never bought into that Spandau–Durany thing.'

The music-press assessment of *Sulk* was nothing less than gushing or ecstatic. Paul Morley wrote in his insightful review for *NME*:

'The Associates – as tactfully as possible – just assume that they're supernatural. They cannot be pinned down, they cannot be caught. If rock music is a slow slow tortoise, the Associates are an elusive butterfly. Billy MacKenzie establishes himself as some kind of master at concealing his sensitivity beneath cryptic layers of coolness and irony, and protects his privacy with sheer hysteria.' *Melody Maker* stated, 'This record has an almost timeless majesty that can only make Billy MacKenzie's rapturous grin grow wider still.' *Sounds* frothed, 'This is a kitchen sink album with gold enamelled taps. "Sulk" makes you wanna invent silly words, hug your best mate, laugh till you cry, cry till you laugh and thank God and MacKenzie and Rankine that you're alive.'

More appealing still to the press was the fact that Billy was becoming something of a gift interviewee. Though by turns proving attentive, seductive, secretive, duplicitous and just plain daft, he became a favourite profile subject among music journalists, who, in return, would buff up Billy's ego both in person and in print. He became hugely quotable, whether delivering grand statements ('In athletic terms, the Associates are a pentathlon'), entertainingly refusing to be drawn on his lyrics ('They're just bad mother-in-law jokes') or nailing his devilish streak ('It's called winding up . . . I wind people up and then I wind down'). In less self-protective moments, he even displayed a certain dissatisfaction with his pop-star guise: 'It's dead boring. Everything. I'm bored with everything we're doing now.'

In his flirtatious, girly conversations with Sunie Fletcher for *Record Mirror*, he would often relate long, lingering anecdotes with no colour spared in the telling. 'I got this letter about four weeks ago from Sharon, a girl I used to go out with in Dundee,' he once said to her. 'It was full of praise, which seemed out of character, 'cause we used to bitch at each other all the time, but it was written on her sort of graph paper. It seemed she was in London, and married, because she signed herself Sharon Sullivan. I wrote back, she wrote again, and I finally went to see her.

'In the taxi on the way there, I was thinking, "What if her husband doesn't like me coming round and gives me a good boofing on the chin?" Well . . . when she came down the hall, her blonde hair was just the same but she'd put on a bit of weight. When she got closer I said, "What have you done to yourself, Sharon Lough?" and she said "No, Sharon Sullivan – I'm a fan of yours." Her mum was shouting, "Do you want a cup of tea?", so I went in, signed her records for her . . . You see, the whole situation brought back the entertainment factor, which is what you go into music for in the first place. That episode brought the simplicity of it back.'

Conversely, admiring the intimidating interview tactics of Siouxsie Sioux, Billy would sometimes take a more combative or mischievous approach in his dealings with the press. On one occasion, when an interview was set up to take place in a pub near the offices of Chris Carr, Billy insisted that before they begin, he and the journalist should line up and down several brandies in quick succession to give the conversation a certain edge. After having knocked back six doubles in less than ten minutes, Billy excused himself while he nipped to the toilet, where he proceeded to climb out of the window and leg it down the street, never to return. Of course, no article proved forthcoming following the meeting, but it certainly fuelled his maverick reputation, whether through calculation or – quite possibly – pure boredom. 'I just like to play pranks,' he later reasoned, 'I get great enjoyment out of that . . . but not really to anyone's detriment.'

In Carr, Billy at least had a publicist who could understand the method behind his artist's wayward frivolity: 'He would pull that kind of caper a lot. He would set it up so that something would happen. The lining up of the brandies was part of him wanting everybody to be impressed with the largesse of any given situation. But his relationship with the press was contentious at times. I'd have to persuade him to do stuff. He was never really totally satisfied with the results and the type of representation he got. It wasn't bad press he was afraid of, it was ineffectual press. He would laugh hysterically sometimes at some of the stories.'

By the middle of June, 'Club Country' peaked in the UK chart at number thirteen (three weeks before, *Sulk* had reached number ten in the album chart) and the Associates were back on *Top Of The Pops* with the single for the second time. The first appearance had witnessed the group joined by new drummer Steve Golding (replacing the sacked John Murphy) and a sultry Billy first summoning up the confidence – or as his detractors saw it, arrogance – to eye the camera directly as he performed the song, knees locked together in a mincing, elbow and hip-led dance that the singer himself breezily described as 'dead Tom Jones-ish'. For his and Martha's duet in the middle eight of the song, Billy produced a second, thin silver microphone for Ladly – who had been pretending to play violin – to use as a prop. Instead of giving it to her, however, he held on to both of them, pointing one in her direction. As she began to sing, though, he turned his back to her and began to march away with both mics in his hands, so that – for those viewers who possibly hadn't twigged – it becomes obvious that she's miming and that Billy is gently taking the piss.

But for this second appearance with 'Club Country' at number thirteen, Billy took advantage of that summer's sexually blurred fashion stances to turn in a performance that can only be reasonably described as 'streetfighter camp': his barrel chest covered in a thin, cruise regulation white vest; made-up, battle-worn scars painted on to his face and arms. On his left, Rankine sits playing the first of two guitars that had been specifically made by Harrods entirely from chocolate, at the cost of £600. During the second verse – surely marking a *Top Of The Pops* first – he feeds it to the audience and then picks up the second confectionery six-string, while Billy bites into the detached neck of the first guitar and kicks a yellow balloon around, visibly in his element, the environment now clearly a playground for the Associates' imagination.

'There was nothing else on *Top Of The Pops* that was remotely like it,' says Rankine. 'Bill was camping it up outrageously. We had all sorts of scams that we couldn't get together in time. I was going to come on in one of these Turkish bath things that your head sticks out of, with my arms sticking out playing a brush or something. The more mental things we get away with, the better.'

In their use of sensuality, hilarity and a certain derailed sophistication, in many ways the Associates seemed to be destined to inherit the mantle of Roxy Music. In the 70s Roxy Music had initially emerged as a cartoon-quiffed glam-rock outfit and –

particularly in the light of Bryan Ferry's subsequent relationship with Jerry Hall and the band's use of top international models on their album covers – had developed into an altogether more *Vogue*-ish proposition. There were clear signals that this was the direction in which the Associates were heading, particularly in the onstage sexual undercurrent flowing between MacKenzie and Ladly. 'There was always that rapport going on between us, although we were never lovers or anything,' Martha admits. 'His whole expression of himself was sexual and I think that was incredibly magnetic for girls and for boys. He was kind of omnisexual – he didn't just see sexuality in people, he saw it in situations and all things really.'

Chris Carr has his own thoughts on the Associates' sexual allure at this time: 'The three of them – Dempsey included – had the lady-killer thing. They could walk into any kind of club at that time and the women would flock to them. There was a posse of women constantly at their beck and call – and it's hard to believe now – but it was beyond groupiedom. It was the start of a sophisticated approach to sex and, to a certain extent, casual sex. If Billy was interested in that, it was to expand. As in everything – his sexual explorations, his mental explorations . . . it was an expanding thing. I mean, you just have to listen to the guy sing . . . he wanted to go all the way there. And they had the élan and the sophistica-tion to pull it off. There wasn't a sexier band that I can think of at the time.'

If the Associates were slowly morphing into Roxy Music, it hadn't escaped the attention of Bryan Ferry. Having seen the group on *Top Of The Pops*, he made an arrangement with MacKenzie and Rankine to borrow their backing band – Ladly, Dempsey and Golding – for the European TV promotion of the singles from the ultra-smooth *Avalon* album. Dempsey points out: 'Billy, of course, loved the idea of Roxy Music's backing band being the Associates.'

Becoming ever more brazen, for the cover of the Associates' next single, a double A-side featuring the exaggerated 60s soul of '18 Carat Love Affair' and a charged reworking of Diana Ross's 'Love Hangover', Billy appeared face down and naked in a full body shot with model Fiona Skinner showering gold confetti on to his naked back. Although initially nervous about releasing such an overtly sexual image as a single sleeve, Billy revealed an adventurousness in toying with his public image at this time by approving the shot. Of his dynamic interpretation of the Diana Ross song, in an interview in *Smash Hits* Billy likened it to a cross-breed between his own singing style and that of archly seductive 70s soul artist Barry White, describing it as 'a big sexy Barry MacKenzie version'.

Out of the vocal performances on all of the Associates' records up to this point, Rankine singles out 'Love Hangover' as his favourite: 'That was a brilliant vocal, the way he stretched it this way and that. I suppose that was helped by it not being our song. That often happens with bands – because it's not their song, they're detached from it in a certain way and they do things that they can't do in their own songs. But I really think Bill was totally on it there.'

Although it sold more disappointingly, stalling at number twenty-one, the Associates again appeared – for the final time in this incarnation – on *Top Of The Pops*, with the single's 'real' A-side, '18 Carat Love Affair'. During the camera rehearsals, however, there was serious friction between Billy and the director. 'We were on the set and for some reason he was drunk,' Dempsey recalls. 'It was very unlike him, because he didn't seem to be drinking at this time, but we were rehearsing and he was fooling around and the director told him to get on with it, and he didn't, and so they said, "Right, that's it, you're off . . ."'

Martha Ladly recalls of the incident: 'For some reason I'd been stuck on the very edge of the stage and if I stepped back one step I was going to be flying into the audience. I started to get quite pissed off about this and they refused to move me. Billy was getting *really* pissed off about the way they'd blocked the shots. So I was moving the piano physically and Billy was sounding off to the cameramen and the director basically tried to kick us off the programme.'

Following a ripple of backstage panic among the Warners television promotion people, it transpired that the BBC's swiftly proposed stand-in act – American bubblegum funk trio Shalamar –

couldn't make it in time, meaning that the defiant Associates had to be brought back onstage. 'We had a reputation for being incredibly difficult by then,' Ladly adds. In the eventual performance, Billy pulled yet another prank on her. In the middle of the song, he motions to hand her a red velvet heart. What directly follows is an intimate and sweetly joky moment that perhaps defines the pair's onstage relationship. As Ladly reaches out to take the heart, Billy snatches it away like a cheeky schoolboy tease and wanders off smirking.

Although now chart regulars, the Associates were perhaps unlikely targets for the teen press. Nevertheless, Rankine and MacKenzie both possessed the requisite sharply chiselled cheekbones, and for a brief period around this time, they became pin-up material. In the subsequent questionnaires he completed for various teenage magazines, the pop star Billy MacKenzie revealed his height (five feet seven inches), weight (nine stone, four pounds), favourite animals (whippets, peregrines, mongeese), favourite clothes (black cotton socks, Italian casual wear 1952–59), favourite films (*Bus Stop, The Sound Of Music, Barbarella*), ambition (four children) and candidly offered his biggest secret ('Not a great lover').

Even if the Associates were at the peak of their musical and commercial powers and Billy seemed to have all the necessary credentials for the classic casting of the misfit-turned-pop star, it was often in these more offhand teen-pop interviews, rather than in the chin-stroking music press, that he was at his most revealing. Shortly after '18 Carat Love Affair', he revealed in *Smash Hits* a certain ambivalence where success was concerned: 'It seems to make quite a lot of people happy, and that's good. It gives you a wee bit more confidence and that, but it's something you've got to handle. Sometimes I can't handle it too well.'

Then, one night at an art-college disco in Dundee with former Associate Steve Knight, Billy made a passing comment with an unequivocal air of foreboding: 'He was saying, "Well, it's all there for me now . . . you wouldn't believe the things that people are saying I could do." Then he said, "But I'm not gonna do it, I'm just gonna throw it all away."'

*   *   *

The first real indication that Billy MacKenzie was starting to feel hemmed in by his own success came in the latter half of July with the beginning of the rehearsals for the tour that was due to follow in the wake of *Sulk*. Propelled by an urgent energy, the chief by-product of their recent triumphs, the Associates set themselves an almost impossible task. Using Basing Street Studios in Notting Hill as their centre of operations, the touring band – expanded to nine with keyboardists and backing vocalists – were to rehearse in the studio live room, and simultaneously, in the control room. MacKenzie and Rankine would set about remixing and updating *The Affectionate Punch*, adding the new digital effects and synthesizer sounds that hadn't been at their disposal at the time of its recording two years before. It would even be an opportunity for Billy to redo some of the vocals that – indeed, like much of the original album – he hadn't been happy with.

The problem was that he seemed keener to spend most of his time up in Dundee and as far away from London and recording studios as possible, resulting in his rarely turning up. In Billy's absence, Rankine carried on the work – and the party – alone, jumping from daytime band rehearsals to night-time remixing. After four weeks of this unhealthy activity, not even Duracells could have kept Rankine going: 'I was sleeping in the studio, I was working seventeen, eighteen, nineteen hours a day. It was heavy shit.'

At this time the Associates' working relationship with Michael Dempsey came to an abrupt end. Billy began to encourage the bassist to take up the offer of producing an album for Dutch multi-instrumentalist Stephen Emmer, who, as a fan of the Associates, had sent the band his experimental, dance-based demo. Whether the duo were perhaps devious in their motives (Dempsey couldn't cope with the horrendous, funky 'slap' style that was required of most bass players in 1982), Billy more than hinted to the bassist that he might be better off forgetting about the Associates. 'He told me that he planned to dismantle the band and I should stay away from what was about to happen,' Dempsey says. 'Whether he was being selective with the truth and trying to spare my feelings, I don't know, but he was almost over-encouraging me to go and do this thing.'

Back at Basing Street, Rankine was becoming frustrated by Billy's prolonged vanishing acts. Even when the singer did turn up for rehearsals, it was apparent to the guitarist that his heart really wasn't in it.

'We'd be rehearsing "Club Country" or "Party Fears Two",' Rankine remembers, 'and Bill would be taking the piss out of them. Singing shite over the top. I think maybe he felt then that he was getting into self-parody. What he wanted most at that time was to go back into the studio and write a whole batch of new songs. But there was a British tour, there was six or seven dates in America, there was Japan and Australia and the whole of Europe all screaming for these dates. I think he felt a tremendous pressure to do the tour and he saw what was lying ahead. I was much more accepting of the rock and roll machine and what had to be done. And if there was something that we began to differ on . . . that was it.'

Rankine, however, insists that there was little room for argument between himself and Billy at this stage: "When he showed up, I'd say, "Where the fuck have you been, man?" and he'd just say, "Been up in Dundee." But then I was thinking, Is he being truthful with me? Has he *really* been there? And that was really something, because if I was ever aware of anything, I'd never been aware that Bill was lying to me. There were times when Warner Brothers were asking me, "Do you know where he is?" And even if I knew where he was in Dundee, I wasn't going to tell them. I thought, If he's got something to work out, he's just got to work it out. I wasn't going to let the record company come between us.'

Meanwhile Tarquin Gotch – as the luckless A&R man in charge of ensuring that Billy made it to the rehearsals – was tearing his hair out. 'One minute he's living in London, the next minute he's gone back up to Dundee,' he remembers. 'So you'd say to him, "OK, where are you living?" and he'd say, "With a friend." I'd say, "OK, can we have a number?" He'd say, "No, he's not on the phone." I remember I got so frustrated, I flew up to Dundee to try to find him and of course the record company was going mad at me. It was a nightmare.'

In addition, it was becoming apparent that the remixing of *The Affectionate Punch* was perhaps a pointless measure. Strapping synthesizer parts on to the songs was making many of them lose much of their initial bite. MacKenzie had re-recorded the vocals for 'Paper House' and 'Deeply Concerned', but to the listener it sounds as if he is merely going through the motions, and as a result the performances are flat in comparison to the original takes. 'It was a big mistake, big mistake,' Rankine now confesses. 'We should never have touched it. It was torturous to do.'

To compound the guitarist's problems, the complex arrangements of *Sulk* were proving difficult to translate to a live situation and the band were still sounding incredibly rough around the edges. Martha Ladly admits that personally she was 'finding it quite difficult to take in all the stuff that I had to know . . . I was making mistakes'. The opening dates of the tour were scheduled to be three consecutive nights in August at the Assembly Rooms during the Edinburgh Festival. The nine-piece group decamped to the Scottish capital, the plan being to enjoy a relaxed sound check at the Assembly Rooms the day before the first gig. Ladly remembers this last rehearsal being 'a bit of a mess'. Alan Rankine, for his part, admits that the band 'wasn't really kicking . . . but if you look at any band when they're about to go on a tour, especially if they haven't played for nearly two years, there's always going to be teething troubles.'

After sound-checking, the unit repaired to the bar at the George Hotel and the alcohol flowed. Mid-way through the evening, MacKenzie, who to the others had seemed slightly preoccupied for most of the day, suddenly announced that he wasn't going ahead with the tour. The rest of the band were slightly disbelieving at first, although their shared reactions quickly turned to shock when it became apparent that Billy was deadly serious.

'By that time everyone was fairly drunk,' Rankine recalls. 'He just said, "I don't want to do it." He wouldn't say any more. All anyone could do then was say, "Right, let's just see whether this irons itself out in the morning." But I knew it wasn't going to because Bill wouldn't say something like that unless his mind was made.'

Edinburgh folklore has it that that night Billy was seen being chased down George Street, closely followed by Rankine, repeatedly hitting the singer over the head with a shoe. Although the guitarist discredits the story, he admits that he might have been spotted battering Billy around the cranium with an item of footwear in the hotel lift.

By the morning, when Chris Carr was due to arrive with journalist Steve Sutherland and photographer Tom Sheehan to cover the Associates' first gig in eighteen months for *Melody Maker*, Billy had cooked up an excuse, claiming that he had contracted pharyngitis, a throat and chest infection that – according to medical dictionaries – can be caused by heavy smoking or an excessive intake of spirits. Since Billy, accompanied by Steve Reid (perhaps his only ally in the circumstances) had gone out the previous night and ended up so leglessly drunk that the pair had briefly fallen asleep under a car, at least it was plausible.

However, when Carr was informed that MacKenzie had lost his voice, he recognized it as being a transparent excuse: 'I said to Tom and Steve, "You sit in the bar and I'll see what's going on." Then I had a bit of an altercation with Billy because I knew he was bullshitting me. At first it was all sign language, but I knew full well, and I managed to needle him enough to get him speaking properly. Then he just fled.' After wandering through the hotel bar to make a token apology to the *Melody Maker* correspondents in a put-on, throaty gruff, Billy jumped into a taxi and asked the driver to take him to Dundee, a journey costing around £50 at that time. As the news leaked out and the session musicians deflatedly wended their way back to London, the legal threats began to fly. Not only had the Associates forfeited their sizeable performance fees in aborting the British tour, there was every chance they were now going to be sued by the promoters. In cancelling the three Edinburgh shows alone, the duo had lost £35,000. For the remainder of the day, Rankine – along with Carr, Sutherland and Sheehan – got very gradually, but stupendously, drunk.

'It broke in such a big way,' Carr says. 'I had all the national papers and music papers coming up to review the shows and all of that had to be called off. Everybody was trying to get hold of Alan, chasing bills. We were constantly moving from one room to another courtesy of the hotel management because somebody would get the room number and Alan was in no state to defend Billy.'

Although not apparent at the time, the reasons for MacKenzie dramatically bailing out of the tour were complex and a combination of his fear of self-parody, his anxieties about being forced on to the road for the foreseeable future, his lack of confidence in the band (albeit not helped by his disappearances during rehearsals) and the terror of falling flat on his face in public, heightened by his tendency toward stage fright. Martha Ladly reckons that Billy 'was really worried – quite legitimately probably – that people were going to come away saying, "That's crap." But I think it would've come right. Whether he got scared or whether he just got bored, I don't know. His boredom threshold was very, very low.'

In the fallout from the cancellation of the tour, a half-hearted plot developed to reschedule the dates, the Associates attempting a handful of rehearsals with a stripped-down, five-piece line-up of the touring band. But as Rankine admits, 'You could tell even then that there was still something wrong and it wasn't going to go away. Bill said he was going to do it, but I wasn't sure whether I believed him.'

It seemed as if – short of counselling – the pair's relationship was now doomed. On the night that Sire Records boss Seymour Stein took MacKenzie, Rankine, Chris Parry and Tarquin Gotch to Langan's Brasserie to discuss the Associates signing to his label for the States, with a head-spinning offer of $600,000, the duo effectively split.

'Seymour was talking about a lot of money,' Rankine recalls of the conversation during the meal. 'He's got the radio stations in place, he's got the tour support organized and he's with us 110 per cent, can't wait to do it. And Bill just says, "No, I don't want to do it. I don't want to tour America, I want to do that later." Naturally this doesn't go down well with Seymour and I can see Parry and Gotch getting a bit nervous.

'After that, we go to the Camden Palace and Bill and I are having words by this time. I'm saying to him, "Bill, I can't handle this, I cannot take any more." And he's saying, "Look, man, let's just record, let's not play live, let's just be a studio band." I said, "Bill, nah, can't do it, that's enough . . . enough." I wanted to tour and I knew that's what was required of us. I didn't know of any other band to use as a yardstick who'd been a studio band, unless you were bloody Steely Dan. Bill was saying to me, "Look, there *is* a way out of this", but to me it just seemed like there was nowhere else this could go.'

In mid-September a mutually frosty MacKenzie and Rankine met up again at the George Hotel in Edinburgh, scene of the ructions only weeks before, to fulfil a photo-session obligation for the sleeve of *The Affectionate Punch* remix. The guitarist remembers there being 'a strange atmosphere, a strained atmosphere. Parry was there because I think he knew there was something not right and he was going to try and patch things up.'

The Fiction boss admits: 'I flew up there to talk to them about things, but there was just no way Billy was going to work with Alan again, and I know Alan found that very disturbing. I was just trying to see if we could get this thing back on the rails again. But it didn't really seem like a possibility and . . . that was the end of that.'

'In the end,' Rankine resignedly sighs, 'it just fizzled out.'

In October of 1982 Rankine informed Warner Brothers that he was leaving the Associates: 'Contractually, it came very quickly. They said, "Are you a leaving member?" and I said, "Yeah." It was a very weird feeling because it was everything I'd worked towards for the last six or seven years . . . everything I'd worked towards since I picked up a guitar when I was eleven. But there was no point in holding a grudge – Bill didn't have any malicious design. Still, for at least six months after that, it was just anger, anger, anger and self-pity and all the rest of it. When we played live in 1980, Bill had seemed to love it, so something had changed, something was different. That fear of the rock and roll machine thing was definitely one of the factors.'

As part of the agreement dissolving their partnership, Rankine handed the rights to the Associates' name over to MacKenzie and 'never really thought about it'.

Fourteen years later, in a frank interview with Garry Mulholland of London listing magazine *Time Out*, Billy – after years of dishing out fluff and wafer-thin excuses to the press – gave his most honest account of the reasons behind the split of the original Associates:

'Drugs. It was just cocaine frenzy. It was practically getting sprinkled on the cornflakes. I got really high and couldn't get any higher and then I would go, "So what? Big deal." I couldn't really get into that self-deception or toxic glamour. I thought it was fucking disgusting. I turned into the bastard son of Frankenstein with it and hated myself. So that was one of the reasons, and also we were unprepared for a lot of things. Nobody ever prepares you for that success and I didn't feel like I was a spokesman for a generation or actually that interesting as a person. I just thought I had an innate ability to express myself through music. But oratory skills . . . my background was such that I had a lot of learning to do.

'It's hip now to downgrade these things and scratch your balls and inject Fosters into your eyeball. But when your icons seemed so kind of supernova . . . you did think you had to match that, and how could you match that coming from a little scuzzy scheme up in Dundee? So there was all that to think about. If I was wanting to carry on just for the money, then I would've done that. Seymour Stein's camp over in America were wanting to take us over there. But then, I'd already sort of travelled the world and created my own little rock and roll lifestyle between 16 and 21.

'It was Alan that basically brought the guillotine down on the Associates. I said, "Yeah, we'll work in the studio together", but I wasn't wanting to tour because we weren't prepared. We'd lost our Australian drummer and there were some techniques on bass that Mike Dempsey wasn't able to do, but we really got somebody in when we shouldn't have.

'Also, I wanted to be able to go to Dundee and inject some energy back into the town . . .'

8

The Sound of Barking

From the outside, at least, it appeared as if Billy MacKenzie had suffered a severe bout of career insecurity and crumbled at the peak of the Associates' success. But if anything, perhaps what he had revealed was an intense fear of the known – the stability of his partnership with Alan Rankine (the bond having been intensified by their success) and the dull predictability of touring life – rather than of the greater unknown. Ever restless and easily bored, up until this point Billy had never shown any real commitment to anything or anyone, aside from his twin devotions to his family and his whippets. In effect, the opposite of the outside theory was the truth – he had grown anxious with the looming realities of career security and musical wedlock. Significantly, from here on in Billy MacKenzie would never be creatively monogamous again and the broader connotations of the Associates' name became increasingly apparent.

If the singer had briefly returned to the relative haven of Dundee to mull over the extraordinary pattern of recent events in his life, he wasn't the only one. Steve Reid, in a situation aggravated by his increasing drug intake, had experienced what he openly describes as 'a complete and utter mental breakdown'. In his fragile state, Reid had made his way back to Dundee and was living with his parents: 'A couple of times Billy would come round and bang on the door shouting, "Are you in?" But I wouldn't answer it because I was feeling like shit. I was insane and I thought it was something to do with me that the Falklands War had broken out. I was a paranoid schizophrenic, dodging imaginary bullets . . .

I thought everyone was after me. I didn't want to see Billy because I thought I'd let him down in some way by starting this big war.'

Eventually, through MacKenzie's dogged persistence, Reid answered the door: 'He came in and he said, "Look . . . all of this is in your head, you've got hobgoblins in your brain and you've got to get them out of there." He was really wise when it came to emotions and mental stability.' As the first step in Reid's rehabilitation, Billy suggested that they record a one-off single together, primarily to provide a path back to reality for the guitarist, and in the process, earn him some cash. 'With Billy being as big as he was at the time,' Reid states, 'we were able to get a good advance for it, about six grand. I was still gone, like, but Billy was great. He understood what was happening and he wanted to help.'

The resulting Reid-penned single, 'Ice Cream Factory', released by WEA in October 1982 under the banner of MacKenzie Sings Orbidöig, was accurately described by Billy as 'the Archies on acid'. A jaunty, off-centre pop track in the style of '18 Carat Love Affair', it was adorned with Bacharach-style brass frills and featured its singer fantasizing about a simple existence that involved marriage and whipping up raspberry ripple for a living. Although a wonderfully skittish pop indulgence, it proved 'a bit too much for people intellectually' in Reid's assessment and, consequently, it failed to set the charts ablaze.

Undeterred, since both had found some sense of creative fulfilment in the collaboration, MacKenzie and Reid decided to return to the studio to record an entire, largely experimental album to follow up 'Ice Cream Factory'. Talking about his desire to work with Reid, Billy said, 'Stevie's the same as me, it's all for the glory of the music and nothing else matters. He's also got the same sense of humour as me, which most people don't understand.' The sessions for the album began in November at Basing Street Studios, scene of the fateful rehearsals four months before for the tour that never happened, with producer/engineer Mark Arthurworrey, Rankine's accomplice in the remixing of *The Affectionate Punch*.

Keen to bankroll what was intended to be Billy MacKenzie's début solo album, Warner Brothers allocated £50,000 to the project, for the block-booking of the studio and the expensive hire of a brass section and string players. In Steve Reid's words, the pair 'let our imaginations run riot'. While employing the multi-layering approach of past Associates material, these recordings, it soon became apparent to visitors to the studio, were swiftly taking on a hysterical, creatively undisciplined edge. The pair would quickly fill up twenty-two tracks of a twenty-four track master tape, copy these on to the two tracks that remained and then proceed to fill up the cleared tracks with more instrumentation and effected sonic treatments, repeating the process until the result was a dense, aural stew. 'We were making this big avant-garde noise,' Reid explains. 'Musically, Billy used really weird minor scales, which I was able to cotton on to just by ear. The way he used melody and structure and counterpoint, it was very advanced stuff in your average pop context.'

Cornwall-born keyboard player Howard Hughes – whose name had naturally stuck in Billy's mind when he was first suggested as a possible musician for the *Sulk* tour – was brought in to contribute to the tracks around a month into the disordered proceedings. He remembers the studio environment being 'a bit like a drug dealer's house, although there didn't seem to be any drugs around. Mark Arthurworrey had this totally other presence. I remember he wore this massive big fur coat when he was sitting at the mixing desk. Billy and Steve would just charge about and there were dogs everywhere. Whatever they said to Arthurworrey, whether it be, "Oh, Mark, we're going to set fire to the room", he would just say, "OK, that'll be fine, we'll put it on these two tracks." It was complete anarchy, but it was very driven. There were no budget restrictions at all. They used tape like it was toilet roll. But very quickly it became apparent that they were prepared to just go on recording for ever. There wasn't really any intention to mix it or to do anything with it.'

If there were doubts whether these tracks could be mixed into anything audibly resembling a major-label album release, then they were well founded. 'Well, we *knew* it was unmixable,' Reid points out, matter-of-factly. 'If you took five tracks out, you had one song. If you put them back and took another five out, you had another song. It was just this kaleidoscope of musical noises and shrieks and bangs.' Furthermore, in the maniacal development of the tracks, nothing was considered a musical step too far. Wandering into the reception area of the studio one morning, Reid was confronted by the security guard's German shepherd barking at him and straining at the leash. Half an hour later, when MacKenzie arrived, the dog was seated upright in the recording room, being conducted by the guitarist to add ferocious, fear-inducing barks to one of the tracks. Typical of their working relationship at this time, Reid recalls, was that 'Billy wasn't surprised or anything. He just said, "Put some echo on that dog."'

One track, 'The Best Of You', written by MacKenzie as a male-female duet, originally featured German cult disco queen Gina X, snapping out her lines in a stern Teutonic howl. Following the subsequent scrapping of her contribution, Annie Lennox of the Eurythmics agreed to record the duet with Billy, secretly impressing the similarly single-minded MacKenzie by insisting on tweaking the vocal melody to her satisfaction. Steve Reid remembers a sudden chivalrous air descending on the day that Lennox visited the studio. 'Me, Billy and Mark Arthurworrey were all kind of after her,' he admits, 'opening doors, saying, "You want a cup of tea?" Everyone was going out of their way to be ultra ultra nice to her. When she wasn't in the room, the three of us were going, "She fancies me" . . . "No, she doesn't, she fancies me." The girl didn't fancy *any* of us, for sure.' In the end, however, when the Eurythmics scored a number-two hit with 'Sweet Dreams (Are Made Of This)', kick-starting the group's subsequent multi-platinum career, RCA Records withdrew their permission to use Lennox's vocal on 'The Best Of You', perhaps concerned that WEA would attempt to release the track as a cash-in single.

Billy's work-in-progress studio cassette of these sessions reveals the lost Lennox/MacKenzie duet to be a half-finished tug-of-war between two wholly complementary voices, the former's seductive, lower-register delivery perfectly offsetting the latter's high-flying histrionics. On the cassette, however, only part of the track still exists, since the tape seems to have also ended up being used by its owner as a notepad for melodic ideas. The tracks are frequently interrupted by the sound of Billy, sitting in the kitchen at Bonnybank Road in Dundee, tapping on a table top and whistling and scatting through ideas for songs including future single 'Those First Impressions' and 'Blue It Is' (not, in fact, released until nearly fourteen years later). The studio tracks themselves are indeed incredibly dense, closer in spirit to a more orchestrated version of *Sulk*, although on the unreleased 'The Moon And Sapphire', Billy performs a quasi-mystical lyric a cappella before the track bursts into an aping of the twangy 60s rock of early John Barry, a musical cross-pollination that sadly would never make it on to record.

Having afforded MacKenzie the luxury of creative control for these solo-album sessions, when Warner Brothers officials first came down to the studio four months into recording, they were reportedly shocked by the material's distinct lack of commerciality (now that the duet with Lennox was unusable) and accused the tracks of being of 'inferior quality'. Somewhere along the line, it had been mutually agreed that the work had ceased to be a Billy MacKenzie side-project and was now the beginnings of the next proper Associates album, and Warners were clearly disturbed by the results.

Billy moaned to *NME* at the time: 'They never questioned the bills when we went in the studio, so we just went out and got the whole LP orchestrated. It did cost quite a bit, but the result is just brilliant. It's the best music I've ever been involved in. But they want something that they think is commercially viable and I just couldn't give a damn. All I wanted to do was better myself with the music that was coming through me.' Warners offered Billy an ultimatum – come up with a radio-friendly single or the album would be shelved. Both MacKenzie's career and creative integrity were now on the line.

Then, fatefully, the master tapes of the album vanished.

Howard Hughes remembers: 'I turned up at the studio one day and Billy just said, "Oh, we've lost the tapes." Warner Brothers blamed Mark Arthurworrey for a while and there was talk that Billy had got rid of the tapes because he didn't like it, he was fed up and he wanted to start again.'

Other theories began to emerge, some plausible, some part of the prankster legend that had built up around MacKenzie. It was said that the poorly labelled masters had somehow ended up in the basement at the WEA offices in Broadwick Street for safe keeping over Christmas 1982 and that it would've taken weeks of sifting through the dusty piles of Rod Stewart and Eric Clapton multi-tracks to recover them. Others claimed that Billy had stolen them from Basing Street and either entrusted them to a friend or dumped them in the Thames. Over the ensuing years, under-standing the theft of £50,000 master tapes to be a serious legal matter, Billy repeatedly protested his innocence and remained evasive: 'Well, *we* didn't scrap it, it scrapped itself. It sort of got lost, so we had to re-record it.'

As a footnote to this mysterious incident, the final resting place of the tapes for the aborted album is known by a handful of Billy MacKenzie's former friends and colleagues. Loyal to the last, however, they keep it a fiercely guarded secret.

Glenn Gregory didn't want a whippet, but he got one anyway. The Heaven 17 singer and Billy MacKenzie were both regular faces on the London club and party scene inhabited by the discerning, free alcohol-thirsty pop star, and as a result the pair had a reputation as ever-ready socialites. 'Whenever I hadn't seen him for a couple of weeks,' Gregory recalls, 'the first thing he'd always say was, "I'm off the drink now." Then you could guarantee that five hours later he'd be off his fucking nut somewhere, climbing up some tree.'

Billy had initially propositioned Gregory with the news that one of his dogs was expecting a litter of pups, adding that the singer would be 'really good with a whippet'. Gregory was adamant that he didn't want a dog, although his wife Sarah was quietly thrilled by the notion. A week later, at a party thrown by Channel 4 and the Comic Strip at the Scala cinema in King's Cross, Gregory and his wife were standing in the foyer sipping wine with the other guests when Billy sauntered through the door. 'He had his big coat and beret on as he always did,' Gregory remembers, 'and he walked straight over and said, "Here, Glenn, I've got you something." He opened his coat and produced this tiny, tiny whippet, and I went, "You fucking bastard, what've you done?" Of course, Sarah instantly fell in love with it. It was wandering around on little tiny weeny legs and everybody in the whole place was doting on this little pup.

'When we were leaving, I asked Billy what I should feed it on and he said, "Well, for the first couple of months you should just give them sardines – they've got all the oils for their coats and stuff.' So for the first couple of weeks, I'm feeding this dog sardines, which it's loving, but its breath and its shit and its farts were outrageously bad, totally disgusting. After a while I took it to the vet to have its injections and I mentioned the fact that I'd been feeding it sardines – thinking I knew all the business – and he said, "You're feeding him *sardines*?" So I immediately phoned Billy up and said, "Did you do that on purpose?", and he innocently said, "No, I feed all my dogs on sardines, Glenn." To this day I still don't know whether he did it on purpose. Since then I've had another two whippets, and I know quite a bit about them. I've read the books and oddly enough, they never mention sardines . . .'

In the early months of 1983 Billy had returned to Dundee to write songs and take stock of the situation with Warners, although he would frequently yo-yo up and down to London for meetings with his label. If Billy's whippet network was growing, then his presence in the fields surrounding Dundee where he often walked his dogs – and usually sang his heart out since there were few people around – was not always welcomed by the landowners and gamekeepers. One day when Billy was out walking Gina, his latest puppy, he first became aware, to his cost, that this small dog had a sheep-worrying tendency. Spying a ram, the young whippet bolted into a field and leapt on to the back of the animal, emerging with a huge tuft of wool between its teeth. 'Unfortunately the incident had been observed by three gamekeepers,' Billy wrote in his whippet diaries. 'As we approached them, I apologized and explained that Gina was only a pup and we were only out for a walk and would keep her under control, [when] one of the men kicked her in the ribs. I lost my temper and swung my fist at him as hard as I could. It took the other two gamekeepers to haul me off.'

Down in London, there was further friction of a different nature. Warners were still insisting that MacKenzie come up with a chart-friendly single and go into the studio with a 'name' producer to keep an eye on him. Martin Rushent, whose production credits included such diverse artists as the Stranglers and the Human

League, was enlisted by the record company to be the session helmsman. Together with Hughes and Reid, in April Billy recorded 'Waiting For The Loveboat', a soaring dance track punctured by sharp electric-guitar stabs, that he had first demoed during his time with Rankine and aired the previous March as part of a Radio One session for John Peel. On hearing the finished mix, Warners, who were under pressure to come up with home-grown hits since the majority of their chart successes at this time were by their American artists, vetoed the track on the grounds that it didn't sound like a hit record to their ears (although eighteen months later they would relent and issue the track as a single). 'I thought we'd done what they wanted,' Steve Reid says, 'but as a company they thought it wasn't like Spandau Ballet or ABC or whoever was in the charts. That's what I made of it anyway. Billy didn't actually tell me a lot of what was going on at that point.'

MacKenzie was privately trying to get to grips with the fact that a tougher new regime was settling in at Warners under the managing directorship of Rob Dickens; Tarquin Gotch having been sacked as head of A&R and replaced by Max Hole, who had previously managed a stable of record producers. While a clearing out of the label's roster had found a number of acts being dropped, MacKenzie – still less than a year after his last hit – had been retained, even if the Associates, label had been dissolved and he was now directly signed to WEA. Max Hole admits he was wary of his new charge: 'He already had the reputation of being difficult to handle from the record company point of view. He was renowned for being naughty.' With no material prepared for release, Billy had been ordered to come up with a new batch of songs to augment the best of the material from the 'lost' album, and for much of 1983 MacKenzie frustratedly remained in limbo.

In September the first negatively angled feature focusing on Billy appeared in *NME* under the banner 'Spoilt Brat, Silly Prat Or Visionary Genius?', accompanied by a photograph of MacKenzie lying in a cobbled street, as if down and out, playing a harmonica as a German shepherd dog lay at his side. The opening sentence simply read 'Whatever happened to Billy MacKenzie?, and in the article, journalist Don Watson asked the singer why – if, as he

Aged sixteen, before the wanderlust set in.

'Boys Keep Swinging' on *Double Hip*, 1979.

Members of The Associates are John Sweeney, Bill Mackenzie and Steve Knight, with Linlithgow's Alan Rankine on the extreme right of the picture.

ALAN AND ASSOCIATES ON THE ROAD TO STARDOM

A Linlithgow student is on the road to stardom . . . with his Associates.

For Alan Rankin of 69 Riccarton Road and his new wave pop group — The Associates — have just clinched a record deal with a top publishing company guaranteeing them three singles and an album over the next 18 months.

The newly-formed band have only played one gig and have visited the recording studio in Edinburgh and London a few times to record their new single, currently in the alternative charts, "Boys Keep Swingin'."

The group are going down to London to discuss the contract with MCA and a publishing deal with Sparta Florida Music Group including plans to rush release the new single.

Before their single the band's members — Bill MacKenzie (22), lead singer; Steven Knight (22), bass guitar; John Sweeney (16), drummer; all from Edinburgh, had a big disappointment when their previous single was dropped at the last minute.

Alan, the group's guitarist, said: "It was a double "A" side — Your double hipness and Logan Town — and the publishing company, Polydor, had second thoughts and dropped it. We were naturally disappointed but carried on.

"This deal is a great break which could lead to better things but we've no idea what the future prospects will be."

He added: "We had 500 records made and distributed them to local radio stations, record shops and newspapers. "Girls Keep Swingin'" reached No. 15 in Bruce's, the record shop in Edinburgh, alternative chart which is a guide to music of the future.

"Our gig seemed to go down very well. It was a small place but the audience responded and we got a few encores."

Alan, a former pupil of Linlithgow Academy, is at college in Edinburgh.

Heading for the toppermost of the poppermost: the *Linlithgow Gazette*, 1979.

With Alan Rankine in full flight on stage in London during *The Affectionate Punch* tour, 1980.

The Associates in the same year. Left to right: Michael Dempsey, John Murphy, Billy MacKenzie and Alan Rankine.

Promotional photo for the contract-nullifying alter ego, 39 Lyon Street, in 1981. Left to right: Billy, Christine Beveridge, Alan Rankine.

39 LYON STREET

Bubble-wrap hell in The Manor swimming pool, Oxfordshire, shooting the cover for *Fourth Drawer Down*.

Rankine in chopsticks and a fencing suit: backstage at *Top of the Pops* for first appearance with 'Party Fears Two', March 1982.

Billy accidentally patents that image: bad haircut concealed under his beret, *Top of the Pops*, March 1982.

Growing in confidence, on the second Top of the Pops appearance for 'Party Fears Two'.

Getting ready to run away with Martha Ladly's mic, performing 'Club Country', May 1982.

Basing Street, summer 1982: in rehearsal for the tour that never happened. Note: no Billy.

The flyer for cancelled show at Ultratheque, Glasgow.

Billy, whippet commander, in the countryside outside Dundee.

1983: Whatever happened to Billy MacKenzie?

Steve Reid, co-conspirator in the unmixable first version of the album *Perhaps*.

The torch singer at Ronnie Scott's, December 1984

Backstage at the Dominion, London, March 1985: Billy trying not to appear afflicted by pre-gig nerves.

With Roberto Soave on stage at the Dominion.

Planned sleeve for 'the great lost album', *The Glamour Chase*, 1988.

Paris in the springtime, 1985.

With Boris Blank of Yello sampling the Zurich nightlife.

Left to right: Billy, Boris Blank, Hubertus von Hohenlohe (co-producer of the *The Rhythmn Divine*), Shirley Bassey and Dieter Meier "Working with her made everything valid with my mum and aunties."

Wild is the wig: video shoot for 'Fire To Ice', 1990.

Doggedly refusing to take the hat off for the record company, in the same year.

A COCKATOO HAS AN O IN ITS OO
JUST LIKE TONTO AND RKLO TOO.
So let's raise our glass to these splendid fellows
Brothers to Gina who read OTHELLO
CHRISTINE'S GANG ON THE MILKY WAY
Still chasing their Tails on there eleven½ Birthday

Birthday poem for Christine Beveridge's whippets.

Billy the happy – but slightly bewildered – shopper, Camden Sainsbury's, 1995.

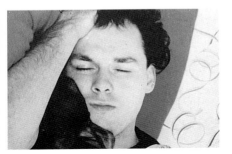

With Tonto II, Kentish Town, 1995.

In a fetching blond wig, witnessing the final stage of the whippet mating ritual.

Christmas 1994. Back row left to right: Auntie Betty, Lily MacKenzie, Billy, sisters Helen and Lizzie.

With collaborator Steve Aungle in the courtyard at 40 Holland Road, 1996.

The last photo session, 27 September, 1996.

modulator . . . that's the way we'll do it." He'd got enough confidence to believe that he knew how records were constructed, and the truth of the matter is that that was never his strong suit. He really didn't know how to fit things together, he just knew he liked individual sounds and he liked that joyous chaos thing, which is a sound in itself . . . but it's not particularly commercial and it tended to bury his voice.

'I tried and tried and tried over about two weeks, and it got to the point where there was just no getting through to him. He would not listen. Really what he wanted to do was to produce the records himself, but the record company – for good reason – wouldn't let him do it. His perception of how the records should sound was different to any kind of commercial producer, and he was already at a point where he was not going to relinquish that control. It was chaos. Fun, but chaos.'

Although the sessions had in fact yielded 'Those First Impressions' and a second song, 'Perhaps', Warners recognized the MacKenzie/Ware collaboration as being potentially combustible and reinstated Martin Rushent as the producer of the album. At the time, Rushent owned an upmarket residential studio replete with tennis courts, Genetic, situated in the grounds of his house on the outskirts of Reading and it was here the new Associates began an eight-week occupancy. Part of the process inevitably involved the re-recording of the 'lost' tracks, which, from Steve Reid's point of view at least, involved a certain amount of drudgery. 'By that time, my heart wasn't in it,' he admits, adding, 'Can you imagine trying to get that German shepherd thing going again? When we did the first version, I was getting my guitar to sound like skyscrapers, but now I was into making my guitar sound like a tortoise. I had to re-create these sounds and it was like, "Have you got a fucking time machine and I can go back and play like that again?" We did it, but I wasn't into it.'

Elsewhere, Soave and Hughes were rising to the unusual musical challenges that would be thrown up by MacKenzie. Generally, he would sing each of the complex parts and the musicians would quickly attempt to translate them to their respective instruments with obscure directives such as 'Give me a historical chord . . . a chord from the thirteenth century' firing from their employer.

'I think the saddest thing about that, of course, is that I entirely understood what a historical chord was,' laughs Hughes. 'Billy was a real perfectionist. He was bouncing off the walls, saying, "Play this, play that." It was like working with a classical composer in the sense that he had that level of attention to detail. He would give you all this grief. He'd get you working over and over one bar and say, "Ah, see that note there, could you try standing up and playing it?" You'd go through this for four or five hours and that's when you earned his respect.' Soave concurs that this was the best way to deal with MacKenzie, who once frankly described himself as 'an expert at psychological warfare': 'The one thing you had to with Bill was stand up for yourself. If you didn't, he would see that as a real weakness.'

From Martin Rushent's perspective, the sessions were torturously slow, chiefly owing to MacKenzie's striving for perfection: 'I tried to get him to open up, saying, "What is it you're trying to achieve?" He'd say, "Oh, Martin, don't you bother yourself about that, you leave that to me." When he first started doing vocals on tracks, it was amazing. You'd say to him, "Billy . . . that was just brilliant" and he'd come back in and listen to it and rip the performance to pieces. Then he'd sing it again and again and again and that could get very boring. You'd finish after this very hard day of singing and Billy would come back in the morning and say he didn't like it and you'd have to start all over again. It was like that in every aspect, with all the band's performances as well. I've always prided myself on being somebody who in situations like that can usually make the artist realize that they're just being too pernickety in their detail . . . but I couldn't do it with Billy. While I enjoyed working with him as a person, artistically I found him very frustrating.'

While there's little doubting that, free of the musical bond with Rankine, Billy's controlling nature was beginning to surface, Howard Hughes argues that the best policy would have been for the producers and record company people to allow MacKenzie to exhaust his ideas, even if it might have been an expensive process: 'With Billy there wasn't any point in standing over him and saying, "I think it should be like this or that." It was never ever gonna work. You had to just let him say, "I want to do this" and eventually he used to run out of ideas and come to you and say, "What do you think?" Everyone thought, He's a great singer, but we know what's best for him. That was a fatal mistake."

During the time at Genetic there were, of course, lighter moments to break up the intensity. One day, when Rushent discovered a trail of whippet shit on the path leading up to his studio, he forced a bucket and shovel into MacKenzie's hands and ordered him to scoop up the offending excrement. As Billy set to his unglorious task, Rushent grabbed the studio camera and surreptitiously snapped a Polaroid of the singer hunkering on the path, shovel in hand. Later this was pinned up on the control room wall, bearing the legend: 'Billy MacKenzie collecting material for his new album.'

By this stage a new Warners employee had been assigned to the Associates. Fresh-faced and twenty-three years of age, John Hollingsworth had worked at the small independent label Cherry Red with a roster of independent acts that included Everything But The Girl, and keen to climb a more corporate ladder, had applied for an A&R post at Warners. In his final interview, Max Hole apparently showed the applicant a printout of the label's current roster and enquired which of the artists appealed most to him. Alphabetically, of course, the Associates were at the top of the list, and the interviewee informed his prospective employer that he had been a huge fan of *The Affectionate Punch* while at college. Hole, already tiring of his day-to-day dealings with the unpredictable MacKenzie, hired Hollingsworth on the spot.

Hollingsworth describes the first weekend he spent at Genetic with MacKenzie as being 'a bit of dream come true. Billy didn't trust me at first, but he liked the fact that I was young. Certainly in regards to dealing with Billy, because I was so immature, I was an easy target for him. There was a big ego thing going down between Martin Rushent and Billy at the time and Max really wanted to get Billy on the phone to have a real go at him because the album was already over-budget. But I said, "Look, Max, it isn't going to help the situation." Max calmed down and said, "No, John, you're right."' Shrewdly, Hollingsworth realized that he was possibly being tested by Billy: 'I was definitely being checked out as to whether or not I was somebody who could be trusted or just a company lackey. At that stage his relationship with Warners was not good.'

When the album, *Perhaps*, was eventually completed, the total cost of recording – at a time when the making of a major label album was considered expensive at £100,000 – stood at a staggering £250,000, once the bills for the aborted first attempt had been taken into account. It was likely that Billy, who had always been in debt to Warners and therefore had never received a royalty cheque, would remain unrecouped for some time to come unless *Perhaps* sold in massive quantities. Nevertheless, even when his advances had been spent (typically in recording contracts this involves a lump sum at the onset of any project, followed by two further payments on the delivery and release of the album), Billy would somehow manage to wheedle yet more money out of the label.

'The project would get an advance, and in true rock and roll style Billy would just go off and invest it in motor cars that he couldn't drive and then he'd have no money left. Then he would go back to Max saying he had tax problems and he'd get paid wads of money in cash. Like a true Scot, whatever happened to his money was certainly none of anyone's business. But then he began to trust me – he would leave cash in my drawer and I would act as a banker for him.'

Having only ever been interviewed on British television with the brief chat on *Friday Night, Saturday Morning* two years previously, Billy wasn't particularly relishing the thought that a camera crew from Tyne Tees TV music show *The Tube* were arriving in Dundee to shoot him discussing the state of the Associates and performing 'Waiting For The Love Boat' on the deck of a ship resting in a dock beside the River Tay. The interviewer, model-turned-actress Leslie Ash, perhaps imagining that she was travelling to a remote Highlands location, turned up wearing a fashionable ski suit. In the footage, Billy, his cheeks visibly pinkened by the cold and his responses delivered in his lilting musical accent, punctuated by cheeky, dimpled smiles, appears as both flirtatious and keen to wind up Ash – particularly following a blunder in which she refers to him as 'Billy Rankine'. Since the finished film certainly showed

Billy at probably his most relaxed ever in front of a camera, the interview is worth offering in its barely edited entirety:

Ash: The place is Dundee, the outfit is a skiing outfit and the location is a boat in a dry dock. And the person I'm on the boat with is Billy MacKenzie.

MacKenzie: Hello. Hi ya.

Ash: What happened to the Associates?

MacKenzie: Well, there used to be about four of them, and now there's about forty. So we've just been adding all year. And they're all over Europe. And some of them are quite interesting.

Ash: Is Alan Rankine or any of the original Associates still with you?

MacKenzie: [Embroidering the truth] Um. I get together now and again with Martha, 'cause she's a nice girl, she's very pretty, and sometimes she plays keyboards and sometimes Michael Dempsey, he plays a little bit of his bass thing.

Ash: Where have you been doing the album?

MacKenzie: [Again glamorizing factual reality] Um. We've being doing it all over Britain really. It's taken up a large chunk of this country. [Turns and points to city] Yeah, there's a little recording studio even up there. You see past that seagull? That seagull up there? Yeah, well sort of past that. So even up there I done something.

Ash: [Slightly bemused] Mmn mn. So when the album comes out, will it be, like, under the name of Billy Rankine?

MacKenzie: [Laughing] Billy Rankine?!

Ash: Billy MacKenzie!

MacKenzie: [Teasingly] Oh, *Leslie* . . . Thanks very much.

Ash: Or the Associates?

MacKenzie: Um yeah, well. I've got this thing about my name, 'cause it just sounds like a sorta sausage advert . . .

Ash: I can't even say it.

MacKenzie: It's like a sausage advert. So yeah, we'll be keeping the name the Associates.

Ash: Well, what can you tell me about Dundee here?

MacKenzie: This is a very . . . well, I'll let you into a secret, right? This is a really, really famous place. Around there [pointing], there's a lot of business goes on – I'll not say what it is.

Ash: Well, what sort of business?

MacKenzie: It's um . . . well . . . this is called Dock Street up here. It's very very famous. Um, I suppose, for the sort of meat markets and things like that. You know what I mean?

Ash: No.

Cameraman: [Laughing] Yeah.

MacKenzie: Yeah?

Ash: What? [Slowly dawning on her that this is the red light district] Oh right, OK then. [Flustered] So you actually . . . do you . . . do you live in Dundee then?

MacKenzie: Once again . . . just over there. Past that spire there. I'm just at the back of that. It's quite a pretty place actually.

Ash: What's this I hear about your dogs? You've got whippets.

MacKenzie: Yeah, well, they're my little pals. And yeah, I do breed whippets. [To camera] So anybody that wants a whippet, contact me through Leslie. 'Cause I'm getting some pups and they're no problem.

Ash: Good. So has your sound changed at all?

MacKenzie: I suppose you'd say it's got a little bit more exotic. Well, somebody told me that and I believed them.

Ash: [Clearly having been fed false information] And you're using literally all different people around the world in the band, yeah? Who? Like, who? Is there names we'd know?

MacKenzie: As I said, there's the famous Howard Hughes. Very talented chap. I suppose they're such cult figures that nobody's really heard of them. And they're sorta into all that paraphernalia. And I'm not really, but I'm able to cope with them.

Ash: Well, I'd like to hear some of this album. In fact, your single. When does it come out?

MacKenzie: Well, I suppose being spoiled for choice . . . You know these record companies you can get? Well, mine is called Warners and [grins] I signed to them because I like Bugs Bunny. But anyway, they're spoiled for choice and they're still choosing between four or five . . .

9

So Precious
Is the Jagged Crown

In the spring of 1984 Jim MacKenzie announced to his family that
he was taking them all on holiday to Palma, Majorca. One afternoon shortly after their arrival at the Spanish resort, Billy, along
with his brother John and Steve Reid (who the others had insisted
should come along) were messing around at the edge of the hotel
pool, the MacKenzie brothers both – for no good reason –
unseasonably bedecked in full-length Crombie overcoats, jackboots and bonnets. Perhaps unsurprisingly, this pointedly over-
dressed party began attracting mocking laughter from a family of
Germans sunning themselves at the pool's edge, and typically, the
MacKenzies began playing up to it. John MacKenzie remembers:
'Billy said, "John, go on and jump in the pool." I just said, "Billy,
no fucking way." So he nudged me into the deep end and started
howling with laughter. But I was nearly dead! I got to the other end
of the pool and I looked up and there was my old man with his
veins sticking out of his neck. So he pulled me out by the hair and
gave us five hundred quid and told us to get out of the hotel.'

Then Billy, as the eldest and therefore the most responsible of
the group, suggested that they take the £500 and find a whore-
house. Steve Reid graphically recalls that on discovering a likely
establishment, the three went inside and 'they paraded a big load
of whores and they were all fat and ugly and really horrible. They
showed us them all and we were, like, "Nah, no thanks."' John
MacKenzie, however, remembers the incident differently: 'We

were all flicking a coin. Steve Reid lost and went upstairs. Five minutes later we heard all this banging. It turned out that he'd taken the girl upstairs, said he was dead shy and could she go into the wardrobe while he got undressed. While she was in there, he locked the wardrobe and fucked off over all the balconies.'

But Steve Reid contests the details further: 'It was John who locked *me* in a wardrobe and I did jump over all the balconies to get away and then I came back . . . we were messing about. But I didn't lock no bird in a wardrobe. After a while, we went to leave to go to a disco and Billy said, "I'll just stay here and have a cup of tea wi' the lassies, right?" because he was chatting away to them and getting on great with them.'

These shenanigans aside, when Reid and MacKenzie arrived back home, there was work to be done. Warners had settled on 'Those First Impressions' as the first release from *Perhaps* and it was accompanied by the Associates' first promo clip, shot in Chiswick House, west London, and featuring Billy being followed up a flight of stone steps by two whippets resplendent in Burberry coats, every inch the fashionable young country squire. In the round of press interviews to promote the single's release in May, Billy teasingly revealed very little about what he'd been up to since his last release, except to say that he'd 'been appreciating old people', had musically thrown himself 'back to the seventeenth century, to flamenco dancers and gypsy dervishes and Hungarian folk tunes' and that the new line-up of the Associates had 'floored me when I first heard them all together'.

Within weeks, however, Billy's working relationship with Steve Reid erupted in conflict at the London rehearsals leading up to the Mark Two line-up of the Associates' first TV engagement as a band, playing live on the Saturday morning children's programme *No. 73*. Reid had arrived at the Nomis rehearsal complex in London with one wheel missing off his amp, the result of roadie clumsiness, and the band were due to rehearse two songs, 'Those First Impressions' and 'Waiting For The Loveboat' during the day, with Billy – slippery as ever – arriving later in the afternoon to check on their progress. Forgetting that it was now three-wheeled, Reid balanced a can of beer on top of his amp, and so when drummer Jim Russell brushed against it on his way to the toilet, the drink was sent flying, spilling dangerously close to one of the power adapters. 'It could've electrocuted everybody,' Reid notes, 'so I ran and tried to turn the power off and basically I lost the head with the drummer. Billy walked in six hours late and during a break, the drummer started complaining about me. So Billy dragged me outside and gave me a big bollocking. I said, "Look, Billy, I'm not fucking into all this anyway. You take the songs, 'cause I've had enough." Then he became really stern and just said, "Look, get your fucking act together."'

On the day before the appearance, the group met at the WEA offices in Broadwick Street to be picked up and driven to Maidstone, where the *No. 73* studios were located. Even in the minibus, the band members remember there being a palpable air of hostility between MacKenzie and the guitarist. 'I was doing loads of heroin at the time, so the band had their gear,' Reid drily points out, 'and I had my own gear.'

After their arrival at the hotel, the evening passed uneventfully for the band, who nevertheless wallowed in pop-star luxury by ordering steaks, followed by Napoleon brandies and cigars, all under the watchful but approving eye of Billy. Reid had previously arranged to trade rooms with the singer, so that instead of, as planned, sharing with John MacKenzie, the guitarist could have some 'privacy'. Once everyone had repaired to their rooms, the band phoned Reid, inviting him to a late-night Subutteo championship. To oil the smooth running of this contest, Reid emptied the entire contents of the mini-bar in Billy's room into two carrier bags.

Three hours later the band were legless and Reid was starving. Venturing down to the kitchens, he found the cupboards padlocked and, suddenly overcome with nausea, pushed open a barred door and stepped outside into the dawn air. 'Then I heard a clink and the door shut behind me,' he says of this comedy moment, unconfirmed by the others, even if the band would certainly witness the repercussions of the incident that followed. 'I was locked out of the hotel,' the guitarist continues, 'so I climbed up the drainpipe and got on the roof and walked around, checking windows, to see what was open. I saw one open, and I thought, It's either that or I'm out here until somebody wakes up, so I climbed in, and it turned out it was a chambermaid's bedroom . . . so she started screaming. The kitchen porter had obviously sneaked into her room and he ran out as well. I was saying, "I'm in room . . . uh . . ." and I couldn't remember the number. They ran away and got the manager and he took me back to my room.'

Very early the next morning, discovering his mini-bar empty, his band violently hung-over and the guitarist responsible difficult to rouse, Billy went ballistic. 'I woke up to all this banging,' Reid recalls, 'and it was Billy. The band were all messed up, they were still staggering, and he had been told it was all my fault. So I said, "Hold on and I'll check my gear." My head was screaming.'

Hollingsworth remembers that the traumatized chambermaid was eventually pacified with gifts of flowers and chocolates, and that Billy, fuming at Reid, was shouting, "'Fucking hell, you're not Iggy Pop, you're just my guitarist!" He realized that Steve was becoming a liability.'

In their altered state, the scene that greeted the Associates at the television studios that morning could not have appeared more surreal. The concept of *No. 73* was that it was a normal Saturday morning in a typical suburban house, although there was always a band – in this case the Associates – rehearsing in the basement. The other guests that week included DJ David 'Kid' Jensen, Professor Stanley Unwin – the lauded master of backwards speech – and an animal expert accompanied by a small pack of sizeable Russian bears, one of which tried to bite Reid when he detachedly poked at it with his finger.

In the opening minutes of the show the Associates announced their arrival by knocking on the door of the pretend house, and staggered in. Impressively, the two songs they performed revealed no real evidence of their alcohol-induced stupor, Billy magnificently contorting the melody of 'Waiting For The Loveboat' to the point where it was virtually unrecognizable compared with the recorded version (a matter that later led to his being ticked off by Max Hole). When the show was over, however, MacKenzie shot Reid a severely disapproving look across the studio floor: 'I looked back and sort of went, "What?" . . . We did *Top Of The Pops* after that, but that was the end.'

As if to fulfil a teenage ambition for Reid, Billy insisted that the guitarist appear with him on *Top Of The Pops*. Even though 'Those First Impressions' had entered the charts at a disappointing number 43, it had been a dull week of non-movers for the charts, and the Associates scraped themselves a slot. Perhaps as a mark of the sobering experiences Billy had gone through in the two years since he had last appeared on the programme, it was very much a straight performance of the song, except for Reid making wind-mill-like movements with his arms while inexplicably dressed as Indiana Jones (possibly to confuse the DSS, since he was still signing on the dole at the time). Still, it was a decidedly muted last fanfare for the partnership between the singer and the guitarist. 'The one thing with Billy,' Howard Hughes reasons, 'was that he was always vain enough to know when things weren't good for his image. If someone wasn't reflecting well on him, then he just wouldn't use them any more.'

In other ways the split with Reid only served to highlight the fact that the singer was now keen to distance himself from any form of drug abuse. At the age of twenty-seven, Billy MacKenzie was beginning to abstain, the control freak within him rarely allowing him to drink and certainly never to take a drug. Still – sober or not – he was continuing to give Warner Brothers the run-around. With Billy as reluctant as ever to trudge through his promotional obligations, John Hollingsworth recalls him seriously talking about getting his younger brother, Alec – who looked very much like a marginally younger Billy – to stand in for him and mime the songs on the various TV shows WEA were arranging. But in Hollings-worth, Billy had possibly found one of the few Warners employees who could outwit him. Early on the morning of one television appearance in Manchester which the Warners staff had taken bets on the singer fulfilling, the A&R man caught a dawn flight to Dundee and was tucking into a cooked breakfast provided by Billy's mum when the singer got out of bed. Like a condemned man, MacKenzie was then taken to Manchester by Hollingsworth in time to make the show.

The A&R man's efforts didn't stop there. When a last-minute appearance opportunity came up at the *Midsummer Night's Tube* in

June 1984, following Paul Young's sudden cancellation because of a throat infection, Hollingsworth hared around Newcastle trying to cut a performance backing tape from a rough test pressing of 'Those First Impressions' (strictly against the union rules of the time), leaving a slightly startled Billy no excuse not to perform. In the end, since there had been no time to contact the band, Billy appeared alone on stage on the live programme, clearly intimidated, shuffling around awkwardly in the instrumental passages, asking a crowd of girls in the front row for a stick of chewing gum, toeing the discarded wrapper into the small crowd and then exiting the stage before the song had even had a chance to play out.

It was increasingly becoming apparent that it was as the piano-accompanied torch singer that Billy felt at his most comfortable in the live arena. Warners, keen to coax him back into live performance on whatever level, arranged a date at London's legendary jazz haunt Ronnie Scott's on 9 December 1984. Billy had not performed live in the capital for four years – in the markedly different form of the post-punk Associates – so there was an inevitable clamour for the 200 tickets made available, although ironically, Warners quickly snapped up three-quarters of the allocation and this key event was witnessed by an audience comprising mainly of record-industry personnel and music journalists. Viewing the existing footage of this half-hour performance was as close as the majority of the Associates' fan base ever got to witnessing the unarguable peak of Billy MacKenzie's live career.

Beautifully shot on 16mm at the expense of Warner Brothers, Lewis Daniels' film of the event holds a strangely timeless quality, with neither the musical or aesthetic fashions of the 80s managing to date the footage to any particular period. Dressed from head to foot in black, the ubiquitous beret pulled down over his ears, Billy at first appears shy and nervous, introduces the set as 'some very, very, very quiet songs' and then launches into 'This Flame' (a MacKenzie ballad destined never to be studio recorded), accompanied by the grey-suited Hughes to his right on grand piano. Within two verses, any rumours of the remarkable extremities of MacKenzie's voice being the result of studio trickery are magically dispelled by the sheer power and controlled vibrato of the rendition. In the moody delivery of Dave Berry's 'The Crying Game' that follows, a photographer's flash pops close to Billy's face and the singer closes his eyes and waves away this intrusion on his concentration. But it is with Billie Holiday's 'God Bless The Child' – a song that MacKenzie had been performing for years – that the set reaches its emotional peak. Billy tackles the melody of the jazz standard with such craft and conviction that there is little doubting that he had every right to take his place among the greats to have graced the stage of Ronnie Scott's.

For 'No' Billy is joined by Roberto Soave and Jim Russell on bass and brushed snare drum respectively, and the introduction is greeted by whoops and applause by the crowd. Following that, the Associates transform 'Even Dogs In The Wild' into brooding cocktail swing. Joined at the end by a string sextet, the Associates offer the first live airing of the classically hewn 'Breakfast', to a torrent of applause.

Elsewhere, however, undoubtedly marking a first for Scott's, John MacKenzie's pet polecat – for no sane reason brought along to the gig – had been left in the hallowed dressing room of the club during the set and was busy crapping in John Hollingsworth's briefcase.

But the hapless A&R man was pushed to the breaking point of frustration the following week when he was sent to Dundee by Max Hole to collect the passports of the five members of the Associates in order to apply for working visas following the booking of two dates at New York's Danceteria. 'I had to drag them to a photo booth and get all their photos,' Hollingsworth says. 'It was all a big game . . . Billy would be hiding under tables away from me. I was almost in tears 'cause I was under so much pressure to get back to London for ten o'clock with all the stuff. Bill would be saying, "Oh, you're not using that photo, it's terrible." Five sets of photos later, he'd go, "Well, that's OK." Ian McIntosh's passport was in Loch Fucking Nowhere at his granddad's and we ended up there at five o'clock in the morning. I got back to the hotel at quarter to seven, got on the plane, landed and made it into Max Hole's office at about quarter to ten. I emptied this Jiffy bag of stuff on his desk and

Max said, "Pay rise? Holiday?" I just said, "Max, I can't do this any more. I joined WEA to be an A&R man, not to be some sort of unofficial manager for the Associates."'

In the end, despite Hollingsworth's efforts, the budget didn't stretch to his accompanying the Associates to New York. Howard Hughes remembers that Billy, terrified of flying, tensely gripped his arm on take-off, although once the champagne had begun to flow, the singer somehow managed to coax one of the air hostesses into letting him try on her jacket. With the first of the gigs on New Year's Eve 1984, the Associates arrived on stage to be met with the sight of an over-exuberant Scottish expat – who was later discovered backstage face down in an ice bin of beer – cheering his heart out and wearing a Celtic FC shirt.

Hughes recalls that on the trip, Billy was less keen to partake in the band's drunken revelry: 'He was reasonably separate, he was always kind of away from things. But I think we were like caretakers for him. It became like a family, it became comfortable.'

Back in Dundee, Billy's own family life had become a huge matter of concern to him with the final, permanent break-up of his parents earlier in the year. The split affected him enormously. As a result, he was living at his mother's house in Morgan Street – described by John MacKenzie as his brother's 'comfort zone'. On Billy's return from New York, in a recorded conversation of 9 January 1985 with his friend Eliz Feeney in his mother's kitchen (intended as an interview for a local unemployment resource centre magazine but never published), he reinforced his current mood of abstention: 'If I was in my wanton, carefree days, I would love to go to New York and get blitzed every night and do this and do that, but I've kind of really grown out of that stage, so I suppose it wouldn't be too much of a playground for me. I've sort of grown out of all that excess stuff. Not that I'm a pure little angel. I've just done that thing to death, all that drinking too much and sleeping around. You just do them and get them out of your system. But it's best to do them when you're younger. Better than waiting until you're forty before you break loose.'

With the bangs and screams of some lively MacKenzie family activity in the background, along with his own constant shooing of omnipresent whippets, Billy also offered his thoughts on the local criticism that still surrounded him: 'Well, you've just got to accept that. I mean, I get a lot of flak. People love to stick their nose in . . . they would say whatever they're going to say anyway. They have and will continue to have some terrible things to say about me and some really quite nice things to say about me, so I just accept it, y'know. As long as I can accept myself, then other people's acceptance can come a lot easier.'

Furthermore, despite the success of the New York gigs, Billy didn't seem any more enamoured of the prospect of life on the road. Although still only twenty-seven, he appeared to be keen to unburden himself, where at all possible, of much his workload: 'It's not that I'm a selfish performer . . . I can't sort of bear that boredom in between the bookings 'cause you're all hyped up and then you've got two days to wait before you do another booking. Being a little bit of a sort of speedy person or a quick person or whatever, this irritates me no end. So that's why, y'know, I think twice about playing now. It's not the actual playing, it's the boring times in between.'

This prompted Feeney to ask: 'But you *are* doing a British tour, aren't you?'

'Well, we're *meant* to be doing a British tour,' Billy replied, mysteriously adding, 'but . . . I'm about to see about that. Tomorrow, I think.'

Nevertheless, counting the accumulated debts going back to the day when the Associates first signed to Warners, Billy was now around £500,000 in the red to the company and so there was little chance of him wriggling out of the forthcoming British tour, already booked to begin in March. Before then, however, he was to confound Max Hole with his criticism of the test pressing of *Perhaps*, which although mastered at a state-of-the-art direct-to-metal cutting plant in Germany, Billy complained wasn't loud enough. Exasperated, Hole picked up the phone and ordered the Warners travel department to book seats for MacKenzie and Hollingsworth for the following day on any available flight to Hamburg, where the album would be recut at enormous expense.

This, it turned out, was one of the many times that Billy attempted to throw away his passport just before an important trip abroad. Cunningly, Hollingsworth had kept a copy of the singer's birth certificate and the remaining photo-booth snaps from the recent passport débâcle in Dundee, so that effectively he had an emergency Billy MacKenzie passport kit in his top drawer. 'Then of course, we'd always be trying to get out to the airport three minutes before the plane left,' Hollingsworth groans, 'so I used to trick him. It got to the point where I used to say, "Right, Billy, the flight's leaving at nine" when it was leaving at ten. So we'd be in the car and he'd be saying, "Och, I don't think we're gonna get there", and he got wise in the end – he'd say, "It's not leaving till eleven, is it?" and I'd say, "Well, ten actually." After that he'd try to call Warners and speak to them about the travel arrangements. I used to have to have all these codes, so people wouldn't tell him the truth.'

The problem with *Perhaps* was that, at fifty-five minutes, it was an extremely lengthy album to attempt to cut to vinyl. On their arrival at the Teldec cutting plant on the fringes of Hamburg, the managing director of the company – feeling slighted that someone should fail to approve one of his test pressings – was there to greet the pair. 'So we're sat in his office,' Hollingsworth continues, 'we're being very well looked after and the record is cut again by his top cutting engineer. I remember the test pressing was still warm when they gave us it. We put it on this incredible hi-fi and Billy's got this very Germanic man in his fifties standing next to him in one of the ultimate cutting facilities in the world, basically saying, "Now, you tell me that this record hasn't been brilliantly cut." So Billy literally listens to about thirty seconds of each side, says, "Oh aye, that sounds great" and goes out to the car. The managing director looks at me and says, "Well, just for your knowledge, John, we cut it exactly the same as we did the last record." This was Billy thinking, How much more money can I waste? How can I delay putting out the record?'

At long last, two and a half years after the first sessions, *Perhaps* was released on 9 February 1985. Billy struck a serious, strong-jawed pose on the cover, wearing a turquoise turtle-necked shirt and tartan jacket that had the possibly adverse effect of making him oddly resemble a *Thunderbirds* puppet. The music was less mysterious and more angular than *Sulk*, with the frequently inspired compositions battling against the over-rounded production values of the day. Yet, despite its sound, much of *Perhaps* has aged well.

Powered by the Linn Drum, the Rolls-Royce of early-80s drum machines, *Perhaps* has a classical, string-laden atmosphere even in its most strident moments, with all the instrumental parts delivered with a clipped precision that betrays MacKenzie's constant search for perfection. In its weaker moments – the flimsy, throwaway pop of 'Schampout', the overworked final version of 'The Best Of You' (eventually featuring Eddi Reader as the female counterpart) – it provided ample ammunition for the detractors who suggested that the Associates' musical magic had vanished along with the departure of Alan Rankine.

In other areas, however, there is a strength of creative purpose and even an intangible nobility to be found on *Perhaps*, particularly in the anthemic 'Thirteen Feelings', the jaundiced romanticism of 'Don't Give Me That I Told You So Look' and the cryptic spiritual searching of 'The Stranger In Your Voice', Billy's personal favourite. In the lyric of the song, which he described as 'new age before new age . . . especially for young men', MacKenzie seems to be tackling the male condition and the unhealthy bottling up of feelings: 'Educate your emotions/Throw away your books/If we can walk this tightrope/It's best that we don't look.' Throughout the album – aside from his developing an interest in exotic, eastern-flavoured chants – MacKenzie's voice has mellowed with age, although there is still evidence of his octave-scaling past in the way that he splinters a single word, a lone syllable rocketing skyward. Still, unsatisfied with the sonic realization of the sounds buzzing around his head, Billy would obliquely describe *Perhaps* as 'a ghost train of an album' and admit that he was not 'a great fan of the productions . . . they've never really done the songs any favours.'

While most of the journalists who reviewed *Perhaps* took into account the troubled circumstances surrounding the recording of the album, they all reached the same conclusion. In his four-star (out of five) review in *Sounds*, Bill Black wrote: 'It's a testament to MacKenzie's vision (a grand word for a grand design) that beyond a brush with the BEF production team and his own lunges at the desk still hum the basic motors of the Associates' sound.'

Steve Sutherland of *Melody Maker*, who had been privy to the break-up of Rankine and MacKenzie and the creative and corporate roller-coastering involved in the fourth Associates album, noted: 'It's hardly surprising that "Perhaps" isn't quite a masterpiece on a par with "Sulk"', although he ended with the more positive statement: 'Confections like this are rare indeed, treats to be savoured, records created for sheer pleasure with no ulterior motive but the ecstasy of existing. There's no perhaps about "Perhaps". It's a definite treasure.' Jim Shelley of *NME* felt that even in its imperfection, *Perhaps* captured the essences of Billy's character: '"Perhaps" is . . . full of sighs, smirks, rage and regrets, the tears and games of love and all his romantic melancholy, nonchalant cheek, his weaknesses and his million and ten emotions. And in that respect, perhaps "Perhaps" is perfect.'

While the album charted at number 23 on the week following its release, the singles that preceded *Perhaps* had stalled at disappointing chart positions. 'Waiting For The Loveboat' scraped to 53 the previous September, while in February 'Breakfast' only reached 49. Max Hole is keen to point out that, since the album had cost £250,000 and eventually sold just 40,000 copies, 'Really it was a failure.'

In the wake of the album's release, the Associates embarked on a European club tour, with an embellished version of the Ronnie Scott's set – they even attempted a jazz rendition of 'Club Country' and a 60s-style reworking of 'Message Oblique Speech' – travelling to Amsterdam, Hamburg, Paris and Brussels, where in true cabaret fashion, they were supported by a magician. There followed a full-band tour of the UK in March for which the five-piece outfit was augmented by two German backing singers, Gert and Udo Scheuerpflug. Introduced to MacKenzie by John Hollingsworth and otherwise known as Die Zwei, the pair, on their arrival in the Associates' rehearsal studio, prompted whispered, light-heartedly jingoistic jokes from the musicians of the 'waiting for the U-boat' variety.

Since he was now solely the band leader, MacKenzie appeared relaxed throughout the tour, which culminated in a sold-out show at London's Dominion Theatre. Albeit self-consciously, he hammed up his front-man role, leading the bewildered and fast improvising band into a reggaefied take on 'Club Country', taking his encore bows with a thunderous cover of Blondie's 'Heart Of Glass', followed by a muted version of 'The Crying Game' where the singer sat atop Hughes's grand piano. When the pianist offered an unrehearsed musical flourish in his part, Billy teased him in front of the packed audience by saying, 'Now, stop showing off, Howard.' In response, the far taller musician remembers: 'I picked him up and carried him offstage, with his little legs swinging in the air.'

Following the relative success of the tour, the Associates were packed off on to the European festival circuit and completed a batch of dates supporting the Cure, during which, in Italy, Billy experienced the dangerous audience practice of showering a band with coins – apparently a mark of respect. In the summer of 1985 the group – joined by new drummer Moritz Von Oswald, a descendant of German aristocracy with a scar on his cheek that Billy had fancifully decided was the result of a fencing accident – travelled to Japan as part of a package tour with Culture Club, vest-wearing MOR funk duo Go West and the Style Council. During the trip Billy still remained isolated from the group, taking cab rides to the beach off Nagoya in the mornings in an effort to counter-balance the Beatlemaniacal star treatment afforded to most American or European groups who travel to the Pacific Rim. 'There were lots of photographers and actually there was groupies,' he coyly admitted on his return. 'That was the first time I'd ever encountered such things to the full-blown extent.'

Even if Billy now seemed content to play the more typical major recording artist game, his love of the creative process and hatred of the promotional treadmill both began to rise again when it became clear that Warners were becoming less prepared to indulge his whims in the light of what they viewed as the relatively poor sales of

Perhaps. John Hollingsworth states that 'there had been all the mischief, but it started to wear a bit thin once that we knew that *Perhaps* really wasn't going to go anywhere.'

'I hate set patterns,' Billy told *Melody Maker*'s Steve Sutherland. '"You've *got* to do this." If anybody says I've *got* to do something, it's like a red rag to a bull with me.'

Where the relationship between Billy MacKenzie and Warner Brothers was concerned, it seemed, storm clouds were gathering on the horizon.

10

The Dark Horse
That Could Win the Race

'I can remember Billy once saying that it felt a bit like being summoned to the headmaster's study when he came to see me,' Max Hole says of the reprimanding role he was having to play in his dealings with the singer post-*Perhaps*. 'I admit I didn't much like the parallel at the time, but I suppose it probably was a bit like that. I was always the one that had to dish out the bad news to Billy. I was the one saying, "There's no more money" or "No, we're not going to do that." But then Billy would come in and smile and be a bit sheepish and I'd forgive him.'

As time went on, however, the upper management at Warners were growing less forgiving. Specifically, there was acute tension between Billy and managing director Rob Dickens, particularly on the infrequent occasions when a matter had to be dealt with above Max Hole's head. Chris Parry, who, as the singer's publisher and unofficial manager, often accompanied him to these financial crisis talks, recalls that Billy, ever sartorially aware, would gleefully mock the MD's dress sense under his breath: 'He'd say, "Look at his shoes! How can I possibly work for a guy that wears shoes like that?" He'd crack up laughing.' Hole confirms that relations between MacKenzie and Dickens were not good: 'They just didn't particularly like each other – life's like that sometimes. Ian McCulloch [singer of Echo and the Bunnymen, another Warners act] and Rob got on great . . . Billy and Rob didn't.'

Even if Hole was often forced to act as the buffer between the MD and his wild-card musical charge, at least Billy was showing a certain willingness to deliver his homework to his surrogate head-master. On the Associates' return home from Japan in June 1985, they entered REL Studios in Edinburgh and completed demos for four new tracks – the balladeering 'You Feel The Same' (which resurfaced five years later as 'Strasbourg Square'), 'You Never Thought (That You'd Be The One)', 'Give' (an early Chic-echoing funk song originated by Billy's Dundee friend and fellow whippet walker Kevin Hutchison) and 'Take Me To The Girl', co-written by Howard Hughes after Billy had sung the melody to him during a cab ride in Utrecht.

Since the demoing had purely been an exercise in attempting to find a likely single to turn around Billy's dwindling commercial fortunes, it was decided that 'Take Me To The Girl', an upbeat dance track with a loungey Euro-flavoured melody, walked taller than the others and was the most obvious choice. Roberto Soave remembers that despite the funding restrictions now being im-posed by WEA, Billy was still splashing out during the Edinburgh sessions – for the most part. 'He'd spend money right, left and centre,' the bassist notes, 'but we'd get a cab home to Dundee and halfway there he'd say to me, "I don't have any change, can you cover this one? You've got one of those cards where you can get money out of the wall." It's was like, "Right yeah, sixty-quid cab bill. Cheers, Bill."

For 'Take Me To The Girl', Warners hooked the Associates up with producer Peter Henderson – an unlikely candidate perhaps, since his benchmark success had been with Supertramp and the MOR sludge of their *Breakfast In America* album six years before – and MacKenzie returned to his old haunt, Morgan Studios to record the track. As if to highlight the extreme shift in his musical direction since the speed-fuelled, pioneering sessions at Morgan for *Fourth Drawer Down*, the gossamer-light Europop production of 'Take Me To The Girl' – despite an appealingly hooky chorus and the wayward playboy-lover romanticism of the lyric ('My flesh was always weak, my tango less than chic/Such grandeur took its toll and left me here a wretched soul') – managed to trivialize what was potentially a great song. The finished result betrayed MacKenzie's eagerness to provide his troubled employers with a hit record, and ironically, on its release in October it became the Associates' worst-selling single from the Warners catalogue, failing even to dent the Top 75.

In their quest to reposition the Associates into the yuppie-led, 'coffee-table' market, Warners had commissioned a video for the song which featured Billy, intercut with shots of sultry female models, sitting on fake-granite steps, delivering the song with exaggerated showbiz nods to accent certain lines. Although he doesn't appear entirely uncomfortable in the promo, when he appeared on satellite music station Music Box, the short-lived British precursor to MTV Europe, on a show hosted by Sunie Fletcher, Billy could be seen visibly wincing as the video ended and the show's director cut back to the studio. 'I don't like watching my own ugly mug on the screen,' Billy confessed, laughing. 'Now if it was a video of my *legs*, then that's a different thing, that's my best point. Nice Scottish white hairy legs.' Fletcher accurately pointed out: 'The Associates' videos have not been their greatest strength up until now.' 'No,' Billy replied, adding drily, 'but then we don't want to appear *too* perfect.'

Around this time MacKenzie's patently camera-shy nature led him to reject the offer of a role as the Wiz in Julian Temple's widely mocked, cappuccino-froth film adaptation of Colin MacInnes' cult 1959 British beatnik novel *Absolute Beginners*, alongside Patsy Kensit, James Fox and David Bowie. 'I never read the script,' Billy offhandedly stated the year after the panned film's release in 1986. 'It was just a pile of Craven "A" rubbish. Crap. But it was nice to have been asked.' Similarly, his stage fright – even if it had partly been quelled by the recent touring – found him instantly dismissing enquiries from Andrew Lloyd Webber's Really Useful Company as to whether he had ever considered branching out into a West End musical career.

In some ways, perversely, it seemed as if MacKenzie's star was in the ascendant in terms of his celebrity, even as his commercial value plummeted. Increasingly viewed by many in the entertainment industry as possibly the greatest white soul singer of the era, if undirected in his career decisions, Billy had put in a performance on *The Tube* the year before that caught the attention of Chris

Blackwell, the founder of Island Records. Blackwell, who was the discoverer of Bob Marley and U2, among many others, was reportedly shocked to learn that the Associates' records, apart from a limited release of a US edition of *Sulk*, had failed to be released in the States.

Blackwell approached Warners with a view to signing MacKenzie to Island in America. This proposal, although unprecedented in terms of corporate policy (since the Associates were still technically contracted to Sire in the US, even if the release options had not been picked up on), Max Hole found appealing. MacKenzie and Blackwell met at Kettners restaurant in Soho to discuss the signing, and over the following weeks the industry machinery lumbered into action, although it was destined to be a thwarted effort. 'I thought Billy was being a bit of a prat on *The Tube*,' reckons Hole, 'but that was precisely what Blackwell liked about it. We were thrilled that he wanted to sign him for America, but I had a lot of politics to get through because we don't have a policy of giving our artists' records to companies outside. But we persuaded the powers that be to let it go to Island, then Blackwell suddenly pulled out for no reason.'

Although drifting rudderless in terms of his career, in 1986 Billy cemented his friendship with Paul Haig, the pair sharing a similar disillusionment with the bureaucratic workings of the music industry, and more importantly, a surreal, childlike sense of humour. With Haig living in Edinburgh, the pair often ate up their idle hours with marathon phone conversations: 'There'd be times where me and Billy would spend four or five hours on the phone talking absolute gibberish. We both invented this character called Osprey who wore a petticoat and boots and had a metallic tongue and would go "Clack" and say, "What you want to do is . . ." It haunted us for years after that. Billy would phone up and say, "Guess what Osprey's been doing. He's sitting on my shoulder, saying, "You want to get out and sing again." Billy would make me laugh so much I'd have a really sore stomach. He would implant this surreal image in my head and we'd just be cackling away for hours.'

On a visit to Glamis Castle on the outskirts of Dundee, a child-hood home of the Queen Mother and magnet for an enormous amount of tourists owing to its reputation as the most haunted stately home in Britain, the pair got caught up in a guided tour and proceeded to caper around like unruly pre-adolescents on a school trip. 'This guide started talking,' Haig remembers, 'and we just started laughing. Billy was prodding me and chasing me around. Then in front of everyone, he went up to the guide and said, "Can we be excused, please?"'

The two began writing songs together, and an Edinburgh pro-moter, on hearing on the grapevine of the collaboration between these two luminaries of the Scottish music scene – which at this time in particular operated in isolation from whatever was going on in London, resulting in the eventual compilation of a Scottish chart that bore little resemblance to the national Gallup statistics – contacted them with the offer of two gigs. Since he was sharing the limelight with Haig, the pair taking turns on lead vocals, the two shows in May 1986 at Wilkie House in Edinburgh and Cardinal Folly in Glasgow witnessed a relaxed MacKenzie. A poorly focused domestic video of the latter performance on 9 May reveals a set comprising both Haig and MacKenzie songs (the only Associates number being a frantic 'It's Better This Way'), augmented by covers of Dundee songwriter Grant McInally's dramatic Scott Walker-like ballad 'The Shadow To Fall', Sly and the Family Stone's 'Running Away' and even Yoko Ono's 'Walking On Thin Ice'.

Haig remembers these first collaborations, both live and re-corded, as involving a shared abandonment of egos, even if Billy would sometimes slip back into his domineering ways: 'I knew that Billy could be a wee Führer in the studio with musicians, and sometimes he would do that to me and then he would go, [sheepishly] "Oh, I'm sorry, Paul." He'd always bite his lip when we were working.' Billy summed up his friendship and working partnership with Haig by simply saying, 'Paul and I just like to sit at the back of the class and throw paper airplanes at the rock business.'

At the time, Billy had invested part of the Warners advance for his next album in a flat in Baldovan Terrace in Dundee, just around the corner from his mother's house. In a neighbouring street lived a local musician, Steve Aungle, a friend of John MacKenzie recommended to Billy by his brother as a likely collaborative partner in the demos for his next album. Aungle had, in fact, first met Billy in 1978 when he had placed an ad in the local paper as a drummer looking for a band. He had received two replies – one from a club band and the other from Billy, at that time looking to complete a nascent line-up of the Associates.

When Aungle visited the singer at the Crypt, he had impressed Billy with his influences (Talking Heads, Devo) and hadn't seemed uneasy with the notion that the Associates were looking for 'a human drum machine', but when he discovered that the band rehearsals were held three times a week in the Scottish capital, the drummer backed out. 'Edinburgh seemed like the other side of the world at the time,' he laughs, 'so I just said, "Can't get through there. Sorry, mate." I went and joined the clubby band instead.'

In 1986 Aungle had an eight-track recording set-up in the tiny spare room of his flat that he referred to as 'the acid chamber . . . it had children's alphabet wallpaper, and if you were in there for more than a couple of hours, you came out with ABCs imposed on your vision.' Providing keyboards and drum programming, he worked on two songs with Billy, the dance-driven 'Set Me Up' and a grand 60s-style ballad called 'You'll Never Know' (never fully realized and released) and recalls the singer being 'really tense and impatient. I'd press rewind on the tape machine and he would be like, [urgently] "Come on, come on, come on, can't you get that to go faster?" He was pretty intense and demanding and it did kind of put me on edge. It wasn't a relaxed atmosphere.'

On his visits south to London, where Billy would somehow manage to convince the Warners travel department to book him a suite in Claridge's, progress meetings with Max Hole would inevitably find the A&R man attempting to push other, better-recognized collaborators in the singer's direction, but to no avail. 'I wanted him to do a track with Peter Gabriel,' Hole remembers, mindless of the fact that the ex-Genesis front man's name would have instantly reminded MacKenzie of his abhorrence of hippie-dom as a teenager. 'Billy looked at me as if I was mad.'

In MacKenzie's mind, WEA were attempting to slowly turn the screws on him until he finally relented and became, as he put it, 'a bland, white soul singer with a safe back catalogue . . . they're music haters and I'm a music lover. I don't adhere to the sweat and toil and workshop attitude of record companies.' Hole admits he was putting certain stylistic pressures on Billy at time: 'I certainly was at him, saying, "Why don't you just take a great song? You don't have to prove to everybody that you're like an opera singer." I was certainly at him at various points to do an album of other people's songs.'

The situation reached stalemate, and for the next two years MacKenzie would be forced to record in sporadic bursts, each batch of tracks that he delivered to WEA being on an exploratory footing as far as the label was concerned. In the summer of 1986, however, he was to forge an important creative relationship that would endure for some years and prove fruitful for all involved. Having kept in contact with his former A&R man Tarquin Gotch, who had since become the musical supervisor for the US film director John Hughes, Billy was brought to the attention of Swiss electronic duo Yello, following the inclusion of their track 'Oh Yeah' in Hughes's teen movie *Ferris Bueller's Day Off.*

Renowned for creating eclectic, cinematic soundscapes that made broad-stroke use of everything from jazz to disco to Latin-American influences in their characteristically pristine sound, both Yello singer Dieter Meier and musician/producer Boris Blank were instantly attracted to the androgynous qualities of MacKenzie's voice. 'The first time I heard it,' Blank confesses, 'I thought it was a girl singing. It was an extraordinary voice, which is very unusual in pop music.'

Although still very much a nervous flyer, MacKenzie made his first trip to Zurich in 1986 at the expense of Yello's record company, Mercury, and was booked into a room at an expensive art-deco hotel in the city. While Blank wanted Billy to create washes of backing vocal treatments for a variety of tracks that Yello were working on for their fifth album, *One Second,* there was one song that he felt might suit the singer's lead vocal, soon to become 'Moon On Ice'. The producer remembers being plainly amazed by the spontaneity of MacKenzie's working methods: 'Within thirty minutes he had the lyric. After half an hour he was already behind the microphone, and we made some test recordings and the song was done in two hours. It was very fast . . . unbelievable really.'

Billy told journalist Allan Campbell in short-lived Scottish music paper *Cut*: 'I felt like some kind of '30s Broadway singer. It's interesting. They've got a very opulent lifestyle. Dieter has this lovely, big mansion and Boris runs about in his Thunderbird car. It's very American. But the music, I suppose, has an essentially European heart. It's definitely European soul music. When I sing the songs, I can actually see my vocal in the track as a landscape, or maybe a really brilliant castle or something, away in the corner of the mix. With Boris, there's a kindred spirit . . . but I tell you it's the most exhausting work I've ever done. Talk about Swiss accuracy.'

Already fascinated by certain facets of European life, Billy fell in love with the slow-lane approach and the breathtaking scenery he discovered in Switzerland. In their breaks from recording, he would hop on the back of Blank's powerful six-cylindered Kawasaki motorcyle and the pair would cruise through the mountain roads, music blaring on their Walkmans. 'In the beginning, he was a bit afraid,' Blank recalls. 'But I'm a very cool driver, not an idiot in the traffic, so after a while he became very trusting.'

MacKenzie made further trips to Zurich as the work progressed. In a track that was later earmarked as the first single from *One Second*, Billy contributed a sky-high diva introduction and falsetto bursts to 'Goldrush'. 'It was always . . . in a way, magic,' Blank says. 'I wouldn't normally use words like that, but it was really always magical working with him.' Strangely, Billy used similar words to describe the producer around the time of these first collaborative efforts: 'Boris is a big kid . . . he just weaves magic in the studio. I think basically he was born with a deep intuitive understanding of musak and music and world music and whatever. He gets the best out of me vocally, that's for sure. When I work with Boris, it's spontaneous. I come in off the plane and the next minute, I've got a lyric sheet out and I've got to write the lyrics and it's just off the top of my head. I very much like to please Boris and make him smile. I would've loved him to be my brother.'

Often when Billy landed at Edinburgh airport on his return from Zurich, he caught a cab straight to Paul Haig's flat. Haig remembers that while MacKenzie was often jittery directly after a flight, he would make light of his in-flight anxieties: 'He just had this look in his face . . . he was completely freaked out and scared and lost. He'd say, "Look at the state of me. I've got Swiss eye." So that became his catchphrase for when he was freaking out.'

On the night of 11 September 1986 Forth FM perhaps foolishly handed over a two-hour radio slot to the tangential anchoring of Haig and MacKenzie, who spent the time spinning mostly easy-listening favourites, including singles by Jim Reeves and Charlie Pride, teasing the back-seat interjections of host Colin Somerville and steering the conversation into choppier waters in terms of broadcasting standards (Billy describes the onions he used to have to chop at the LA burger bar as a teenager being 'like somebody's prostate' and is halted in mid-flow by Somerville with a cautionary 'Steady on, Billy . . . steady on').

Although the pair's improvised dialogue often veered into dangerously self-indulgent territory, there were genuinely funny moments. On admitting that the pair were severely hung-over, MacKenzie colourfully noted: 'I feel like I'm a burst crisp bag. My eyes feel as if they've just come out of a Hoover bag. I feel as I'm on the end of somebody's fishing line and I'm just going to give up and get caught.' When introducing an Andy Williams record, he comically mused: 'I'd give my eye teeth to see Andy Williams filling in Tony Bennett in Las Vegas. I thought Tony was a farce . . . those big grizzly sideboards. Can you imagine the locusts and everything that must've been in them? 'Cause it's hot in Las Vegas.'

Just under four months later, however, Haig and MacKenzie would pull off perhaps their most subversive broadcasting coup. In a hare-brained move by STV to update their hogmanay show from the tired kilt and bagpipe format of old, a new approach for the station's New Year's Eve television celebration was devised by broadcaster Muriel Gray to accommodate Scottish alternative music. Together, on the live show, Haig and MacKenzie contrib-uted a radical reworking of 'Amazing Grace' that began as a deceptively faithful rendering – sweetly delivered by Billy to a shimmering backdrop of tinkling bottles and the sampled sounds of popping balloons – before the track erupted into industrial punk. At the song's ebb, the audience – mostly the same pensioners who would normally have been attending a more traditional gathering – offers a ripple of polite applause, mildly stunned and with bewildered looks on their faces.

On the night that followed the day that Billy MacKenzie spent in the company of Shirley Bassey, he dropped to his knees and serenaded her in a crowded hotel lobby in Zurich. Early in 1987 he had returned to Switzerland to witness an important development in the recording of *One Second*. Having received Billy's unsolicited vocal demo for a new track, 'The Rhythm Divine', co-written with Yello, the Welsh superstar had agreed to perform the song.

The magnificent realization of the sophisticated European balladeering influences that Billy had been toying with since 'Those First Impressions', 'The Rhythm Divine' is a noir torch song steeped in drama and mystery. The echoes of the orchestral grandeur of John Barry that had always been detectable in the Associates' sound were sharply focused by Bassey's typically emotive delivery of the lyric – hungering and shaking for her absent lover, as she searches for him in far-flung, exotic locations such as Warsaw and Rome. In essence, Billy MacKenzie had written his Bond theme.

While 'The Rhythm Divine' unarguably spotlights his talent as a songwriter even when working within the classic tradition, the writer was not, in fact, present for Bassey's recording of his song. Keen to direct the superstar in her performance, although too nervous to do so, Billy was introduced to Bassey in the studio and then announced that he was going take a walk for half an hour while Blank recorded the singer warming up. Of course, by the time he returned, Bassey – ever the seasoned professional – had completed her vocal tracks, ghosted by haunting backing vocals that Billy had earlier recorded.

Following dinner that night – 'a real warm evening', as Blank recollects – the party repaired to the exclusive Hôtel Baur au Lac for a nightcap, where an alcohol-emboldened Billy performed his a-cappella 'God Bless The Child' party piece for Bassey. 'She was so attracted by his voice,' the producer remembers, 'that afterwards she sang a few lines of the song, and people were in tears around the table. It was an absolutely great moment.' An enthralled Billy later spoke of the event in *NME*, describing the singer in terms that could easily have been applied to himself: 'She's a prankster . . . 50 going on 18, she's hilarious. To me, Shirley Bassey had always been one of those otherworldly creatures.' He further added that, naturally, this collaboration with a bona fide legend had galvanized his reputation in the eyes of his relatives: 'Working with her made everything valid with my mum and aunties. It's smoothed out those family wrinkles.'

At the same time as Switzerland, with his increasing visits there, was becoming a creative haven for MacKenzie, away from the reminders of his low commercial capital and massive record company debts in London, he was also retreating further into rural Scotland. Billy had made a typically dramatic promise to his brother Alec, then expecting a child with his girlfriend, that if the baby was a boy and he named it after him, he would gift his brother the flat in Baldovan Terrace. When the boy was born and named William James MacKenzie, Billy honoured the deal.

Using an advance for his projected fifth album, provisionally entitled *The Glamour Chase*, Billy started viewing different properties in the village of Auchterhouse, seven miles outside Dundee, at the foot of the Sidlaw hills where he often walked his dogs. In fact, he ended up buying one property and renting a second: the first was a luxury flat situated in a renovated hospital building where he would live and build a work room on the upper level; the latter, Rose Cottage, was where he planned to build kennels for his ever-expanding platoon of whippets.

Taking the idea one step further, out of £20,000 that he had left, he invested £15,000 in the formation of the Dundee Whippet Rescue Society, based at Rose Cottage, which would provide a sanctuary for any stray or unwanted whippets that found their way into the other kennels in Dundee. Employing a couple of friends to run the venture, he stocked up on crates of dog food and kept a sly check on the whippets' diets and weights, to make sure that they were being fed and walked properly. After the pedigree ones had been bred, the litters would be given away to prospective owners through local papers – never sold, although it would likely have proved a lucrative business. John MacKenzie explains that this served 'as a communication link' for Billy and that 'he would always find out what the whippets were up to'.

Additionally, Billy harboured plans to build a recording studio of his own in Auchterhouse. This would be a rural base where he could work spontaneously and, of course, on his own terms, but the plan was never realized. At this time he talked to *Blitz* about the method behind these seemingly isolating manoeuvres. 'Remember . . . a lot of money has passed through my hands,' he pointed out, 'and I gleefully squandered just about every single penny of it. But I was always an enterprising bugger. I realized that to survive, I'd need some kind of fortress. So I took what money remained and invested in property. I couldn't have anyone getting the upper hand on me, you see. The only way they could get to me was by cutting off my allowance, which they had tried once.

'The record company basically regard me as a pain in the neck,' he added, 'because I won't come down to London and get a flat off the Edgware Road. They view me as a dark horse that could possibly win the race. That's fine by me. I don't have to play their game.' In addition, Billy hinted that he planned to quit his musical career on his upcoming thirtieth birthday and begin studying to become a veterinary surgeon. 'I'm getting tutors in to help me . . . I can do it better now because my concentration is much better,' he said, although this idea never reached fruition.

Work on *The Glamour Chase* continued as random pockets of tracks recorded with different producers in a variety of locations – with Tears For Fears producer Chris Hughes at the Wool Hall in Bath, with Peter Henderson in London and with Boris Blank in Zurich. Since it was a favourite of the Associates' live set during the 1986 tour, MacKenzie had agreed to record a more techno-orientated version of Blondie's 'Heart Of Glass'. Perhaps inevitably, in the first indication of a climate that exists to this day of launching new artists – or indeed relaunching ailing acts – with a cover version, Warners Brothers were soon making enthusiastic noises about the track being the next Associates single.

There is a lingering argument that Billy was bulldozed into releasing 'Heart Of Glass' as what was inevitably regarded as a comeback single, since it was an unspectacular retread of the original (although, unbeknown to him, it became a cult floor-filler on the New York club scene). Certainly, at the time, he was unshakeable in his defence of the track, although when it limped to number 56 in the week following its release in September 1988, he perhaps realized that it had been a weak move and instantly denounced the single as being a folly on the part of Warners.

'Being totally honest about it, it was the record company's choice,' he told *Melody Maker*. 'I'm still about half a million pounds in the red and they've never got anything back so, although it was a mess, I thought, "Why not?" When the tape came back [from Chris Hughes], it sounded like early Can, early electronic music, so I started enjoying it a bit.' Max Hole still insists that the company didn't railroad MacKenzie into releasing the single: 'You couldn't force Billy to record a song he didn't want to record. It came out and it wasn't a hit – we all thought it was going to be Top Ten – and then I think Billy went off the idea.'

The accompanying video for 'Heart Of Glass' – which even Hole admits was 'terrible' – didn't help the cause. Adhering to a lumpen storyboard that involved Billy wandering in and around a set depicting a caravan park full of circus performers, the singer offers an agonizingly stiff and uneasy performance, as if recognizing the whole scenario around him to be slightly ridiculous and hugely embarrassing. 'When I saw that video,' Paul Haig admits, 'I just knew how angry he was, I could see it in his face.'

Indeed, in the round of interviews for 'Heart Of Glass', there were other clear indications that Billy was growing severely disillusioned, not only with his present predicament, but with his past glories as well. Of "Party Fears Two", he wearily stated, 'Oh, I never liked that. How could anybody get in such a fucking state when they were singing? That's what gets me.' Of his lack of any major success since, he claimed, 'I'm not really that bothered because I've always had a problem about earning money from music anyway. I've always felt strange when the cheques flew through the door . . . I always feel it's never been warranted and I got this cheque for doing something I love. So to get maybe a million out of it or something would make my skin crawl. I'd just have to distribute it to different members of the family first probably and then earn my money properly in another sort of way. I just don't need to upgrade my life through money. I get it through other things.'

In the light of the events that followed 'Heart Of Glass', *The Glamour Chase* would remain unreleased. As the cult surrounding Billy MacKenzie has grown over time, it remains the Associates' great lost masterpiece, its legend having grown among those who have never heard it – although their numbers have dwindled down the years as the album has been widely bootlegged from Warners' advance promos issued to the press at the time.

In reality, if viewed through the distance of time and calculated in the old vinyl-album money, *The Glamour Chase* reveals itself to be very much be an album divided by its two sides. Three of the tracks destined to make up side one – 'Reach The Top', 'Terrorbeat', 'Set Me Up' – are hewn from the light funk typical of ABC in their weaker moments, and as such, sounded sorely dated in 1988, with the emergence of acid house and dance culture diverting the attentions of the pop buyer, along with the factory-pre-set production line of Stock, Aitken and Waterman. The fact that 'Heart Of Glass' is programmed into the middle of these tracks only serves to reinforce the awful truth that – even though Billy would probably never have admitted it – Warners were winning hands-down in their battle to reshape him into a bland white soul singer.

However, for the remainder of the album, Billy launches a counter-assault with no little amount of panache. While there were persistent rumours that much of the lyrical content of *The Glamour Chase* focused on a bitter attack on the music industry, there is only any real evidence of this in the 40s swing of the Boris Blank-produced 'Snowball', with Billy ruminating on the fate of the fading star 'when the box office falls' and the treadmill role of the puppet performer: 'We're all just clowns for hire/Walking on the high wire/Miming all desire/So sweetly inspired by yesterday's fire.'

But by far the most notable aspect of *The Glamour Chase* is the development in Billy's singing style, the voice that had once ached with edginess and paranoia now mellowing into a seductive croon, particularly on the album's two balladeering high points, 'In Windows All' and 'Because You Love'. In the epic, eastern-influenced 'Empires Of Your Heart', MacKenzie blends the musical essence of 60s spy-movie soundtracks with an emotional vocal, providing the stand-out track of *The Glamour Chase*. This number, he later admitted, was his own favourite on the album, not unreasonably boasting that it was 'as good as David Bowie's "Heroes".'

But it is 'Country Boy', a cover of a song written by Gert and Udo Scheuerpflug of Die Zwei, that remains the strangest recording of Billy MacKenzie's entire career. Driven by synthetic double bass and an echoing single drum augmented by a rigidly precise beatbox, it features the Scheuerpflug brothers harmonizing a showtune chorus that is stylistically lifted straight out of the Rodgers and Hammerstein songbook circa *South Pacific* in 1949. In direct contrast, the verse lyrics reveal a rites-of-passage tale involving a young man with a rural heart who leaves his home to be 'free and strange' and becomes embroiled in a high-society city life, surrounded by 'pretty virgins' in fake furs. With no real post-rock 'n' roll reference points to pin it down, the track is both unhinged and magnificent, but unarguably commercial suicide. Stirring up the conflict with Warners – perhaps by this time simply for his own corrosive amusement – Billy insisted that it be the single to follow-up 'Heart Of Glass'.

Former Associates publicist Chris Carr confirms that at this time Billy confided that he saw little future for himself at WEA and was purposely winding up the label's bosses: 'He said to me, "I'm gonna break these fuckers. They're going to get so tired of me, they're going to shut me off."' At the same time, Warners sought advice from Carr on how to deal with MacKenzie: 'I would always say the same thing – "You give him space." With Billy, if you put it on the table and said, "That's it – that's the A to Z of the music industry'', he would go, "OK, I'm interested in D to P and S and T, and the rest of it, let's find somebody else to do it." I would say to Warners, "Get somebody to spend some time and understand him." They'd say, "We don't have the time to. Do you know what the bill is?'''

Following the not inexpensive recording of *The Glamour Chase* and the sizeable advances he'd received during the period, Billy was unrecouped to the tune of around £750,000 in his Warner Brothers contract. Understandably concerned about the deficit, Max Hole even considered capitalizing on interest from producer Trevor Horn in signing Billy to his record label ZTT, with a portion of the advances from this new deal going to repay at least part of the alarming debt.

Horn remembers a preliminary meeting with MacKenzie to discuss the terms of the deal and the direction of any future album they would make together as taking on a slightly surreal twist after the producer made a perhaps tasteless joke: 'We went out to lunch somewhere just off the Portobello Road and Billy was telling me about how he had gypsy blood . . . making a fairly big thing of it. I said, "Why don't we call your album *Gyppo* then? That way you can face that whole thing head on . . ." He was a bit nonplussed by that. Then he started to tell me about this idea he had for a television show that featured a goat called Goatie 1 and how it would sit there with its little hooves crossed over. So then I had to sit through the rest of the meal keeping a straight face while he went on about this goat.

'I liked Billy, but after the lunch, I said to everyone at the record label, "We can't do this, because I know what'll happen. We'll make a really great record and he'll disappear." He wanted to do some of those big show tunes, a real Shirley Bassey thing, but I could see that he was going to be difficult to pin down.'

Horn's worries were compounded by the fact that in February 1988 ZTT had been successfully sued in a contract dispute with Holly Johnson, lead singer of Frankie Goes To Hollywood, with whom the producer had experienced fleeting, if record-breaking, success earlier in the decade. 'I'd had very bad experiences with flaky artists,' he insists, 'and even though I liked Billy, I just didn't want to knowingly go into a situation with somebody who was going to be flaky again. The problem is that you put in so much effort and you invest an enormous amount of money and if the person up front can't sell it or can't be relied on, believe me, it makes your life a misery. But I always sort of regretted it a bit that we didn't sign him, because who knows what kind of an exciting record we could've made together?'

In a desperate, directionless move, Warners pressed up 5000 copies of 'Country Boy' as the date of Billy's contract option loomed – the point where a record company can decide whether or not to renew a deal. Since the promotion of *The Glamour Chase* – an album that the Warners executives didn't consider as being a particularly commercial proposition – would have obliged them to commit at least another £100,000 to the marketing budget, a corporate decision was made. Eight long years after his signing in 1981, WEA dropped Billy MacKenzie in January 1989, an act that typically clears the artist of any responsibility for their debts and, of course, caps any further spending on the label's part. As a result, the plans for the release of both 'Country Boy' and *The Glamour Chase* were scrapped.

'On a number of occasions,' Max Hole admits, 'I'd said, "Billy MacKenzie is an undroppable artist – he's somebody that is too great to not indulge on your label." He was the kind of artist that, even if we didn't make money, was a good advertisement for the label. It's like Tom Waits made certain artists want to be on Island, and I felt the same about Billy. But we were so unrecouped . . . we decided to drop him. Really I was under pressure from Rob [Dickens] and the finance people, and to be fair to them, it was actually the right thing to do. In a way, I needed to be told, actually.'

Hole clearly remembers breaking the news to MacKenzie over lunch in a Kensington restaurant: 'I said to Billy that I thought it might be good for both of us if we called it a day, and that the relationship wasn't really going anywhere from his point of view, as well as from ours. There was too much history. There was too much of a negative [feeling] about Billy in the building. I felt really miserable and he was so sweet. He actually said to me, "Oh, Max, you look so sad" and he sort of put his arm around me. He was cheering me up, and I was the one that was dropping him from the label.'

After lunch, Billy returned to the Warners offices for the last time, casually asking Hole if he could perhaps book one final cab on the label's account to take him home. Of course, owing to the heavily emotional nature of this last request, Hole agreed.

When the VIP car pulled up outside the WEA building, Billy got inside and – in an ultimate, conclusive act of opportunistic defiance – told the driver to take him to Dundee.

11

From Fire to Ice

In Billy MacKenzie's mind, it was as if someone had finally unlocked the door of his cell at the end of a seemingly interminable eight-year stretch, an impression followed by the rush of conflicting emotions that come with any sudden change and period of rehabilitation. While there's little arguing that this wilfully difficult inmate had taken great delight in baiting his captors, by the end, the walls had begun closing in on him. Although he was suffering from mixed responses of trauma and loss, freedom and possibility, the dominant feeling that Billy was experiencing in the fallout of being dropped by Warners was one of growing bitterness.

During a decompressive visit to Zurich to work with Yello, Billy and Dieter Meier – a dabbling art-house film director then working on the unscreened film *Snowball* – concocted a fanciful scheme involving the singer writing the script for a remake of *Theatre Of Blood* as an anger-venting exercise. In the 1973 film, Vincent Price portrays a Shakespearian actor who exacts absolute revenge on his critics by systematically murdering them; in this imaginary version, Billy would fake his own death by throwing himself in the Thames and in the aftermath, the voting panel of the Brits Awards, who – as the plot had it – had always failed to merit MacKenzie, would mysteriously be bumped off, one by one.

Although never realized, this blackly comical notion mirrored Billy's darker thoughts during this period. 'At the time,' he later admitted to *Melody Maker* of his sour feelings regarding the situation with Warners, 'if I'd seen any of those people, I'd have killed them. They were affecting my creative personality and anybody who does that – Warners, friends, family, anybody – honestly, I could kill them. I'm luckier than most people because, when I laugh, I laugh hard. I'm very happy with things at the moment but I'm still torn at any different time of the day. Sometimes my life is like a really beautiful painting and then something will come along and put a great big huge rip through the canvas.'

Spending most of his time in Auchterhouse, with the daily needs of his family and dogs providing ample distraction from his own problems, Billy found his unbridled enthusiasm for his music – never repressible, even in bleaker times – eventually buoying his spirit. Particularly during his long walks with the whippets in the silence of the hills around Dundee, where passers-by often discovered him loudly singing to himself on the footpaths, ideas for new songs began to tumble around in his mind.

In his eternal search for new collaborators, Billy called Philipp Erb, a Swiss programmer living in London, inviting him to Scotland to work on the pre-production of these new tracks. Billy had first encountered Erb engineering on 'Cinemas Of The World', a Europop track by the obscure French group Uno that the singer had guested on in 1987. Keen to re-explore his love of electronic music, Billy recognized that Erb – who suggested they also enlist the talents of his musical partner, female American keyboard player Blair Booth – could, with his programming skills, help provide an re-entry point for him. But even if the singer seemed keen to get this new project underway as quickly as possible, his behaviour was unpredictable.

When Erb and Booth arrived at Dundee at the end of their long train journey from London King's Cross, Billy, who had promised to meet them both at the station, was nowhere to be seen. 'We were standing there and all we had was a telephone number,' Erb remembers. 'Eventually we managed to get in touch with him through about fifteen friends and he picked us up and put us in his flat in Auchterhouse. He left us there for about three days because it turned out that the studio in Edinburgh where we were supposed to be working had already been booked by someone else . . . it was all a bit mad really.' Erb hadn't been able to bring all of his equipment up with him on the train, but Billy proved that his squandering ways had not deserted him when he used up a sizeable chunk of the Fiction Songs budget for these publishing demos to hire for the programmer a vast array of state-of-the-art keyboards, more than Erb or Booth would have ever been able to use.

Strangely, Erb recalls that Billy then seemed to quickly lose interest in the tracks: 'He came and did some vocals, and then he just said, "Oh, you finish it off." That was the last we saw of him until the tracks were finished.' In reality, through technology, Billy, who was never fond of the laborious recording process – apart from during his high-jinksing days with Alan Rankine – had perhaps found his ideal working method. Through the program-ming medium, Billy could communicate his ideas to Erb and Booth, disappear for three days and then return, when the work was completed, to tinker with the results. Given his low boredom threshold, it was an arrangement that suited him perfectly.

When the tracks were finished, Billy began looking for repre-sentation, having realized that his past difficulties in dealing with the music industry were partly a direct result of not having had a manager to soften some of the financial blows he would inevitably inflict on any record company. At Chris Parry's suggestion, he met up with Bob Johnson, who in his time had managed such diverse artists as the Ruts and Frankie Goes To Hollywood. An easygoing Londoner with renown and clout within the record business, Johnson had often bumped into Billy in the Warners offices over the years, and there had been talk of him managing the Associates during the *Perhaps* period. At the time, Johnson already had two acts on WEA, Roddy Frame and ex-Special AKA singer Stan Campbell. Acknowledging that taking on a third might pose a conflict of interests, the relationship came to nothing. Now that Billy was out of contract, it was a different matter, and in their preliminary meeting in the summer of 1989, the singer and the manager hit it off immediately. 'He's really quite grounded and quite normal,' Philipp Erb says of Johnson. 'He's got his whole family life, which I think Billy quite respected because that was what he valued up in Scotland.'

Finding a new deal for the singer was never going to be the easiest of tasks for Johnson. Naturally, Billy already had a reputation as one of the most difficult artists operating within the business, having been through four deals in ten years. However, this notoriety was counterbalanced by the huge weight of respect within the industry for his vocal talent, and so there was still a pocket of A&R personnel who felt they were up to the challenge of resurrecting MacKenzie's career. In pole position was Ashley Newton, who had cut the one single deal for 39 Lyon Street back in 1981 and who was now the A&R director of Circa Records, a recently formed subsidiary of the Virgin group. From MacKenzie and Johnson's shared perspective, this proved to be the most attractive offer. From the former's point of view, it didn't hurt either that Paul Haig, who had also recently signed to the company, would be his label mate.

'It was a small label,' Bob Johnson says of the reasoning behind Billy's subsequent singing to Circa, 'so we'd get a lot more input, a lot more time and care taken over it. In the large corporate thing where you've got nearly two hundred acts, it was very difficult for someone like Billy to keep to a schedule and then to wait until the corporation had the time to put out his record.'

Perhaps shrewdly – knowing of Billy's financially excessive tendencies – Ashley Newton made a modest offer of £40,000 for the first album, plus recording and marketing costs. 'It wasn't a very expensive deal,' the A&R man admits. 'The reason that I refused to indulge in high advances was that I knew it was going to cost a lot of money to record, although it didn't escalate out of control. But I knew that Billy was not a cheap date. He was lots of fun and you knew that you were going to go on another great journey with him, but he wasn't a cheap date.'

Circa had recently set up their official headquarters in Soho's Wardour Street, where, in keeping with the tail-end of the design-obsessed 1980s, Newton was keen to present what he termed 'the aesthetic of the label'. As a result, the interior of the Circa offices featured bleached wooden floors and expensive furniture shipped in from Italy. 'It really was beautiful,' Newton says, 'and we'd only been in there for three or four days when

Billy came down. He brought in his two whippets, which, of course, walked in the office and immediately pissed and shat everywhere. The girls in the office, who always watched from afar with their arms folded at me being such a fussy wanker, just thought this was hysterical.'

For Billy, it was business as usual, then. But Paul Haig remembers him offering a distinctly cynical view of the Circa deal from the outset: 'He said he thought they'd signed him because he'd be a bauble on their Christmas tree . . . a shiny Rolls-Royce that gets polished once a year.'

Nevertheless, Billy was now re-energized, if not still a little battle-scarred. Since the deal with Circa had been cut with only four new demos, he threw himself into the task of writing the other songs for his sixth album, often employing highly unusual methods. In this period the singer had faced up to the obsession that would lead him to spend an average eight hours a day on the telephone, and he had dealt with it by temporarily denying himself a home number. Bob Johnson remembers: 'If I wanted to get hold of him, I'd phone a pay phone in Auchterhouse and try and get whoever picked it up to cycle up to find Billy.'

At the time, MacKenzie didn't even own a basic tape recorder to use as a musical notepad, and so, if he came up with an idea for a song while walking in the hills, he would stop off at a phone box in Auchterhouse and sing the vocal and instrumental parts on to his manager's answering machine in London. 'He was the only writer that I've ever dealt with that actually couldn't play an instrument,' Johnson points out. 'So he used to write at this time by filling up my answering-machine tapes – singing the words and the drumbeats and the horn parts on to them. Then he'd make me transfer the ideas on to cassette and send them back up to him.'

Before long, it was becoming apparent that it was going to be virtually impossible for Billy to fulfil the obligations of this new contract from such a remote location and that a move back down to London was the only real solution. Seven years after he had last had a permanent base in the capital, Billy moved into a two-bedroom house in Hampstead (where his distinguished neighbours included Dame Peggy Ashcroft), taking with him a friend from Dundee, Steven Phillips, whom he employed as his PA with a loose job description that involved all of the more typical organizational tasks but stretched to include house-cleaning and whippet-walking duties.

A producer was found for the still-untitled album. Julian Mendelsohn, who'd served his apprenticeship with Trevor Horn as a mix engineer, was a forthright, plain-talking Australian who Circa had decided was well equipped to deal with the creatively demanding singer. 'Julian wouldn't take anything from him,' Erb notes. 'He'd say, "Just shut up, Billy." He was quite bolshy with him and in some ways it worked, although he was a bit overpowering.' Howard Hughes, brought into the sessions to provide additional keyboards, confirms that there was a certain amount of light-spirited friction between the producer and the singer: 'Billy once got Mendelsohn to lie down behind the desk when he was doing a vocal. He said, "I can't sing 'cause you're so ugly, Julian. I can't stand looking at your face." Julian just went, "Oh, all right, Billy", and lay down on the floor.'

Instilled with a certain urgency following the agonizingly protracted recordings of both *Perhaps* and *The Glamour Chase*, the new album was completed in a relatively painless eight weeks at Sarm West in west London, reasonably within budget, although a procession of top-level session musicians were wheeled through the studio. Having lost none of his love for extravagant one-upmanship, when Neneh Cherry's husband/manager Cameron McVey visited Sarm West one day and happened to mention that her recent single 'Manchild' had featured thirty string players, Billy jokingly insisted after he had left that the track the team were currently working on should employ thirty-*five* orchestral musicians. Moreover, the passing of time had not dimmed Billy's intensity in the studio. Philipp Erb recalls of the sessions: 'It was just "Go go go" and he would be too impatient for the tape to rewind. It was just like, throw it all down, as quickly as he could, and that always seemed to work best.'

On its completion, the album was entitled *Wild And Lonely* – not so much an insight into the desolate, barren state of MacKenzie's soul, but instead, simply the name of a whippet that he had encountered. 'The unsuspecting critics and public had no idea that the title was taken from the name of the dog,' Billy wrote in his whippet diaries. 'Most of them thought that it was my windswept and romantic idea.' In *Melody Maker*, he enthusiastically attempted to describe the process of making the album: 'It was thrown up in the air and we juggled with it and shaped it and twirled it about and kicked it off the wall and pummelled it and panel-beated it and spat on it and chewed it up and pissed on it and slept with it and loved it and licked it and . . . d'you know what I mean?'

There was one major stumbling block in the planning stages of the marketing of *Wild And Lonely* – Billy's refusal to take his hat off for any of the album's photographs. While everyone around him understood his sensitivity regarding his receding hairline, the singer would never admit to this insecurity, instead inventing grand theories designed to underline the importance of his head-wear. 'I remember the beret becoming an absurdly big issue,' Ashley Newton states. 'It was one of those classic record-business conversations and Billy would go into these surreal depths of how significant it was whether he wore the bloody hat or not.' In the end, for the album's sleeve, which featured Billy in black leather jacket and corsage of ivy and roses, posing in front of a specially commissioned painting by Colin Williams depicting a drunken male figure – possibly intended to be MacKenzie himself, although there's little real resemblance – passed out in a deserted bar, the photograph of the hatless singer is tactfully cropped just below the hairline.

A separate marketing argument of more pressing importance centred around whether the album should be released under the name of Billy MacKenzie or his group's trading name. Billy's opinions on this subject apparently veered back and forward on a daily basis. After much deliberation, *Wild And Lonely* became the sixth Associates album, released on 24 March 1990. In the week of release, Circa threw a themed launch party for the album at Wimbledon greyhound track, where the assembled journalists frittered away their money, wagering on the races. 'I think most people there had never been to a dog track in their lives,' says Judy

Lipsey, the Associates' publicist at the time. 'Of course, Billy knew his way around like the back of his hand. We had food and drink and nobody was interested, they were so busy asking Billy which dogs they should bet on. Everybody had a really great time and lost loads of money. He loved it because he was completely the centre of attention.'

The following week, however, *Wild And Lonely* charted at a massively disappointing number 71. Significantly, the album's long-term fortunes weren't aided by the fact that nine months after the release of the album, WEA issued *Popera*, a seventeen-track retrospective of the Associates' recording career, in the process likely tempting away many casual record-buyers. In her dealings with the press for *Wild And Lonely*, Judy Lipsey – who now handles the Spice Girls and David Bowie – remembers there being a huge amount of attention from both the music press and the broadsheet newspapers, and mercifully little tabloid interest in MacKenzie, eight years on from his last Top 40 hit: 'With Billy, people were interested in him and his voice and his history and the new music . . . they weren't really interested in who he was shagging. At the time, nobody knew if he was gay or not and he would never, *never* talk about it. He was so practised, I think, with not answering questions directly about his private life.'

If MacKenzie was expert in deflecting an unwanted line of questioning, then he seemed ready at this stage to reveal more of his past, even if it involved slightly dramatized accounts. Talking about 'Fever', the first single pulled from *Wild And Lonely*, in a wide variety of interviews from this time, Billy explained how the song was about him losing his virginity to a twenty-two-year-old prostitute whose child he would babysit for at the age of fourteen. 'I was sexually very aware at the age of about 12 and I seduced an older woman, basically. It was very traumatic for her. She thought it was all her fault, but I was able to cope with it even though the roles were reversed. She couldn't handle it. It fizzled out.' In further discussing lyrical content, Billy offered carefully rendered insights into his sexuality: 'I'm always very honest in my lyrics. It's got to go beyond stereotypes, beyond male and female, beyond genitalia.'

But the truth was that *Wild And Lonely* was not a great album, largely a result of its sterile production. In an attempt to perhaps produce a more sophisticated record for an older generation, modelled on the solo Bryan Ferry, the Associates' music had been sapped of its mystery – an ingredient that, arguably, Boris Blank could have added to the finished result. At points Billy sounds completely detached, his thoughts a million miles away from the task at hand. If many of his vocals on *Wild And Lonely* still effortlessly surpass the best work of many other singers from his peer group, then it is only a measure of the distance between MacKenzie and his contemporaries. These were the sort of performances that he could deliver in his sleep, and true to form, the listener can almost picture him yawning in between the lines.

Tellingly, it is the more timeless, balladeering tracks that prove most effective, where there is less evidence of the lumpen 80s-style production that lingers throughout. Both the title track and 'Strasbourg Square' echo the introspective grandeur of 'The Rhythm Divine', and elsewhere 'Just Can't Say Goodbye' – if imagination strips it of its upbeat pop arrangement and replaces it with a string-laden mid-60s treatment – could easily have fitted into the catalogue of Scott Walker. In its far less cohesive moments, 'People We Meet' matches an emulation of Kraftwerk's 'Tour De France' with an over-light, nursery-rhyme melody and 'Calling All Around The World' presents the absolute nadir of MacKenzie's entire recording career. Over a perky programmed Motown beat and cheesy horns, Billy vainly wrestles with a melody that is part Dusty Springfield, part Buck's Fizz, the overall effect reminiscent of Stock, Aitken and Waterman's illustrious work with Jason Donovan, or worse, the theme tune of the daytime soap opera that spawned him.

The reviews of the first Associates album for six years were mixed but fair, MacKenzie's past glories ensuring he would be spared a savaging by the press. 'His distinctive voice is in danger of getting lost amongst Julian Mendelsohn's (over)polished production,' Jane Phillips noted in *Record Mirror*, 'sounding uncomfortably smooth and controlled. With this album Billy isn't taking too many commercial or personal risks, but he still retains one of the most spine-tingling voices in pop.' In *Melody Maker*, Simon Reynolds was even kinder: '"Wild And Lonely" is no "Sulk": the volcano of MacKenzie's purple hysteria remains dormant. But this album is a thoroughly aristocratic return for one of our last pop heroes.' Judy Lipsey remembers: 'When the reviews came out, people were still expecting the kind of histrionics of the early Associates stuff. Well, he was thirty-three at the time, and of course, the voice matures – you can't still sing in that crazy, high octane way that you did when you were twenty-two. But I think people felt that he hadn't moved with the times. Some people felt that the arrangements were a bit dated.'

Neither of the singles from *Wild And Lonely* had managed to revive the Associates' chart career, both 'Fever' and its follow-up, 'Fire To Ice' floundering outside the Top 75, despite lavishly expensive videos, produced for in the region of £70–80,000 each and craftfully styled by Michael Nash Associates, the design company who now number Harvey Nichols among their upmarket clients. The former features Billy performing the song in close-up, intercut with shots of body-painted models swimming in underwater shots, a succession of images that might have merited use on the cover of any of the Roxy Music albums. The other video is similarly glossy, but finds MacKenzie in an absurd black, quiffed Elvis wig and 60s dark glasses, playing roulette and laughingly flirting with a trio of waif-like black models in matching blonde wigs. While beautifully stylish, the high budget values of these videos – each of which might easily have been used to finance the recording of an entire album – only served to magnify the relative failures of the singles.

In the years that followed, Billy would admit that he considered *Wild And Lonely* to be his weakest album, while equating it with Hollywood film stars 'allowed' their one bad film. 'I thought it would be a relief with "Wild And Lonely",' he said six years later, 'to just do a sort of bland album as a safety net for the creative insanity that does go around in my head. It was actually to see if I could just do something . . . [laughs] boring. And I don't mean that in an arrogant way. But my natural preference is for things to have a real cracked element.'

* * *

As if unwillingly shoved from the wings into the spotlight, Billy agreed to fulfil one live appearance with a full band in support of the album at the Big Day, an open-air festival-styled gig held on 3 June 1990 in Glasgow's George Square, designed to highlight the Scottish music scene. The Associates were slotted in to perform just before the headliners, Wet Wet Wet, and the day's events were televised live by Channel 4. For four weeks before the show, with the amount of effort and planning normally afforded to a full-scale world tour, a six-piece band led by Philipp Erb and Blair Booth was rehearsed in preparation – Billy turning up on the last day and singing through each song only once. On the Saturday afternoon of the appearance, Erb remembers the singer being incredibly nervous, a reaction intensified by the fact that the event was running late and the Associates might be hard pushed to fit their set into their allocated televisual half-hour.

In the footage from the event, Billy appears comfortable, if not wide-grinningly relaxed, as he fronts the band in blue crushed-velvet jacket and ever-present beret, his eyes shielded behind aviator shades. Five songs in, Bob Johnson, watching from the side of the stage, was informed that the TV production crew were going to be forced to cut the appearance short and go into an ad break. With the seamless, programmed nature of the set, however, the close of one song segued directly into the beginning of another and the programme's director flipped. Cameras were laid down and the stage crew rushed to switch off the band's equipment, while the manager grew furious. 'Me and the tour manager had to physically keep them off the stage,' Johnson remembers. 'I was saying, "You unplug that – £80,000 worth of equipment – and we're gonna sue you."'

For the European promotion of *Wild And Lonely*, Billy embarked on a lightning five-city media tour, taking in Hamburg, Amsterdam, Paris, Rome and Barcelona, the exhausting itinerary of each day involving a flight, followed by what is accurately known as a 'grip 'n' grin' meeting with the representatives of each separate wing of the record company and then a concentrated schedule of press, TV and radio interviews. Each morning Circa boss Ray Cooper remembers Billy arriving for breakfast, having spent the previous night on the tiles, declaring that he was immediately moving to the city – every city – 'lock, stock and barrel'.

In the US, where Billy was facing his first album release since *Sulk*, Virgin had revived their ownership of the Charisma imprint – which, ironically, had boasted Genesis as its most successful act in the 70s – for the release of *Wild And Lonely*. Beforehand, Bob Johnson travelled to the States to assure the record company that Billy would make himself available for a media promotional trip similar to the one recently completed in Europe, although privately he was having doubts whether MacKenzie could stand the long-haul flight to New York. To lighten the load, Circa agreed that Steve Phillips could accompany Billy as the trip's co-ordinator. 'I actually got him on the plane to New York pretty easily in the end,' Johnson recalls.

To his surprise, a strong cult following of the Associates had built up in New York over the years, with even the less successful singles of MacKenzie's recent past, such as 'Those First Impressions' and 'Take Me To The Girl', proving enduring floor-fillers, particularly in the gay clubs, along with the new house remix of 'Fire To Ice'. At a party thrown by Charisma in his honour on his arrival in the city, Billy was approached by Naomi Campbell – who had been a massive Associates fan in her youth and at the time was considering a musical career as an alternative to her modelling day job. Billy said of the meeting: 'It was all kisses and cuddles. She was just saying that she wanted to work with me because she liked my voice.'

One night in the near-legendary Roxy club, MacKenzie was accosted by what he described as 'this Leigh Bowery effect who came across and was like, "Hi there, Billy, how are you?" and "Oh, you're so wonderful and so special to me." All this kind of caper. The next minute he'd roped me in [to perform] . . ."Please will you do something for me? It would make my dreams come true" . . . and all this kind of Judy Garland stuff.' Flying on brandy, Billy performed a series of karaoke-style numbers including the Lemon Pipers' 1968 psychedelic hit 'Green Tambourine'. Another impromptu gig occurred at a Red Hot & Blue AIDS benefit in a club called the Saint, where Erasure pulled out at the eleventh hour and MacKenzie filled their slot with a rendition of 'Heart Of

Glass'. 'It was to about five thousand gay men,' Billy explained. 'There was this big winged-angel effect above me and its wee nummy looked quite . . . y'know, extended, and I was like, "Christ what's happening here?" It was swinging above me! I says, "Well, I can't sing if you allow that to swing above me, so would you take that down and stick it in the corner?" But it went down really really well.'

For three weeks MacKenzie and Phillips enjoyed the first-class, stretch-limo treatment as they travelled to a number of cities, among them Boston, Chicago, Washington, Miami, Dallas and San Francisco. All was going well, in fact, until their arrival in Los Angeles. It was the first time Billy had returned to the sprawling West Coast city since the days of his short-lived marriage. As a teenager he had been intoxicated by the atmosphere of LA. Now, in his early thirties, it made him feel unbearably claustrophobic. 'I was there for one night and I just *freaked*. When I was seventeen, I was oblivious to the real sort of undercurrent and underworld feeling of the place. I never noticed the social cripples on Sunset Boulevard when I was seventeen. I thought they were interesting and quite glam actually. But the reality hit me and it was really quite scary.

'The overwhelming feeling was that the place was just gonna explode. That was before [the 1992 riots] and I got really quite frightened for people. I just thought, I don't know how this place exists without the whole lid just blowing off the gaff, y'know, and I was frightened. I thought it was the most horrible, disgusting, tacky dump and I just said [to Phillips], "Right, we're out of it." We had plane tickets to go back to New York, but I says, "I'm not getting on another fucking plane, that's it, we're going on the bus." I wanted to see if I had the bottle to do it, after all that sort of high-flying.'

The pair dragged their bags down from the Four Seasons Hotel to the local Greyhound bus depot, where they called Bob Johnson in London. 'Billy said, "I can't get on the plane, I need a holiday,"' the manager recalls. 'He convinced me that he couldn't stand the eleven and a half hours back from LA. Then Steven came on the line and said to me that the seven hours to New York had been enough and he didn't really want to get on the plane with him either. I was telling Billy, "Just take some tablets, knock yourself out and you'll wake up when you get here." But he couldn't do it and he promised he would keep in touch.

'I told Steven to phone me collect from wherever they were and I think the first call I got was from Arizona or somewhere. I was like, "All right, where are you going?" and he said, "New Orleans." In the end they went all the way back to New York on the Greyhound bus. I managed to convince the record company to cash in the return flights.'

But then, when Phillips called Johnson from New York, he informed the manager that Billy was still too nervous to fly back to the UK. 'Billy had worked out that the *QE2* was actually sailing in about three weeks' time,' Johnson says, 'so if I could keep him in a hotel in New York until then and get him a *QE2* ticket, he'd be fine. But I couldn't convince the record company to do it, since I'd just managed to get a new lot of tickets out of them and so I had to tell Billy that he couldn't wait for the *QE2*. His excuse was that he couldn't stand a flight that was any longer than four hours, so I worked out that it was only four hours to Reykjavik. They flew there, stayed the night and then came back to London.

'After that,' Johnson says of the conclusion to this eventful series of incidents, 'it was almost impossible to get him on a plane again.'

12

Cosmic Space Age Soul

In the final analysis, *Wild And Lonely* had tallied up around 30,000 sales – not a disastrous reckoning at the end of the day. Still, Circa Records were now forced to concede that it might take a second album to fully rebuild MacKenzie's career and to recoup the £250,000 outlay for this first album.

Typically, at the beginning of 1991 Billy's attention was divided, his thoughts scattered everywhere. There were dozens of planned and imagined projects in the pipeline, every one of them needing to be realized immediately, if not before. There was the ongoing plan to record more material with Paul Haig, another to work with his brother Jimmy MacKenzie – who was now heavily involved in the club scene and working as a part-time Scottish A&R man for ZTT Records – on some dance tracks at a studio that had just opened in Auchterhouse. There were murmurings that the many unreleased tracks that Billy had recorded in Zurich over the years might be issued as an album by Mercury under the banner of MacKenzie/Blank. There was even a plot to open up a shop in Dundee selling art-deco collectables; this was to eventually materialize, although it closed three years later because of a slim local demand for such an enterprise. Furthermore, it appeared as if a collaboration with Sparks – Billy's former leading musical lights – was likely, since the Mael brothers had contacted him to express their admiration of his voice.

While most of these potential musical manoeuvres were destined to remain in the planning stages, this explosion of rejuvenated energy signified the extent to which Billy was now revelling in his musical freedom, the torturous limbo of the Warners years now dimming in his memory. Around this time, he began to talk of the 'utter, psychotic frustration' that he had experienced in the past, equating it to 'being Boris Becker at peak fitness, unable to play a match'. Now, paradoxically, there was more to be done than time would actually allow.

The only extracurricular project fulfilled in this period was MacKenzie's contribution to the British Electric Foundation's *Music Of Quality And Distinction Volume 2* – a soaring, sweetly performed offering of Deniece Williams's 1977 number-one hit 'Free'. Nine years on from their last collaboration, Martyn Ware noticed a marked change in Billy: 'He wasn't as wild, he was much more reflective about things. But you'd ask him what he was up to and he was always doing a million things at once. I suppose I wanted him to do a soul classic because I'd always regarded Billy as a soul singer. But he was really self-conscious about it – which wasn't a trait I was familiar with in him. He had such deep respect for these kind of songs, he did genuinely think he couldn't improve on them.'

One real benefit of this side-project was that it reawakened Billy's interest in his soul roots. Alongside his current passion for the more ecstatic, Balearic-derived area of dance culture in 1991, he had designs on blending the two influences to create what he grandly coined 'cosmic space age soul'. Pre-production for the next album began at the house in Hampstead, with Philipp Erb and Steve Aungle providing the musical input. The work rate was fairly intense, although Billy rarely hung around during these programming sessions, leaving the pair to churn out the backing tracks, underlining the somewhat battery-chicken element of the musicians' role. Erb remembers there being increasing friction between himself and Billy during the progress of this work: 'It got more difficult. He was being very impatient. He came up with new songs and a lot of them weren't that good and it was hard to tell him. He just wasn't very open to criticism sometimes.'

As Billy's publisher, Chris Parry recalls experiencing similar frustrations at this time: 'He could talk endlessly about how good something was that he'd done, and it was very difficult to get through to him that, y'know, "It's not *that* good, Billy . . . it's OK." He didn't have any rationale for what was good and what was not so good – it was all great, everything was great. He couldn't see the wood for the trees or measure his own work. It was a devil's job to try and get him to face up to the fact that things weren't as good as they could be.'

If these older associations were becoming sour, then MacKenzie and Aungle were building a friendship, even if the pair would often visit a nearby Hampstead café for a coffee and then sit together in complete silence for lengthy periods. 'Every so often,' Aungle recalls, 'Billy would say, "You're really quiet, Steve. Have you not got anything to say?" Then he'd ask you loads of questions like, "What pictures do you get off that track?" Now, I don't really visualize music, I just hear it as sound. But he was the opposite – he had a lot of visualization going on with the songs. So I just had to make stuff up to keep him happy. I'd say, "That makes me think of the Sphinx" and he'd say. "Oh, that's great, Steve." He was always trying to draw interpretations out of people to maybe give himself a different angle on something.'

Before long, the 'cosmic space age soul' project was being drawn towards Berlin. For years, something of a co-influential synergy had existed between MacKenzie and the German underground music scene. Billy's interest in both the country's electronic pioneers and the experimental fringes of Krautrock had surfaced in the Teutonic edges of the early Associates sound. This in turn inspired a clutch of German bands such as DAF and Palais Schaumburg, the latter having featured Moritz Von Oswald, who served as the Associates' drummer for the 1985 tour.

As it happened, in 1990 Von Oswald and former Palais Schaumburg member Thomas Fehlmann had been approached by Warners to remix 'Waiting For The Loveboat' and 'Club Country' for release on *Poperetta*, an EP to promote the accompanying retrospective compilation. Rather than being riled by the discovery that his old label had commissioned remixes without his consent, Billy was intrigued to hear the results and was indeed happier with these new productions than with what he viewed as the 'abysmal, really awful' attempts to remix Associates' material in the past. As Billy evocatively put it, he became 'like a hound on a truffle trail', tracking down Von Oswald and Fehlmann with a view to working with them on the new album. When Circa consented to financing three tracks on an experimental basis, in the summer of 1991, Billy travelled to Berlin to begin work on what would eventually become *Outernational.*

In comparison to the sterile, pine-furnished, top-flight recording environment that had been the setting for *Wild And Lonely,* Von Oswald's studio was a compact programming suite, not even boasting a separate vocal booth. But in some ways this down-grading appealed greatly to Billy, since it was in very similar environments that many of the more cutting-edge dance records that he currently loved were being created. The location further added a certain glamour to the situation, since Berlin had been the setting for the trilogy of David Bowie albums that had endured as Billy's favourites since the time of the Associates' 'Boys Keep Swinging' début. 'This time,' Billy later said of the most frugal recordings he had been involved in since the Situation 2 singles, 'there were no whims. Except Häagen-Dazs ice-cream. I put on about a stone eating that.'

The German team rose to the challenge, even if this inevitably involved tackling the singer's unusual musical requests. Thomas Fehlmann recalls: 'He came up with the most obscure suggestions of having a Chinese female choir in that corner of the mix or something. He could be quite challenging in that way, asking you for something that you definitely didn't have. It was all a bit of a game, but then it wasn't as if he came up with an idea and insisted on having it done. It was more like throwing all of the ideas into the pot. Also, with programming as opposed to working with a band, you can very gradually build the track up. The songs developed quite naturally on their own and it flowed very well.'

At the close of each day's work Billy would disappear into the Berlin night to absorb the city's vibrantly decadent club culture, although he was always guarded about the details of his exploits if quizzed by the others in the studio the next day. 'He wouldn't say, "I came back home at two o'clock at night,"' Fehlmann recalls. 'He'd say, "I came back at two o'clock in the afternoon." When you asked him where he'd been, he would always say, "You don't wanna know." I've still got this video footage that I shot of us working in the studio, where he walks in in the morning and I ask him, "How's it going, Billy?" He laughs and says, "I've got a bit of an eye infection. I think I've seen too much in Berlin." I say, "Was it very disturbing?" and he says, "No no, it was very educational actually.'"

As work on *Outernational* continued in Berlin with Fehlmann and Von Oswald, and in Zurich with Boris Blank, Billy decided to give notice on the house in Hampstead and move back to Auchterhouse. This meant that on his visits to London, he booked himself a room – and another for the dogs – at the Gore Hotel in Knightsbridge, recalling the excesses of the Warners years. It was in this way, rather than in the actual expense of recording, that the budget of the album began to soar. 'The cost of making *Outernational* just escalated out of control in terms of the hotel bills,' Bob Johnson remarks. 'You can imagine how much a hotel in Zurich costs, and he could be there for three or four weeks just doing three tracks with Boris. You're looking at £250 a night – spending nearly two grand a week in hotels alone, and that's before he's even had breakfast. Sometimes Billy would fly in and spend half an hour in the studio doing the vocal with Boris . . . but we were still in Zurich for a week.'

'It wasn't sound business practice, but Billy's enthusiasm was infectious,' the manager admits. 'He was probably spending the same amount of money, but Circa were a lot nicer about it. They kind of thought if Billy had a good idea, they'd run with it. Whereas with Warners, everything always seemed like an extravagance because they didn't want him to do it . . . and because they didn't want him to do it, he *doubly* did it. He did have that kind of them-and-us thing that he'd obviously had with Warners, but he didn't *appear* to be extravagant because he wasn't making a fuss. In reality, he was still travelling first-class on the train.'

What's more, Billy's collection of vintage cars had recently expanded, with the purchase of an elegantly expansive 1967 Volvo Estate that the singer bought with the dual aim of accommodating his whippets and travelling in style – even though he couldn't drive and was in the habit of paying friends to ferry him around. At one stage Billy lost the keys to the Volvo for a whole year and it lay outside his flat until the tyres sagged. But Johnson shared his love of classic motors, and when the manager was forced to put his beloved Bristol into the garage for repairs, Billy promised that he would lend him a car. 'I had to meet his brother and his uncle somewhere in Hampstead,' Johnson recalls, 'and they took me outside to give me the keys, and sitting there was this Rolls-Royce Silver Shadow. I said to them, "Billy can't drive . . . what's he doing with a Rolls-Royce?", and they just said, "Oh, he swapped it for the Mercedes Convertible." To be honest, I was a bit embarrassed to drive it.'

On the completion of *Outernational*, it was decided, after a little deliberation on the singer's part, that it would be released as Billy's first solo album. When questioned about this, Billy simply said, 'Ah well, it stops everybody asking me what happened to the Associates. I just wanted things nice and clear that this was very much a Billy MacKenzie album in the direction that he wanted to go in and not to confuse the issue.'

The fact that Billy had musically aligned himself with club culture resulted in these new efforts falling victim to the transient fashions of the dance world, where beats become passé within mere months. By the time of its release in August 1992, more than a year after its conception, the light grooves offered on *Outernational* had been overtaken by the new, harder-edged techno style. This posed a dilemma for MacKenzie – his desire to keep apace with the developments in dance music would have been better suited to low-budget, independent releases, where there is a quick turnover. But in order to maintain his lifestyle, Billy had to be signed to a major label, where releases are often delayed because of lengthy procrastination over marketing and strategy.

As a result, none of the singles lifted from *Outernational* succeeded in either igniting the dance floors or registering in the Gallup charts. Throughout this, Billy remained philosophical about his lack of mainstream success, telling Allan Campbell in an interview on Forth FM, 'I think it's more important for people who like me for me to have a hit. But I'm content with the situation at the moment. If people think that hits mean quality material, then I'm quite prepared to just wing it and roll with the punches.'

In many ways the choice of the singles from the album was possibly misguided – the unspectacular pop of 'Colours Will Come', the tired retread of Stevie Wonder's 'Pastime Paradise' – for, in creative terms, *Outernational* was undoubtedly Billy's greatest achievement since 'The Rhythm Divine'. Criminally, 'Baby', the first single released from the album, was the most likely hit record Billy had penned in some years. A towering ballad with an expansive, Spectoresque production, 'Baby' is performed with real force and emotion by the singer, whose voice cracks and distorts with passion as the dramatic strings threaten to engulf him at the powerful conclusion.

In his attempts to describe the music on the album, Billy talked in terms of 'glacial beauty' and serenity, describing the title as being an imagined concept of 'total outer body experience . . . it means you can stay at home and be "Outernational".' Wryly, addressing his ambivalent attitudes to travel, he added, 'If you're international, you've got to be on planes and trains and buses . . . and oxen and such.'

For the meandering title track, driven by a rhythm that is evocative of both Kraftwerk and *Station To Station*, MacKenzie offers an otherworldly travelogue through the human emotions, delivered in a ghostly tone, arriving at its destination of 'inner calm'. In 'Opal Krusch', over a house beat and bubbling synthesizers, the vocal is wafting and heavenly, pinning down the nocturnal atmosphere of the album. In many ways *Outernational* found MacKenzie striving to create the perfect soundtrack accompaniment to a comedown night drive through the darkened city streets – the chorus of police car sirens that introduce the disorientated European travel diary of 'Sacrifice And Be Sacrificed' only intensify the effect.

Frustratingly for Billy, the press response to *Outernational* remained as mixed as it had been for *Wild And Lonely*. As the struggling publicist for the album, Judy Lipsey explains that the PR objective had been 'to take him into other areas – for instance, we did a very beautiful fashion spread with *GQ*. But by then, he wasn't hip and trendy enough for the *Face* and he wasn't cutting edge enough for the *NME*. Billy would get very black and white and be quite bitter about it and say, "Well, fuck them, they don't know what they're talking about."'

Chris Parry has his own explanation for MacKenzie's waning relevance in the music industry: 'The press started to think that he wasn't the same character and the music wasn't as strong. He wanted to become an artist free of the trappings and the bullshit and the razzmatazz of the music industry. You can do that kind of thing – y'know, Neil Young, Van Morrison, they're two long-standing artists that just drop the stuff out and they may do an interview or they may do nothing. He could've been that kind of person, but he just needed to play the game a bit to sort of establish himself as more of a household name. But he was making so many moves that didn't seem to make much sense and he was having to defend things a lot of the time . . . it entrenched him.'

Behind the scenes, corporate reshuffles were conspiring to trip up Billy's career once again. Twelve months before the release of *Outernational*, Circa had been absorbed into the Virgin group and its bosses, Ray Cooper and Ashley Newton, put in charge of the whole roster of Virgin subsidiary labels – including sideline imprints Ten, Siren and Caroline – leaving them to oversee the fates of around one hundred and seventy signed acts. In what Newton describes as a 'pretty savage' rationalization, these were whittled down to around fifty.

When the release of *Outernational* triggered an option in Billy's contract, at the same time it was announced that Richard Branson had sold Virgin to EMI. As a result Circa was effectively defunct as a semi-independent entity. Newton and Cooper had no choice but to drop MacKenzie, whose debts at £700,000 were now on a par with the deficit he had left behind at WEA. *Outernational* had fared dismally on a commercial level and since there had been no hit in the UK, the album failed to achieve release outside of Britain, which, for such Euro-influenced music, was ironic at least. The crippling reality was that the estimated sales for *Outernational* were no greater than five thousand, and may in fact have been as low as three thousand.

'If *Outernational* did five thousand copies,' Bob Johnson admits, 'I'd be very surprised. I think Virgin stuck with it as long as they could, until the accountants got their hands on it. Billy didn't mind really. He was pretty fatalistic about it . . . realistic really. I'd explained to him what the second record meant, that it was make or break really. He knew how many records we'd sold, so it wasn't as though it was a great shock or surprise to him. It wasn't like the shock that I think maybe the Warners situation had been, where he'd gone in to make a record, finished it and was then told they weren't picking up the option. We knew that if *Outernational* didn't sell x amount of copies, then we had a problem on our hands.'

Ashley Newton says of the circumstances surrounding Circa's dropping of MacKenzie: 'We did it on a very personal basis. It wasn't at arm's length through lawyers, although we probably had to back it up with that. He knew that we'd committed a lot of money and heart, but culturally and commercially, it wasn't happening.'

Still, the fact that he was now once again out of contract did little to blacken Billy's creative outlook. Within a handful of months he had borrowed an eight-track from his friend and management stablemate, Aztec Camera's Roddy Frame, and was working on two new tracks at his Auchterhouse flat – 'At The Edge Of The World' and an unreleased instrumental entitled 'A Mood For All Seasons' – as part of a new co-writing collaboration with Steve Aungle.

In the meantime Billy was confronted by another, major distraction, which, although it may have seemed hugely insignificant to some, affected him deeply. Valuing his sideline dog-breeding career as highly as his musical endeavours (he once claimed that his ambition for one of his dogs to scoop a winning prize at Cruft's probably outweighed his desire to have a number-one record), he was troubled and incensed when he became the target of a witch-hunt from within the whippet-breeding community.

The pedigree line he maintained along with his friend Linda Wren, known within dog circles as the MacArthur strain, had been performing exceptionally well in whippet-racing trials, many of his dogs becoming national champions. As a result, a whispering campaign was mounted by his rivals, speculating that he was cross-breeding his dogs with greyhounds – the equivalent of fraud in whippet racing. Eventually a flood of accusatory letters were written to the whippet regulation board, the WCRA. MacKenzie and Wren were then forced to present four generations of the MacArthur line to the body's committee for tests and inspection, and in the end the pair were cleared of the allegations.

Billy wrote of the incident in his whippet diaries: 'We were saved the hangman's noose, but I was quite prepared to go to court to clear our name. A public apology was accepted, but it took a long time to regain enthusiasm for our sport. If by singling me out as a whipping boy deters others from under-handed dishonesty, then I hope something good has been brought out of this attempt to discredit us.' Furthermore, he noted: 'My life experience when any form of success enters the picture has always been highs and lows in equal measure.'

For some eleven years there had been virtually no contact between Alan Rankine and MacKenzie. Significantly, however, in his three-star *Q* review of *Outernational* in September 1992, Martin Aston, having been fair to the album, concluded with the suggestion that it was 'time, perhaps, to rethink, or to give ex-Associate Alan Rankine a call'.

'I'll admit I had a wee smile when I read that,' Rankine admits, 'but five days later Bill did call. He just said, "Hey man, it's Bill. Do you want to do some music?" I was like, "Aye, fair enough." It wasn't anything more than that – it was just, "Let's do some recordings." But I admit I was really keen.'

In the intervening years Rankine had found work as a producer, initially through sessions with the Cocteau Twins, Fiction Factory and Paul Haig. This had led in 1987 to a permanent tenure as house producer for Belgian label Les Disques du Crépuscule (at the time generously funded by Island) and a relocation to Brussels. In time he released two solo albums – *The World Begins To Look Her Age* for the Belgian label in 1986, followed by *She Loves Me Not* for Virgin in 1987. Both showcased a languid pop, fronted by the musician's breathy singing style, but led to Rankine eventually admitting to himself that he had no real confidence in his own vocal capabilities. Instead he released an instrumental album, *The Big Picture Sucks*, in 1988, in an attempt to attract offers of film soundtrack work, which, considering the cinematic qualities of the Associates' early music, was not entirely out of the question. When no offers presented themselves, he spent periods in both Tokyo and San Francisco, before relocating to Bath for a year and then drifting back home to Edinburgh.

Since the passing of time had proved to MacKenzie and Rankine that their partnership was unarguably greater than the sum of its separate parts, it made sense for both of them to seriously consider a reformation of the Associates. Of their first meeting for over a decade, Rankine remembers: 'There was no strangeness and no barriers that we had to get around. It really felt like I hadn't seen him for two months, not over ten years, and we just quickly got back into it.'

Energized by their reunion and both doubtless eager to find out if the spark of the partnership could be rekindled, Rankine and MacKenzie rapidly penned nearly twenty songs over two weekends at the latter's flat in Auchterhouse. After this, they began the process of auditioning musicians, although Rankine remembers that Billy's distinctly rural approach – letting his whippets roam in the fields and then trail their muddy footprints through the singer's tastefully pastel-interiored flat – left a striking impression on a bassist and drummer who arrived from London. 'This whippet came in and started puking on the carpet,' the guitarist recalls, 'and up comes this half-eaten rabbit. These guys were up from London they were obviously sitting there, thinking, Fucking hell.'

Recording began at the studio in Auchterhouse, with at least the light, playful nature of the classic Associates sessions still evident. One memorable night the work collapsed into a cabaret session of covers by David Bowie and the Rolling Stones, where Billy adopted his little-heard throaty rock vocal. Rankine remembers the singer 'camping it up, Mick Jaggering it up . . . it was just hilarious.'

By May, six tracks of new MacKenzie/Rankine material had been completed. Retrospectively, the most musically startling and lyrically intriguing of these is undoubtedly the insistent glam rock of

'Stephen, You're Still Really Something'. In the early 80s Billy had forged a fleeting friendship with Morrissey, which had allegedly ended with MacKenzie stealing a Jane Stein novel and a favourite shirt from the singer's Manchester flat. The music industry rumours that the two had enjoyed a brief affair were fuelled by the release of the Smiths' sixth single, 'William, It Was Really Nothing', in September 1984. If then, 'Stephen, You're Still Really Something' is more than likely MacKenzie's response song, it is nothing if not lightly affectionate, with even the vaguely threatening 'outing' line 'If I'm going down, I'll do you down with me' sweetened by the coupling 'And I loved the way you sent your poetry'.

Of the other tracks, both 'Gun Talk' and 'Mama Used To Say' are both ineffectually funky pop, while 'Fear Is My Bride' powers along on a spiralling beat echoing Bowie's 'Look Back In Anger', MacKenzie's voice at its paranoia-racked best. 'International Loner' returns to the theme of the isolated traveller, albeit cloaked in more magically mysterious tones ('Who were you having for breakfast in L'Escargot?/What were doing in downtown Tokyo?/ Why were you disguised as Dieter Meier?/Why were you outbidding Gore Vidal?') over a strident, funk groove. Elsewhere the duo's rendering of 'At The Edge Of The World' – which Rankine says that Billy had forgotten to inform him was co-written with Steve Aungle, causing discord for the guitarist on its eventual release – sails off into sonic territories initially charted by Pink Floyd.

Even if the tracks seemed slightly over-produced in the context of the stripped-down sound prevalent in the early 90s, then at least there was enough substance to suggest that there might be a future in the Associates' reunion. Having funded the recordings, Chris Parry took the tracks to the Polygram group, which funded Fiction, but received little interest. Then, having toyed with the idea of continuing with Bob Johnson as their manager, the duo decided that – since they were now both based in Scotland – they would do better to look for representation closer to home.

At the first of the two Celtic Park dates of U2's *Zooropa* tour in Glasgow in the summer of 1993, Rankine and MacKenzie bumped into Bruce Findlay – the one-time owner of a chain of record shops who, back in 1979, had bought up stock of 'Boys Keep Swinging' and had subsequently managed the lucratively successful career of Simple Minds until 1990 – and slipped him a tape. 'I loved it,' Findlay admits. 'At the same time it was a very lavishly produced demo and I thought it could have had more cutting-edge elements to it. But I did see it as a fabulous demo – so good, in fact, it was worthy of release in its own right. I sat them down and said, "Look, I know you guys and I'd love to do anything to help, but to do it in any semi-official capacity, I'd want to know that you'd be prepared to tour."'

Considering the circumstances of the Associates' collapse in 1982, it was a sticky point. MacKenzie and Rankine had already privately discussed this delicate matter, the guitarist recalling that Billy had eventually admitted that the split had been partly been caused 'by the kind of macho shit that he just hated about touring. He just said to me, "I didn't want to do that type of gig. Would you've wanted to play to five thousand people in a gay disco?" And the answer is no.' Nevertheless, Billy assured Findlay that he would tour in support of the Associates' reunion. Rankine claims that he 'believed him sixty per cent'.

When Findlay began touting the new Associates' tracks around the London record companies, the response was partially disappointing, if typical. 'They liked it but they wanted to hear more,' Findlay explains, 'and since I was going in with the promise that they'd be playing at some point, a lot of them were saying they wanted to see them live. Billy, of course, didn't want to audition. Then if they *did* say they would do an audition, he would come up with some funny idea of how they could do it. I could tell it was beginning to become a bit of a piss-take.' Eventually, both Findlay and Rankine simply held their hands up in defeat. 'You just walked away from it,' the manager reasons, 'and thought, Och, typical Billy.'

If there was perhaps a more cynical, financial motive behind the duo's reformation, then Findlay admits that he sensed it: 'Yes, there was an element of that and I smelt it. I could smell that they were just cashing in on the Associates' name and it did worry me. But then again, any band that gets back together again, you question their motives. Maybe Billy's motivation was guarded at best. He was maybe thinking that it was quite good to have the Associates' name to get a record deal, but then he could've gone on and done his own solo project.'

In fact, this appeared to be the crux of the problem. Fearing that he was perhaps becoming musically tied to this collaboration alone, Billy had sneakily begun to let the manager hear some of his collaborative efforts with Paul Haig, which, in his own words, he felt had 'more of the original essence of the Associates'. Rankine decided that MacKenzie's creative promiscuity was unlikely to stop here, and because of this – and, of course, their conflicting views on touring – the partnership once again began to crumble. 'To me,' Rankine argues, 'if you're going to try and make a comeback in some sort of form, then the public isn't going to swallow that you're doing it, but you're still doing all these other things. They need to have something that they can identify with . . . but Bill just didn't see it that way.'

'When we got back together,' Billy told German journalist Gilbert Blecken,' it was uncomfortable for both of us, [even if] there were still some things that were good. The picture was more intricate than that. Other things were going to reveal themselves which were more important than the music. Alan just wanted it to be us and no one else, and I couldn't have that. He didn't like the fact that I was doing some other stuff with Paul Haig. He might have found that threatening. But there was nothing threatening about it. I certainly wasn't going to be held to work as a duo for the next five years. It was just too shocking.'

By November, any hopes of a full-scale reunion of the Associates were dead in the water.

'Only at the end of the day did we discover that Billy's heart was not absolutely into it,' Findlay states. 'They got back together and they realized they'd drifted too far apart.'

13

Amused As Always

Like some time-warped period piece, the flat appeared to have remained untouched since the 1960s. The carpet was of the type of swirly-patterned, kaleidoscopic hue that only really made sense in that mind-expanding decade. The walls in the hallway were adorned with the finest Formica. There was frosted glass in every internal door, even the bathroom, doubtless fitted with the kind of permissive thinking that doesn't find the sight of a live-in partner parked on the toilet even mildly off-putting. Of course, Billy MacKenzie – never one to cheat on the cheese – loved the place and moved in immediately.

Following the Associates' aborted reunion, in December 1993 the singer relocated to 31 Great King's Street, in the New Town area of Edinburgh. Before long the new tenant of this possibly difficult-to-let property, in his quest to furnish the flat with suitably high-grade tack, stumbled upon the perfect addition to his new surroundings – a prime example of the tasteless bed designed for the swinging bachelor in that permissive age. Among the bed's features were a huge suede-upholstered headrest, integral tables at either side topped with bendy-framed lamps, and a compact, cassette-based 'music centre' for those intimate moments where a little mood music may be required.

Before the move, Billy had galvanized his musical partnership with Steve Aungle, when together in Auchterhouse they had completed a new batch of uncompromising electronic material that the latter describes as 'techno Goth, pretty discordant, nightmarish and dark, real thumping, in-your-face stuff. I thought this was a great direction to go in and so did he.' As the disturbing result, he feels, of one track '14th Century Nightlife', Aungle suffered a panic attack in the middle of recording: 'I had to go up the hill because I was hyperventilating. Billy was just casual about it and said, "Oh, I get that all the time."' When the musician returned to London to complete work on the track at his flat, he found that the music was having a similar effect on his girlfriend: 'She took me aside and said, "I really hate it, it's doing my fucking head in." When I told Billy that, he said, "That's great, Steve. That's a really good sign. Whatever you're doing, just take it to the extremes."'

In February 1994, when it was mutually decided that the collaboration needed a concentrated period of work, Aungle slung his belongings into the back of his car and drove to Edinburgh, where he settled into the spare room at Great King's Street. Not least for their shared eccentricities, the pair proved to be wholly compatible flatmates. In their entire time spent living in the flat, there were no pots and pans in the kitchen, only a champagne bucket, once used to whip up a vat of tuna pasta by the visiting Jimmy MacKenzie. Billy would rarely empty the teapot of used bags, simply throwing in another couple and brewing up endless cups of tar. The sole teaspoon owned by the two would frequently go missing and turn up in the most ridiculous places. 'Once I found it in the bottom of the toilet bowl,' Aungle recalls. 'I said to Billy, "Why did you put that in the toilet bowl?" and he just said, "I don't know anything about that. Honestly it wasn't me." It didn't matter how much you interrogated him about it, he would never let up.'

Later another highly unusual domestic pattern developed when both found themselves sonically addicted to the soothing qualities of the 'pinging' sound emitting from the timer on the old-fashioned cooker in the kitchen. 'It was just this hypnotic ping that you could hear from any room in the house,' the musician remembers, 'and you got so used to hearing it, if it stopped and we were right in the middle of something, I'd go, "Oh, the pinger's stopped" and Billy would run down and put it back on again. We never analysed it, but I suppose it's mental really. Then, Billy used to try to get me to make all the tea. He said, "Steve, you might think this is a bit weird, but I think the kitchen's malevolent and I can't go in there any more." Then I'd find myself doing everything in the kitchen, thinking, Wait a minute.'

Aside from the distractions of this cartoon existence, the musical alliance with Aungle was proving to be MacKenzie's most intensively prolific time since the early days in Edinburgh with Alan Rankine eighteen years before. Within five months the duo had written thirty complete songs and another twenty unfinished sketches, MacKenzie sometimes waking Aungle up in the middle of the night to fire up the equipment if there was an urgent, sleep-depriving idea buzzing around in his head. Stylistically, the music was becoming incredibly diverse – some of it stripped down and acoustic, some of it electronic, or 'eclectotronic' as Billy termed it – with the only constant being the distinctive vocal.

For the duration, however, the duo were forced to lead a simple existence, since both – as if harking back to MacKenzie's penniless but musically magical Situation 2 days – were hellishly broke. Paul Haig, living just around the corner, remembers that often when Billy visited him, he'd wander off in the direction of the kitchen, returning to say, '"Paul, that quiche looks like it's going off to me . . . I better eat it." So I used to take him out for his tea a lot.' Aungle was constantly badgering a reluctant MacKenzie to sign on the dole, which despite the singer's continual promises, he conveniently never got around to actually doing. On one occasion Aungle got as far as dragging him down to the local DSS office: 'We walked up to the entrance of this huge building and he was almost cowering, saying, "Oh, I don't know if I can go in there." Then we got in this lift to take us up to the claims section, and he was sort of talking to himself, saying, "Well, Billy, you're not in the lift going up to the fourth floor of the Savoy any more, you're going up to fucking sign on."'

In the claims office, Aungle offered to fill out the requisite forms for Billy, so that the singer had only to add his signature. In the end, MacKenzie couldn't even bring himself to do that and the balled-up form was thrown into the nearest bin as the pair left. 'It was a pride thing,' Aungle reasons, 'the fact that he'd have to sign on every two weeks and stand in the dole queue and be really conscious of someone maybe recognizing him. He didn't want to give the impression that he was skint. He eventually got on insurance benefit for his back and that was all right, because he would get the cheques sent to him. Still, if there were any letters about it lying around the house and we were expecting a visitor, he would hide them all. But even when he was skint, he handled it really well. He would just shrug his shoulders. It probably did him good. It gave him a bit of humility and respect for money.'

In the summer of 1994, four years after his last public performances in New York, Billy was invited to appear at an elaborate party being thrown at the George Hotel in Edinburgh – drawing him back to the scene of the Associates' sudden split in 1982 – by Sebastian Horsely, an artist and millionaire friend of Paul Haig. Once Billy had agreed to perform, the shadow of his abject stage fright returned to haunt him, manifesting itself in a prolonged spell of anxiety lasting for three weeks. As part of his regular afternoon ritual whereby he would go back to bed, crawling under the duvet with the comfort of his whippets, he spent endless hours on the phone talking to his friends about his dilemma. 'He was trying to find any excuse under the sun not to do it,' Haig notes.

Eventually Billy announced to Aungle that the only way he would appear was in a disguise similar to the one he'd used in the 'Fire To Ice' video – black Elvis wig and thick dark glasses – although this was, of course, a futile ploy since as soon as he opened his mouth to sing, everyone would instantly know who he was.

When the night of the event arrived, no expense was spared by the host, with a limousine arriving to collect the performers and transport them the short distance from their flat to George Street. In front of a select audience – indulging in free Bollinger for the entire evening – which included Lily MacKenzie and assorted relatives, Billy appeared in this outlandish guise. Accompanied on piano by Aungle and local guitarist Kenny Brady, he delivered a loungey set of songs including 'Breakfast', the newly completed 'Blue It Is' and 'Wild Is The Wind' – the crooner standard made famous by David Bowie and for one night only drily rechristened 'Wild Is The Wig'. Despite Billy's acute pre-gig fears, the event was a success, and when they left the stage, the trio were approached by journalist-turned-broadcaster Allan Campbell to repeat the set on an STV arts programme, *Don't Look Down*. The party moved on to Horsely's house, where the champagne continued to flow by the crateload. Billy awoke, the next morning, lying in a flower-bed.

As a return match, it was decided to stage a themed 60s party, echoing MacKenzie's regular activity back in the Dundee punk days, in the suitably gaudy environment of 31 Great King's Street. Determined to outdo himself in the surreal overdressing stakes, Billy, along with Aungle, spent an afternoon at a local theatrical suppliers, annoying the assistant and trying on 'various noses and Afros' as the latter recalls, until the singer finally unearthed a mop-topped wig to his liking. On the night of the party, the guests were treated to the kitsch strains of Mantovani and Henry Mancini, the host's chosen wig complementing an outfit involving drainpipes, Chelsea boots and a T-shirt depicting the young Cassius Clay. 'He put on all this stuff,' Aungle says, 'and just became this different character, charging around the rooms and talking surreal nonsense.' In the midst of these mildly demented proceedings, MacKenzie's pregnant whippet Sophie, bedded in an airing cupboard, gave birth to eight pups, raising the total number of dogs in the two-bedroomed flat to ten.

Work on the new self-financed demos – Billy's share was covered by the reviving of the creative loans from Jim MacKenzie – continued in earnest at both Seagate Studio in Dundee, for the band-based material, and at a programming suite in Edinburgh for the electronic tracks. In the latter setting, in particular, Billy continued to display the impossible, if descriptive, requests that were a staple of his work methods, once memorably asking the engineer if he could give a certain sound 'the Cecil B. De Mille treatment'. Subsequently the already over-pressurized technician scrambled around for an eternity, trying to approximate this sonically, while the increasingly wound-up Aungle looked on. 'I used to think,' he reflects, 'Oh, you're just testing out this guy to his limits.'

In this way, MacKenzie had quite likely found his collaborative match in Aungle, who had quickly grown wise to the singer's tricks: 'He'd purposefully have a go at something like a bass line when it was perfectly fine. He'd say, "Oh, I don't know about that bass line, Steve. I think you could maybe do a bit more work on it." So I'd say, "OK, Billy, I'll work on it tonight." The next day I'd put it on again, having done nothing to it whatsoever, and say, "What do you think now?" and he'd say, "Oh, it's much better, Steve. Much, much better."'

Attempting to front up the project in a managerial role, Billy began mailing tapes to the various record-company contacts that he still had in London. The music's wide-ranging diversity prompted a blanket response from labels – it was lacking in direction. From here on in, Aungle and MacKenzie began to 'list out', loosely arranging the material by genre. Although there were probably four or five distinct albums' worth of songs, two separate band concepts emerged as front runners: the first was Winter Academy, for the album of piano-led, torch songs; the second was Outerpol, the name under which the electronic tracks would be flagged.

As a physical group, Outerpol was planned to consist of MacKenzie, Aungle and Haig. When the project attracted the attentions of Radio Scotland and a crew was dispatched to Haig's flat to interview the trio, the proceedings were interrupted by apparently poltergeist-like behaviour that MacKenzie claimed was his responsibility. 'Billy was convinced that he brought a presence to Edinburgh,' Haig states. 'During this interview things just started happening, like the TV came on by itself and the light bulb in the hall somehow unscrewed itself and was found lying on the floor. So on my behalf, Billy wrote to the parapsychology department at Edinburgh University and I got this letter back saying they'd like to come down and do some tests. But I must admit I never took them up on it and nothing like that ever happened again.'

In the end the Outerpol project was sidelined by sheer economics. Since the Winter Academy material, by its very nature, would be far cheaper to record, it was on this that the MacKenzie and Aungle concentrated their efforts, booking two days at Palladium Studio in Edinburgh to record seven songs – including 'Blue It Is' and 'Nocturne VII' – and two instrumentals. Aungle recalls of these sessions: 'Some of Billy's performances were just outstanding. I'd never heard him sing so delicately.' In the end the recording ran over by a day, the bill for which neither of the two could afford to pay. Billy told Aungle not to worry, as he would negotiate a deal, and invited the studio owner back down to the flat to view some antiques he would give him in his exchange for the studio time.

'As it turned out,' Aungle explains, 'the guy obviously knew absolutely nothing about antiques and Billy just totally ripped him off. But it was really funny the way he did it. Billy said, "I've got this really nice painting for you. It's an original and it's called *The Huntress.*" It was just some print that he picked up for a tenner and he got £100 off the bill for that. Then he gave him some chair that was worth fuck all and he convinced him it was an antique. In the end the guy drove off in his Rolls-Royce with all this junk. Billy was just using his background, the gypsy second-hand thing, as a weapon. I must admit I was really impressed.'

The greatest irony of this was that Billy did indeed own certain items of antique furniture and crockery during his stay in Edinburgh, although these were ritually destroyed one afternoon when a mood of frustration turned into a childlike destructive spree. Haig and Aungle were sitting in the front room of the Great King's Street flat, when Billy walked in and, saying nothing, wandered over to an antique chair valued in the hundreds and forcefully hammered his foot through the seat. For an encore, he smashed an expensive decorative plate over his head.

Following that, he encouraged the others to join in, which – although slightly bewildered, they did, keen not to further deepen the singer's apparently black mood – smashing up hundreds of pounds' worth of antique crockery and lamps in the fireplace of the front room, while Billy cackled hysterically at the contorted faces that his friends were pulling mid-throw. Later Billy dismissed this unusual outburst of personal-effects vandalism to Aungle: 'He said, "It helps you to get perspective, Steve. It's a perspective exercise." He thought that, even if you're broke, you shouldn't get too attached to things that are worth a lot of money.'

The time in Edinburgh was as creatively fulfilling as it was commercially frustrating, and finally the duo agreed that they would have to move back to London if they were ever going to secure a deal. By the time they gave notice on the Great King's Street flat, there was very real visible evidence of their, and more importantly, the whippets' stay there. The doors were scratched with claw marks, there were the beginnings of tunnels that the puppies had begun to burrow in the skirting boards in an effort to escape the airing cupboard, and the floorboards were warped, due to serial whippet leakage. On their departure, Billy left behind all the bizarre 60s furniture – including the dandy bed complex – to compensate the landlord. In reality, considering the damage, it was worthless.

Then the financial bombshell dropped. Over the years, Billy – having displayed no firm grasp of day-to-day monetary realities – had grown completely out of touch with his finances. Before his hand-to-mouth days in Edinburgh, all of his outlay had been dealt with by standing order. If something had to be paid urgently, one of his friends or family members would write out the cheque, leaving Billy just to sign it. Then, around this time, he discovered that the standing order for the mortgage payments on the Auchter- house flat that he still owned had lapsed, leaving him £19,000 in arrears to the Royal Bank of Scotland, while he had remained unaware of the warning letters. Almost simultaneously, he was presented with a bill for £30,000 in unpaid taxes from the Circa period, a matter that Billy claimed he thought Bob Johnson had dealt with – not realizing that ordinarily this isn't an aspect of the manager's role. It hadn't even occurred to Billy, in his limited understanding of his personal finances, to employ an accountant.

Billy MacKenzie, it appeared, was effectively bankrupt. 'He told everybody he was bankrupt,' Aungle explains, 'but one time I said to him, "Look, Billy, let's just go through what your assets are and tell me how much you owe the bank." When I looked at his finances – what he owed and what he owned – there wasn't a deficit. He just said, "Aw right. Maybe I'm no' bankrupt then."'

By this stage, it was too late, however, and the Royal Bank of Scotland had begun proceedings to repossess the flat. For the remaining blacklisted years, Billy would never again be eligible to hold a bank account.

The incident was eventually reported in the Scottish *Sunday Mail* on 2 April 1995, under the typically weak punning headline 'Pop Goes Billy's Fortune!' Detailing what was in essence a phantom bankruptcy, the unintentionally dry article read in part: 'The action was granted against the singer-songwriter after a court move by the Royal Bank of Scotland. Following the hearing at Dundee Sheriff Court, officials confirmed they were still trying to contact him'.

14

Before the Autumn Came

Billy was in London, weathering the relentless burn of the blistering summer of 1995. To his eyes, the skies were not clear and blue, but polluted and white. On the days when he would arrive at Steve Aungle's flat in Chiswick to work on new songs, he often insisted on closing the curtains to block out the daylight, claiming, 'It's like Hiroshima out there . . . it's like radiation.'

It was a hard year for MacKenzie, the most trying in recent memory. Living on money borrowed from his parents, he was lodging in his friend and former PA Steve Phillips's small, one-bedroomed flat in Notting Hill, the first time since the Associates' early days in London that he had no real space of his own and was constricted in his movements. While the pair enjoyed a close friendship, Billy's general inability to function on a daily domestic basis ensured that there were plenty of trivial matters for the two to bicker about – the singer wouldn't take the rubbish out or he'd leave an appliance switched on all day – and frequently Billy stormed off in a huff, his belongings stuffed into two huge suitcases that he would haul on the tube to Aungle's flat in Chiswick and then only have to drag back to Notting Hill the following day when the argument had inevitably cooled.

In one way, at least, Billy's presence in the capital had allowed him to rebuild the bridges of a friendship from the past. In 1984, owing to the tangled mess that had led to Steve Reid being slowly marginalized in the *Perhaps* line-up of the Associates, Christine Beveridge had sided with her then guitarist boyfriend and she and Billy had suffered a severe falling out. Two years before, in 1993, out of the blue, Billy had called her from Edinburgh: 'One Saturday night, I went to bed and dreamt about him. When I got up, the phone rang and I knew it was him. I picked it up and somebody said something like "Lyon Street" in a Chinese accent and I thought, I'm going mad. So I hung up. Then immediately he phoned again and said, "It's me, Christine, it's Billy." After that we were on the phone for three and half hours. We never even discussed the fact that we'd fallen out.' When Billy arrived back in London, Beveridge travelled to the Notting Hill flat to see him for the first time in eleven years: 'We just took each other's hands and it was the most natural thing in the world. It was like I'd seen him yesterday. We just picked off from where we'd left off.'

At the time, owing to his living circumstances, MacKenzie was unable to bring any of his dogs down from Scotland. In their initial phone conversation two years before, he had sounded quietly amazed and not a little touched to discover that Beveridge still had the two whippets, Riglo and Tonto, that he'd given her as puppies and as such, they served as an additional link. Before long Billy had been given a spare key to his friend's flat in Kentish Town, and one evening, Beveridge arrived home to discover him – uncharacteristically on his best behaviour – with his hands in the kitchen sink, washing the dishes. Soon the flat became a regular home from home. One day, another friend who held a key to the flat let himself in and caught the singer lying in the bath while loudly vocalizing along to Beveridge's old vinyl copy of *The Affectionate Punch.*

When Beveridge had to travel to Scotland on a work trip, she entrusted MacKenzie to take care of the flat and look after the dogs. On her return, she discovered that Billy had nearly burned the house down, having left a tub of margarine on top of the blazing cooker grill and then gone out. Worse, too lazy to walk the whippets one day, he had simply opened the door to the flat and let them wander out – a habit that was perhaps fine in the open countryside surrounding Auchterhouse, but not in the traffic-congested environs of NW5. Before the dogs were eventually found, neighbours had reported sighting MacKenzie running up and down the street in a dressing gown, calling out for the whippets in flustered, swearing tones. 'Having Billy around,' Beveridge states, 'was just like having a kid in the house.'

Similar to the old married-couple routine that he played out with Steve Phillips, the relationship between MacKenzie and Beveridge – both stubborn, feisty and strong-willed – was inevitably full of petty, if affectionate, quarrelling. 'We did talk about the fact that we'd get married just for the company,' Beveridge admits. 'Then we started talking about having a kid. I wanted to have a kid and we agreed that if I hadn't met anyone by the time I was forty-two, then we'd have one together. He got completely carried away with this idea and told everybody.' Although in their discussions, Beveridge attached firm conditions to the arrangement, in an effort to ensure that Billy – whose flighty nature was unlikely to find him ever sustaining any kind of long-term relationship – would always be there to provide for the child, it was never to happen. For her part, Beveridge was under no illusions as to how Billy might have coped with fatherhood: 'He would've been fucking hopeless.' Even Phillips was worried about the prospect that as 'Auntie Steve', he would possibly be the one left holding the baby.

In terms of music, 1995 saw the beginning of the developing pattern that found the deal-less MacKenzie being invited to provide cameo vocal appearances on other artists' releases. In April, a month after his thirty-eighth birthday, Billy bumped into Barry Adamson, the ex-bassist with both Magazine and the Bad Seeds, who, now a solo composer, had released a series of lauded albums showcasing an atmospheric, filmic sound. Adamson invited MacKenzie to his small programming suite in an industrial block in Kensal Rise to hear a piece of music he'd been commissioned to write for an aborted Martini commercial, with a view to Billy adding a vocal to the track.

On their arrival, Adamson recalls: 'I was really worried because I was having to load up the sampler and digging all the bits out and letting it play, and he just started to sing. It was kind of amazing. Just hearing him sing that in the room was really quite incredible.' Days later MacKenzie returned with the completed words to the song, 'Achieved In The Valley Of Dolls', and provided his smoky, jazz-flecked vocal over the track's hip-hop beat. 'With Billy, he liked to keep going over it and over it,' Adamson notes of the singer's perfectionist streak. 'Knowing that he has this amazing voice, I was quite surprised that he wanted to do it so often, although, in the end it sounded great.' When the resulting album, *Oedipus Schmoedipus*, was released, Billy's appearance was welcomingly received in several of the reviews – despite the more distracting presence of Nick Cave and Pulp's Jarvis Cocker elsewhere – with *Q* commending MacKenzie for his 'sterling vocal performance'.

Tellingly, however, in the writing credits on the album, Billy's publishing rights were listed as 'Copyright Control', the basic Performing Rights Society tag for a writer out of contract. A few months before this, MacKenzie's sixteen-year publishing arrangement with Chris Parry and Fiction Songs had collapsed. 'We reached a point where we couldn't get him a deal really,' Parry explains, 'and we had to either carry on and take up another publishing option or make some sort of decision on it. I felt by this time that I couldn't offer anything more to Billy's music, so it just felt appropriate at that point to terminate it. I thought that may give him the kick to do something different.'

In November, Billy finally set down roots again when he – along with Steve Aungle and a Glasgow friend, Lorna Fisher, nicknamed Lady Kuku – moved into a large, three-bedroomed basement flat at 40 Holland Road, the main traffic route between West Kensington and Shepherd's Bush. 'It was such a relief for him to get that place,' Aungle says, 'because he had to have his own room and his own space.' Within weeks, however, the musician remembers there being a slight return to the shenanigans of the Edinburgh days: 'One of the first things that Billy said after we moved in was "Steve, that doorbell, I hate it." It was really loud and it rang in the kitchen and it rang in the hall. All of a sudden it didn't work. Then I discovered that someone had removed all the batteries . . . and I knew it wasn't Lady Kuku. So I put a notice on the door saying the bell wasn't working. It disappeared after a day and I found it screwed up in the bin in the kitchen. I tried to talk to him about it, but I never got to the bottom of it.'

During his days in Holland Road, Billy's day-to-day existence was often one of acute boredom, owing to the fact that he was sorely lacking in funds. The flat was so spartan that there wasn't even a television in the living room and since it was still impractical for him to bring any of his dogs down from Dundee to live in such built-up surroundings, his mornings and afternoons were spent lazing around on the settee or talking long walks around the area, his gypsy instincts resurfacing when he began to return home bearing found objects. 'There was one occasion where I'm sure he interrupted a burglary and didn't realize,' Steve Aungle says. 'He came back with a hi-fi, a stack system with all the wires clipped at the back, which is a sure sign that it's hot. He said, "Oh, I was just passing this house and I saw it sitting outside . . . maybe they were chucking it out." He also found some really nice clothes sitting outside someone's house. He was on a mission to get all this stuff and none of it was junk.'

Still, whatever spare cash MacKenzie had was rarely spent wisely. At this time he was indulging in an idiosyncratic health kick, rarely drinking or smoking a joint (ever visually driven, he complained of 'getting the grids' in front of his eyes if he did), while experimenting with combinations of vitamin pills and obscure foods, once returning home with a pound of what he insisted to his flatmates were 'kangaroo sausages'. His living partners marvelled at his mildly obsessive hygiene and beauty routines: using an entire tube of toothpaste in one single brushing, spending an eternity rubbing lotions into his skin before he would shave. At one point he invested in an expensive 'clicky sparky gadget' purporting to emit electrical pulses to relieve back pain, and excitedly informed the others that while experimenting with it, he'd begun applying it to a bald patch in his eyebrow and the hair had now miraculously grown back. As sensitive about his appearance as he had been as a twenty-five-year-old pop star, he often fished for compliments from the others. 'He'd say, "I just look like an old woman, don't I?"' deadpans Steve Aungle. 'So you'd be forced to say, "No, no, you're looking great, Billy."'

Just as Billy was settling into the diversions of this new life, at the beginning of 1996, the news arrived from Dundee that Lily MacKenzie had been diagnosed with terminal cancer of the stomach. This shook Billy more than anyone could have realized at the time, his emotions soon turning to anger, since his mother had sought medical advice the year before for stomach pains, and the severity of her condition had not been diagnosed at that time. While those close to MacKenzie witnessed him breaking down over the matter on a handful of occasions, they claim that within hours he would always put on a braver, stronger face. Around this time, having never have been a confirmed smoker, Billy suddenly developed a thirty-a-day habit. In offloading his emotional baggage, he would often wake Aungle or Fisher in the middle of the night, just to quietly talk and unburden himself of his thoughts.

In an attempt to block out his serious concerns for his mother, Billy threw himself into his work and plans for his future career, regularly picking up the phone and launching into a prepared spiel to shop the new demos around the record companies. Apart from some initial interest shown by German label Logic – who had recently signed Sparks and subsequently booked time for MacKenzie and Aungle in a low-budget studio in Clapham for some preliminary recordings that the company failed to pick up on – the response was much the same as it had been in Edinburgh.

However, after Billy spent an afternoon at the Primrose Hill home of Martyn Ware, the producer happened to mention to former Heaven 17 manager Keith Bourton that MacKenzie had visited him. Ware then hooked the pair up, with a view to their working together. When they met, as Bourton recalls: 'He gave me a twenty-track cassette and all the good stuff was right at the end of it. It took me quite a while to get to it, to be honest, so at first I wasn't all that impressed. It was a bit hit and miss. But the piano ballads were extraordinary. I wanted to work with him anyway, but that's what really swung me.'

As there was little else to do in Holland Road, working on new material became more of a pastime than anything else for MacKenzie and Aungle, their writing still split between programmed electronic tracks and the acoustic songs penned at the latter's piano, recently installed in the front room. Aside from this, Billy's extracurricular collaborative work continued in earnest. Michael Dempsey, now living near the East Sussex coast and composing incidental music for film and TV, invited MacKenzie down to his home studio to add vocals to two independent film themes. 'His voice was always so cinematic,' Dempsey states, 'and these days you can get a song placed in a film – and in particular a voice like *his* placed in a film – and suddenly there's this huge market again.' Encouraged by the results of their efforts, the pair hatched a plan to record an entire album of soundtrack music, although apart from a handful of demos, this remained unrealized.

With the arrival of spring 1996 came two other guest appearances that would help to raise Billy's profile in what, for the record-buying public at least, was his wilderness period. A connection was made with a German electronic duo, Loom, initially as possible demo producers. They presented Billy with a thirteen-minute ambient track that welcomingly reminded the singer of the bubbling analogue 70s soundscapes of Tangerine Dream – probably the only hippie group that, in his youth, MacKenzie could ever stomach. Lying in the bath at Holland Road one day, Billy began singing the melody to the still-unused 'At The Edge Of The World' along to the cassette of the Loom track and the two seemed to mesh. Within half an hour of visiting the duo's studio in Portobello Road, MacKenzie had recorded the vocal for the track, now entitled 'Anacostia Bay (At The Edge Of The World)', which was released in September on the German imprint Millennium Records, in the quick independent turnover that Billy had longed to achieve with *Outernational*.

In addition, MacKenzie's links to the dance world were underlined by his contribution to the London collective Apollo 440's *Electro Glide In Blue* album, with the aching eight-minute ballad 'Pain In Any Language', which was reminiscent of the spacious epics of his time with Yello, but with a languid hip-hop undertow. Group founder Noko recalls that at the sessions for the track, Billy seemed to enjoy being directed by the other musicians, something the singer hadn't experienced since his work in Zurich: 'There was already a melody and words and so it was like he was a musician that day, but he really, really got off on it. His brother told me that this went back to his grandmother, where he would be singing something and she'd say, "No, no, that's wrong" and give him a slap round the head. You'd sing a vibrato envelope to him and he'd just copy it exactly. It'd come back exactly like you were programming a drum machine, it was fantastic. It was like standing in the room with Pavarotti.'

By far the most unusual request for Billy's vocal talents at this time was when he received a phone call from the Scottish Football Association inviting him to perform 'Flower Of Scotland' a cappella on the pitch at Wembley Stadium before the Euro '96 England v. Scotland match. Jittery about the prospect, he refused to confirm, asking if he could have time to think about it. Then, suddenly exhilarated by the thought, he tried to call back and accept the offer. According to what he then told his friends, at least, the line was engaged for two hours. By the time he was eventually connected, the organizers had unceremoniously replaced him with one-time Marillion singer Fish. 'He wouldn't discuss it after that,' says Paul Haig. 'I think he was a bit pissed off.'

In their journeys north to Edinburgh, MacKenzie and Aungle began working on electronic tracks at the studio of former Fini Tribe programmer John Vick. In the same way that Aungle could deal with Billy's creatively conniving ways, the musician remembers Vick fielding MacKenzie's more obtuse musical instructions with a certain cool panache: 'Any time Billy said something like, "Can you make that sound like an Egyptian pyramid?", John would just say to his assistant, "Right, can you plug in the Egyptian pyramid machine, please?" And then he'd turn around and say, "Right, Billy, anything else?"'

Still, this was mere child's play compared to the elaborate windups that Billy could spin. At the beginning of one block session, Aungle was a day late in arriving at the studio. The next day, with MacKenzie conspicuous by his absence, Vick began to quiz a bemused Aungle about his previous day's no-show, asking him if he did any alternative work, maybe within the realms of psychology. When the musician appeared baffled, Vick suddenly twigged and laughed. Aungle says: 'It turned out that Billy, trying to invent some new identity for me that I knew nothing about, had told John that the reason I was a day late was because I was in Barcelona treating Annie Lennox and that I was some sort of psychologist to the stars. He'd told him it straight up, as if it was fact.'

One of these trips to Scotland involved a planned weekend at the T in the Park Festival, held near Glasgow that year, although Billy's concern for his mother had recently been heightened by her increasingly delicate condition. When he told Lily MacKenzie that he planned to forget about the festival to be with her instead, she insisted a number of times that he go there and not worry about her. As it transpired, the weekend outing did Billy's morale no end of good, as he was frequently accosted by fans and stumbled into old acquaintances from his past. Billy Sloan remembers that MacKenzie 'looked fantastic and kept on talking about the fifteen different projects he was working on simultaneously with all these weird and wonderful characters'. Chris Carr observed that 'Billy was so much back on form, as though a lot of the demons had been exorcized. I kind of had really great hopes for him and we had a chat about old times.'

Subsequent reports in the music press that Billy spent his time at T in the Park tripping on acid and regaling anyone who would listen with tales of his sexual exploits with three Cuban boys were imaginative but wildly erroneous and doubtless part of some lingering journalistic desire to paint him as the seemingly decadent creator of *Sulk*. The far less tantalizing truth was that, aside from the imbibing of some potent grass, MacKenzie spent most of the weekend in the dance tent, and backstage, re-establishing old musical contacts, including one with Siobhan Fahey of Shakespears Sister, their meeting leading to the recording of a duet in London shortly afterwards.

Midway through the Sunday afternoon, an announcement was made over the PA, asking Billy MacKenzie to come to the information centre. Coincidentally, 'The Information Centre' had always been his pet nickname for his mother's house, since on his visits home, the fad-driven and inquisitive Lily MacKenzie would always excitedly tell her son about her latest discovery, whether it be magnetic shoes or some new psychic revelation she'd read about. This afternoon, however, the MacKenzie family had been forced to call the festival office and locate Billy when his mother took a serious turn for the worse.

On receiving the alarming news, Billy waded through the crowds, urgently trying to track down Aungle, desperate to be driven back home to Dundee. By the time the two arrived at Lily MacKenzie's home just over an hour later, an undertaker's car was already parked outside, bearing an empty coffin. When he was struck with the horrible reality that he hadn't been there for the death of his mother, Billy suddenly found that he could barely walk and had to be led into the house by his friend.

According to those close to him, the shock that Billy suffered with the death of his mother manifested itself in his inability to show real grief. In essence, he bottled up his emotions, perhaps feeling that, as the eldest son, it was somehow his duty to maintain an exterior strength. In grand MacKenzie style, the wake that followed Lily's funeral had an almost celebratory edge, however, with Billy taking a turn on the stage to sing 'The Night They Drove Old Dixie Down'. John MacKenzie confirms that even the bar staff at the venue for the wake seemed genuinely taken aback by the spirited atmosphere: 'They actually started phoning up half the bars in Dundee, saying, "You won't believe what's happening – we're at a funeral, but we've never been to such a party."'

Back in London, Billy's new comfort zone away from Holland Road became Steve Phillips's flat, where he would spend long periods of time. Otherwise, as he had done before, the singer attempted to busy himself with work. As MacKenzie and Aungle's new manager, Keith Bourton had, in fact, managed to stir up interest in the new demos far swifter and more successfully than any of Billy's own attempts, the new front runners being Sony Publishing and Nude Records, the latter having built up a fashionable roster from 1992 onwards since their signing of Suede.

Nude boss Saul Galpern had first encountered MacKenzie as a Scottish expat working in a London record shop frequented by the Associates' singer during the Situation 2 days and had gone on to A&R for a number of labels including Island, Elektra and RCA. Periodically Billy called Galpern in an effort to secure a new deal post-Circa. The A&R man, not particularly fond of MacKenzie's output after *Sulk*, admits he was always disappointed with the material: 'He would let me hear stuff and I just thought, Nah. But I had a massive amount of respect for him as a songwriter. I suppose it was just a matter of time before he did something that was right.'

Still, even when Bourton first approached Galpern at Nude with the new songs, the label boss admits that he was less than keen, having to be coaxed by his A&R aide, David Laurie, into hearing the tracks. Of Nude's initial response, Bourton recalls: 'I made the mistake of giving them the whole tape of twenty songs and Saul rang me about a week later and said that he quite liked it but he wasn't that mad about it. Then about a week later, David had got to the end of the tape and found all the other stuff.' Specifically, the piano ballads of the Winter Academy project appealed greatly to Galpern in particular: 'It really blew me away. I just thought, Scott Walker . . . it's fantastic.'

Responding to the interest from Nude, Billy invited Galpern and Laurie to Holland Road to hear some other new songs. On their arrival, the pair were expecting MacKenzie and Aungle simply to play them a cassette; instead they were treated to a live, piano-accompanied performance in the living room. Galpern recalls Billy continually offering to play them even more songs: 'He kept saying, "Just thinking about it, I've got another one I could play you", and then they did this totally amazing song called "MacArthur's Son". I was sitting there thinking, This could be a huge hit.' Keith Bourton is in no doubt that the performance secured the subsequent offer from Nude: 'That's what really did it. A voice like that in the same room as you, it could melt an iceberg.'

The terms of Nude Records' contractual offer to MacKenzie were modest to middling if compared to standard signing advances in 1996. The budget set aside for the recording of the album was £80,000, with the singer being personally advanced £20,000 on signature, followed by two further payments of £10,000 on delivery and release of the first album. While there had been interest shown by Epic Records, Nude's was the only firm offer and Billy was advised by everyone to sign it. Notably, it was only when they arrived at the lawyer's office to complete the deal that MacKenzie finally admitted to Aungle that Nude were signing him alone as a solo artist, not the two of them as a duo. Aungle admits that he was initially narked by this revelation: 'Yeah, I was. It wasn't discussed and I kind of assumed that I'd be signing it as well. I said to Billy, "What's going on here?" and he said, "Well, they wanted to sign me as a solo artist and we'll sign a publishing deal together." I was happy with that.'

From the perspective of Galpern and Laurie, at least, the securing of the deal was an incredibly painless process. There were few negotiations between the lawyers representing the individual parties and within a mere eight weeks of the offer being made, the contract was legally completed, in the latter half of October. Following this, Galpern, Laurie and MacKenzie began discussing the finer details of the singer's return. 'It was all very optimistic and we were really looking forward to working on it,' Galpern states. 'I really did think he had two or three singles that would've worked and I was pretty confident we would get them on the radio. When I mentioned that we'd signed Billy MacKenzie, people thought it was a cool idea.'

In reality, Billy had been privately agonizing before putting pen to paper. While the singer was undoubtedly desperate for both money and an outlet for this new music, he admitted in one of his phone conversations to Paul Haig that he was nervous about stepping back into the promotional light: 'He said that he didn't want to have to go through the interviews and the concerts and the videos. He was fearful of it.' Aungle remembers the immediate days after the inking of the Nude deal being 'a bit anticlimactic. We kind of realized it was a mistake soon after the event. But we needed a cash injection from somewhere. It was just down to hard cash, basically.'

From the outset, the division between Nude and the duo was over musical direction, the one constant in MacKenzie's catalogue of difficulties with record companies. Galpern, of course, favoured the piano ballads and the Motown-style pop of 'MacArthur's Son', and began to voice his dislike of the electronic tracks, a matter that might have been obvious earlier considering Nude's solely guitar-led roster. For his part, MacKenzie felt there was no challenge for him in pursuing the direction of the torch songs, and still energized by the new developments in dance music – his favourite record at the time was the Prodigy's 'Firestarter', which he claimed reminded him of the sonic assault of the Situation 2 singles – he secretly began plotting with his partner to concentrate on the electronic material nonetheless. 'We were just going to go in the electro direction and not tell the record company until it was all mixed,' Aungle admits. 'It basically would've been an electronic album with a couple of orchestrated ballads. The truth is that they probably would have freaked and the album wouldn't have been completed.'

There was talk of Billy being reunited with veteran Associates producer Mike Hedges, who over the subsequent years had gone on to achieve further success with Manic Street Preachers and McAlmont & Butler, but this proved impossible owing to the producer's prior commitments. Instead, Apollo 440, who under their pseudonym Stealth Sonic Orchestra had already proved their talent for string arrangements, were commissioned to produce four tracks for the forthcoming album. The names Outerpol and Winter Academy were revived as possible contenders for the project, along with Billy's suggestion of Case (the plan being that the design of the CD booklet would list words and phrases – 'suitcase', 'nutcase', 'in which case' – that incorporated the group name). There was even serious discussion about a touring line-up that included Jimmy MacKenzie, Billy admitting to his brother that he had always longed to work with one of his family members in the past: 'Billy said, "I wish I'd had somebody there with me all the way through. I had never had anybody and it's good that you're coming down to get involved."'

In his seeming urgency, Billy spoke of releasing three albums in quick succession, an idea that Keith Bourton considered unrealistic: 'He actually wanted to put out an electronic album, an acoustic album and a rock album. I kept saying to him, "I just don't see how we can do it, but we can maybe try to work towards it." To be honest, I never took it that seriously. I'm used to artists talking about things like that. Coming back after four years and talking about putting out three albums at once . . . it was a typical Billy mega idea gone mad.'

Two weeks after the death of his mother, Billy conducted his last significant interview, with Garry Mulholland of *Time Out*, in the light of the rekindled interest following the Loom and Barry

Adamson releases. In their recorded conversation, Billy is serious and subdued (he admitted to the writer that the bereavement had precipitated a period of 'self-analysis' for him), his voice audibly nervous in parts, as he undergoes his first major profile since *Outernational.* Questioned about his continuing work, Billy jokes that it is perhaps part of a pre-destined fate ('Somebody up there still wants me to work. Or else I would be drowned in a pig sewer back up in Scotland, the way that I was going'), points out that his whippet obsession was 'pre-*Parklife*' in reference to the greyhound-race cover shot of Blur's key 1994 album, and makes light of his lack of commercial success post-*Sulk.*

'I didn't mind getting two and a half minutes of the fifteen minutes,' he dismissively stated, before breezily adding, 'some people say, "Oh, you haven't realized your potential musically and you should've been playing Knobworth or whatever." But that wasn't the reason for me doing music, to have maximum exposure. And sometimes I think that brings a whole set of different problems anyway. The main thing is just to connect with people and always be honest and true. If [I] went into the studio, it wasn't just, "Oh fuck, I've got to go to the studio today and this is a bore." It should basically exhaust you . . . once you've come out of the studio, you should have a nervous breakthrough. I never took that lightly. For other people's sake, I'm not the sort of person to take up a self-pitying class and go in and become professional and neurotic.'

Further pressed, MacKenzie admitted that he had been a reluctant star, blaming his lack of confidence on the canyon-wide divide between the circumstances of his upbringing and his aspirations to the apparent glamour of fame: 'In many ways, I was born self-confident. Circumstances imbued low self-esteem with me. I didn't have that narcissism that you need to be a figurehead.' Elsewhere he expressed the view that it was perhaps still too early to gain any real perspective on the bland music and unbridled avarice of the previous decade, although he strongly felt there was a connection between the two: 'From '84 onwards . . . the corporate belts started tightening. Then it was, "Sing properly and become Luther Vandross and we'll all be fine." Obviously I reacted intensely against that and didn't want things to be diluted. It was synonymous with what was happening in Britain under the Thatcherite regime . . . the politics at the time definitely swept away what was happening from the high streets to the docklands to the backwaters. It glossed over a lot of real issues and it really wasn't acceptable to be doing a "Firestarter" around that time.'

Bravely, Mulholland then raised the question of Billy's sexuality, explaining that 'as a fan and a follower of yours, I'd always assumed that you're gay . . . I've never read anywhere that anyone's ever asked you or you'd particularly talked about it'.

Billy slowly replied: 'Well, it's something that . . . how would you say? My background is that I'm more interested in individuals and if I've got an affection towards them, then I don't really see hang-ups or boundaries coming into things. So if you're honest and you like either sex, if you're comfortable with that, that's OK. I've never witch-hunted myself in that area, but others have done that for me, y'know. It's something that I don't have to justify to myself.'

Mulholland continued by asking, 'Have you been genuinely hassled to come out by the press or any groups?'. Billy stated, 'No, not really . . . I've been pretty much well left alone,' before readdressing the initial question. 'It's what's behind somebody's gender that appeals to me,' he tentatively remarked, 'and what they are in essence. So, y'know . . . it's a very individual thing for me, as for most people. [Laughs] So has that skirted round the issues? Your knob can get you into trouble, regardless, can't it?'

In publicly admitting his bisexuality after all these years, MacKenzie managed even to surprise a handful of his former friends and colleagues, for whom the singer's sexual persuasions had always been an issue that he fiercely guarded and went as far as attempting to bury. For others closer to him, it had never been regarded as an issue of any import. The fact that Billy appeared to harbour a fear of relationships and commitment outside of his family and inner set of friends inevitably led him to the casual sexual freedom of the gay lifestyle, rather than the protracted manoeuvres of the heterosexual mating ritual. In the end, it seems, his deepest relationships were with his family and closest friends, not his lovers. The fact that he was largely unwilling to admit to his bisexuality can probably be regarded as the guilt of his Catholic upbringing and the knee-jerk homo-phobic attitudes prevalent in small-town life.

In keeping with this, a week after the article was printed Billy called Mulholland at *Time Out* to somehow be reassured that he hadn't 'come out' in the interview. In the conclusive quote printed in the feature, Billy had perhaps revealed the true nature of his sexuality to be one that was blind to gender.

'I'm just waiting for the day,' he laughed, 'when we're all what we were intended to be . . . hermaphrodites.'

Still numbed by recent events, Billy entered Red Bus Studios in London with Steve Aungle in October to record the next batch of piano ballads, including 'And This She Knows' and 'Beyond The Sun'. 'He was talking a lot about the fact that he hadn't grieved properly for his mother,' Keith Bourton remembers. 'He did go straight into the studio and get on with the work, which is another reason why I think the vocals he recorded for those songs were quite astonishing in their emotion.' Delivered in delicate tones, the opening lines of 'Beyond The Sun', perhaps only in reflection, ring with an ominous foreboding: 'There must be a pill/That can make you turn back/Far from this world/Close to a violet spark.'

In spite of the dark clouds that must have been gathering in Billy MacKenzie's mind at this time, there were still glimpses of the devilish twinkle in his eye. Christine Beveridge recalls one occasion in this period where the pair were sitting in a Notting Hill café and MacKenzie used his obtuse humour to baffle the waitress serving them their food: 'When it came, he went, "Oh?" The woman said, "Is there something wrong?" and he said, "Well, this is a 60s hamburger, I really wanted a 50s hamburger."'

Another day in Holland Road, when Aungle was working on a track with his singer friend Caragh McKay, Billy popped his head around the door, asking the two if they'd mind if he got involved. When the pair were encouraging, Billy disappeared to the shops and returned five minutes later, his arms laden with bottles of champagne. Vanishing for a second time, to his room, he reap-peared wearing a fur coat and his old mop-top wig and initiated an afternoon of drinking and dressing-up with the others, recalling the louche, playful recording behaviour of the Associates' peak, fourteen years before. 'It just one of those one-off magical days,' Aungle states, 'and he instigated it. We were being quite workman-like and he just lifted it into another realm.'

In late October, Billy flew to Berlin to visit Thomas Fehlmann and Moritz Von Oswald. By the former's account, he seemed 'in fairly excellent condition' and effusive when it came to the details of his musical work back in London, although it was only later that Fehlmann discovered that Billy's mother had died, as the singer had never once spoken of it during the trip to Germany. On his return to London, it was agreed by the co-inhabitants of Holland Road that the fact that their lease was due to expire at the end of November and they were being forced to move on should be celebrated by a party. Shortly before the first guests arrived on the allotted Saturday night, Billy called Paul Haig and feigned mock anguish: 'He was saying, "I just don't want to have this party . . . do you think I should wear the wig though?"'

At the party, Billy's socializing skills returned as he circulated the room, smiling and laughing and talking to friends from his present and his past. Later, in the small hours, a group of them relocated to one of the bedrooms, where Billy was – as always – eventually coaxed into singing by his fellow revellers. Lying flat out on the floor, his head of cropped, blond-dyed hair resting against a mattress, he opened his mouth to sing the opening lines of 'Gloomy Sunday', the song he had first heard as child and that had gone on to become the emotional centrepiece of *Sulk*.

While MacKenzie had first encountered 'Gloomy Sunday' through the version recorded by Billie Holiday in 1941 that – along with 'Strange Fruit' – remained one of the dark show-stoppers forming a significant element of her repertoire, the song has a morbid history that stretches back to pre-war Hungary. Rezro Seress composed the mournful song in 1933, the lyric expressing a feeling of futility and helplessness following the death of a loved one, unusual in that it is directed at that person, the narrator detailing numberless shadows and conveying thoughts of suicide. The fact that there is a twist in the song's bridge crescendo, where the previous lyric is revealed to have been a dream, was often fatefully overlooked by its listeners.

Over the years, folklore determined that the song was cursed. The first reported death associated with 'Gloomy Sunday' was that of Joseph Keller, a Budapest shoemaker whose suicide note in 1936 quoted the lyric. In the Hungarian capital alone, seventeen other similar deaths apparently followed, bearing some connection with the song: a couple were said to have shot themselves while a gypsy band performed 'Gloomy Sunday'; there was talk that a fourteen-year-old girl had thrown herself into a river clutching the sheet music. The song was eventually banned in Hungary, although even these days the occasional piano rendition is performed in the Kis Papa restaurant in Budapest where Seress first aired the song.

The legend of 'Gloomy Sunday' grew as its apparent effects became further reaching. In New York in the 40s, there were reports that a typist gassed herself, leaving instructions for the song to be played at her funeral. In London, a policeman was alerted to the fact that a recorded instrumental of the song was being repeatedly played by an unseen female neighbour who, when her flat was entered, was discovered to have overdosed on barbiturates while an automatic phonograph played the song over and over again.

Doubtless these tales have been embellished over the years in an effort to emphasize the myth surrounding 'Gloomy Sunday', but certain facts remain: the BBC ban imposed on the song in the 40s has not been lifted to this day; Holiday suffered a tragic premature death at forty-three from heroin-related liver cirrhosis in 1959; Seress, the song's composer, himself committed suicide in 1968.

That is not to dramatically overplay the significance of 'Gloomy Sunday' in the events that followed in Billy MacKenzie's life, but certainly his personal grief at the time imbues the song's lyric with an uneasy resonance that could not have escaped him. As he lay there singing in the early hours of the Sunday morning following the party, Billy alternated the line 'Let them not weep, let them know that I'm glad to go' with his own lamenting alternative: 'Let them not weep, let them know that I'm sad to go.'

15

Close to a Violet Spark

As autumn turned to winter, the flatmates of 40 Holland Road began to move out their belongings. From the beginning of December 1996, Billy was once again without his own home and dividing his time between Steve Phillips's Notting Hill flat and the cottage that his father was now living in near the singer's old flat in Auchterhouse.

It was from this point onwards that Billy started to fade away. Some friends state that rather than a specific shift in his general mood, he seemed preoccupied at times and prone to making odd statements. The last time that Michael Dempsey saw MacKenzie, he sensed an intangible emptiness in him that he had never experienced before. The two had met up in the West End for an evening discussing the plans of their cinematic album, and as they were saying goodbye to one other at Piccadilly Circus, Dempsey remembers: 'He said, "I don't want to go home yet, I'm just going to walk around." It did make me think that he was incredibly lonely at that point.'

Following the sudden untethering of one emotional anchor with the passing of his mother, Billy even appeared to be drifting away from his music, the other constant and comfort in his life if ever he found himself sailing through rougher waters. Keith Bourton admits that at this time he found it strange that when the Nude deal had been inked in October, Billy was determined to get into the studio as soon as possible, in spite of his bereavement; now within a matter of weeks, he had lost interest in the new contract and the recording of his first album for the label. Apollo 440 were due to begin work on the preliminary four tracks they had been given by Nude, but in a phone conversation from Scotland with his manager in December, MacKenzie insisted that there was no need for him to come back down to London since the producers had all the vocals they needed from him already: 'He suddenly went volte-face from bugging me everyday to get in the studio to saying, "Let them finish the tracks they've got and I'll do the rest in the New Year."'

In the seven weeks following his leaving Holland Road, Billy in fact travelled by train between Scotland and London six times. John MacKenzie, who accompanied him, says that during those long, six-hour journeys, his brother seemed to want to talk about little other than the death of Lily MacKenzie: 'All he did was talk about our mum. He felt he'd let our mum down.'

If it was clear that Billy was suffering from some form of depression in these last weeks, then there was no way at this stage that even those closest to him could have determined just how deeply it had taken root. In talking about his own fragility, nine years before, Billy had almost foreshadowed his current state: 'Externally things affect me a great deal. Empty moments have come, but I've side-stepped them. I could never give into them. If I ever start closing down, it will mean I've contracted some kind of mental illness.'

In the aftermath of the events that followed, it was widely assumed that Billy had been prone to depression over the years. The reality appears to be that his mood swings were no more dramatic than the average mentally healthy individual. In fact, as many of the key incidents in his past serve to highlight, his one emotional recurrence was a certain steely resilience in the face of adverse conditions, whether they be his career struggles, his financial difficulties or otherwise. Perversely, his own insight into his psyche was to prove more accurate than anyone could have predicted. Somewhere amid the irrational guilt and confusion of the last weeks of his life, Billy suffered a swift and severe nervous breakdown. From that point, he lost his will to live.

Over Christmas and New Year, Billy was with his father at Scotstoun Cottage in Auchterhouse, his restless state troubling

Jim MacKenzie so much that he made the decision to stay in over the festive period and cancel any other arrangements he'd previously made. 'He wasn't keeping well at all, couldn't sleep,' his father admits. 'I was supposed to go out, but I wouldn't . . . Billy was bad. He didn't want me to leave him, didn't want to travel, didn't want to do anything.'

On New Year's Eve, Billy went to bed early, taking with him a bottle of sleeping pills that he'd been prescribed for the acute insomnia he'd been suffering from. That night, it appears, he took an overdose of the pills in an attempt at suicide. Once discovered, he was rushed to Ninewells Hospital, where he was revived on a ventilation machine. Afterwards he tried to convince his family that it had been an accident. Partly due to his excessive nature – if he ever decided to do something, it was never by halves – his protestations that he'd mistakenly taken too many of the pills were, to a certain degree, reasonable.

Deeply distressed by the incident, however, his father tried to insist to doctors that Billy be taken into the care of the hospital's psychiatric ward, although it was clear that his son was terrified by the prospect and so determined not to comply with it that he even managed to convince the hospital psychiatrist that there was nothing gravely wrong with him. In the end Billy was simply prescribed anti-depressants. 'I tried to get him kept in,' Jim MacKenzie says. 'But [the psychiatrist] said, "Oh, there's nothing wrong with him." He was a great actor, Billy, and he didn't want to stay in the hospital. I said, "Look, I would prefer if you could keep him in." She just said, "I don't think it needs that, he can go." They wouldn't listen to me.'

Understandably, it wasn't until later that anyone outside the immediate MacKenzie family grew to learn of this apparent suicide bid. To the majority of his friends, even if it was worrying, Billy merely seemed distracted and uncharacteristically low.

When the music industry's wheels ground back into action again at the beginning of the new year, business drew Billy back to London. On 15 January he travelled to the capital for the signing of a new publishing agreement with Sony Music that had been negotiated in the wake of the deal with Nude. When the singer arrived at the lawyer's office, Keith Bourton and Steve Aungle noticed that he was looking drawn and pale. Billy explained that he was suffering from flu and was running a temperature.

After the deal was signed, MacKenzie dismissed the others' suggestion that a celebration was in order, claiming he was too unwell. On reflection, both can now see that Billy's behaviour at the meeting was strange, even knowing. Aungle states: 'I do remember him asking the lawyer at least two or three times, "Is that money going to come through in twenty-four hours?" It was as if he wanted to make sure that I would get my money and everyone else would get their money. It was almost like he was tying things up. As we left, he just said, "Oh, I'll phone you" and that was the last time I saw him.' Bourton says: 'I remember now that he said goodbye in a really peculiar way . . . he said it about three times and made sure I saw him waving. Since then I've had this strange feeling in the back of my mind that he really was saying goodbye.'

For the following days, back in Scotland, there were times when, according to those around him, Billy seemed to return to a more balanced state and others where he still seemed unsettled and lost. Always, as night fell, he was at his lowest. He was still having real difficulty sleeping, and it reached the point where he insisted on either his father or one of his brothers being in the same room as him during the night. In telephone conversations with his friends, Billy now seemed disturbed, saying that he felt as if his sense of humour – the element of his character that helped him survive so many highs and lows in the past – had now deserted him. By the end, he just couldn't laugh any more.

Worse, he was now suffering the more extreme symptoms of clinical depression, telling both Aungle and Haig on the phone that he was experiencing hallucinations, particularly if he tried to watch TV, the horrible recurring visions involving flashes of the carnage and mutilation of medieval battles. Regression experts might argue that at this point Billy was perhaps tapping into subconscious memories. Years before, the singer – always fascinated by the psychic paranormal – had claimed to have been regressed and learned that in a past life he had been a Catholic heretic put to death in seventeenth-century Spain. While this is a fanciful aside, had Billy admitted these hallucinations to a psychiatrist, the more common diagnosis would surely have been that he was in a dangerously unbalanced and overloaded state.

Both of the friends that he talked to about these visions say that because Billy's thought process would often fly off on a surreal tangent, alarm bells didn't ring. 'I knew it was bad,' says Haig, 'but I always thought he'd pull through.' Aungle further admits: 'He'd told me he'd had stuff like that before. We'd both talked about playing around with insanity, which was tied in with all the dark stuff in the music. Against all that, when he started saying to me that he was hallucinating, I just thought it was another of these episodes. If it had been anyone else, I might've thought, There's something really wrong here, they need treatment.'

In the days that remained, Billy contacted a handful of his friends by telephone. Christine Beveridge received a message on her answerphone from the singer on Sunday 19 January: 'He was very low, I could tell by his voice. He just said, "Love you, doll", and that was it.' Paul Haig last spoke to him on Monday the 20th: 'I just said, "Look, Billy, I'm coming up to Dundee or you come to Edinburgh and we'll sort this out." He just said, "Yeah, I'll phone you back" and he never did.' In his last conversation with Steve Aungle on the same day, Billy seemed to have lost all his motivation: 'He was just beside himself, he didn't know what to do next. I said, "Look, Billy, come back down to London." He just said, "But what will I do when I come back down?" I thought, Why's he asking that question? It's obvious – you just live your life and get on with things. I said, "Well, you've got a bit of money now, you can go and get yourself a nice wee flat, get a couple of dogs." But he was just totally without any enthusiasm for anything. It was just, "Oh well, yeah, I'll maybe do that then."'

On Monday MacKenzie visited his grandmother in the old people's home where she lived and ended up giving an impromptu performance of Hank Williams's 'Jambalaya' in the residents' lounge. Jim MacKenzie, who accompanied his son on the visit, notes: 'You wouldn't think anything was bothering him.' On Tuesday afternoon Billy was dropped off at Scotstoun Cottage by a friend, saying that he planned to take his father's dogs for a walk. There was a report that a local farmer later saw Billy walking across the nearby fields alone with a duvet draped around his shoulders, although this claim seemed odd since the neighbour stated that MacKenzie then turned back and headed in the direction of the shed behind Scotstoun Cottage where he sometimes kept his whippets. If this was his intended destination, the detour across the fields would have been unnecessary.

What is certainly true is that on Tuesday afternoon Billy had left a note for his father in the cottage, saying that he'd gone to visit friends in Dundee. By the following evening, when Jim MacKenzie returned home to Auchterhouse and there still hadn't been any further word from Billy, he began to grow worried.

He recalls: 'I was sitting in the house and thinking, It's not like him. He wasn't well and he didn't want to leave the house. So I phoned around the family, even phoned over to Edinburgh, thinking, Maybe he's just jumped on the train. But something kept on bothering me, so I thought, I'll away and check the huts. It was dark in the hut and I was just fumbling about and I suddenly felt his hand.'

Jim MacKenzie detailed the discovery of his son's body to reporter John Dingwall of the *Daily Record*, the first paper to break the news of Billy's suicide: 'He was wrapped in a duvet clutching a photo album. I felt his hands and went into a panic when I realized how cold he was. I must have screamed because a neighbour came out. He phoned for an ambulance and the police.'

Shortly after 11pm on Wednesday 22 January, the police and ambulance crew arrived and Billy MacKenzie was pronounced dead, having taken what the post-mortem determined to be a massive overdose of prescribed and over-the-counter pills, including paracetamol, beta-blockers and the anti-depressant amitriptyline. Beside the body lay a suicide note. 'He never said why he did it,' Jim MacKenzie told Dingwall. 'He just said sorry to his family.'

A statement issued by Tayside Police read: 'The body of a man was found in a shed behind Scotstoun Cottage, Auchterhouse, late on Wednesday night. Police were alerted just after 11pm and the man was pronounced dead at the scene. He has been identified as William MacKenzie. There are no apparent suspicious circumstances.'

On Friday 24 January, the front page of the *Daily Record* bore the blunt, attention-grabbing headline 'Pop Star Billy Kills Himself'.

Nine months later Jim MacKenzie sits in the back room of one of his second-hand shops in Dundee. The day after Billy's death he burned the shed to the ground. 'You don't know what your emotions are at all,' he says softly, trying to express his feelings in the aftermath of the tragedy. 'You don't get over it, you learn to live with it. If somebody gets hit by a car or falls off a building and dies, you could understand it . . . but Billy was the last laddie you would've thought would take his own life.'

He admits he is still angry that many of the reports of his son's death in the newspapers stated that he died of an unspecified 'overdose', giving the misleading impression that Billy's death was perhaps as a result of illegal drug abuse. 'They can talk about what they want, his problems or whatever,' he states, 'but if he just got to sing and do his thing, he would've been all right. It was the business side that killed him. He used to tell me that the music business was "rotten to the core".'

Inevitably, in the emotional fallout of a suicide, one of the greater anguishes is the thought that the death could have somehow been avoided or that it might have been a cry for help gone drastically wrong. In this way, for those close to Billy, there is at least some comfort to be taken from the knowledge that his death was not the result of an impulsive act, the circumstances of his initial failed suicide bid serving to reveal how he was somehow – for his own deeply felt, deeply hidden reasons – determined to end his life.

In addition, of course, there is always the agony that perhaps the person concerned could have turned a corner, psychologically. For his part, John MacKenzie is in no doubt as to the one real solution to his brother's problems. 'The door back for Billy would have been if he'd been sedated for a month,' he says. 'He needed to be put out for a month and nobody was willing to do that.'

In the end, often what is left behind is a frustrating search for reasons and answers. John MacKenzie believes that Billy's real problem was 'having to feel like you're performing all the time. To take something away from you where you don't need to perform – which was my mum – that was what did it. When that was taken away from him, he thought he had to perform all the time, and he couldn't take it.'

While the death of his mother was unarguably the catalyst for Billy MacKenzie's eventual fate, some believe that although this was a significant part of the equation, the sleeping pills and anti-depressants that Billy had been prescribed slowly erased his personality, eventually closing down his whole being. Others state that Billy often seemed to shoulder too much in the way of responsibility for those around him – the fact that he was regarded as a tower of strength only made his suicide all the more shocking – and that, running out of energy, he couldn't admit to the vulnerability he had felt after Lily MacKenzie was gone.

The tragic conclusion is that there are no clear answers and that the true reasoning behind Billy MacKenzie's suicide died along with him. In many ways, throughout his life, the child within Billy had refused to be suppressed, and therefore perhaps it was his fate never to grow old. Years before, he had admitted as much to his brother.

'He knew,' John MacKenzie says. 'He told me that when he was thirty-nine, that's when he was out. He just knew that he was out at that age. He said, "I won't let anyone puncture me or take my energy away."'

16

Beyond the Sun

The fact that Billy MacKenzie died thirty-seven days short of his fortieth birthday only deepened the tragedy. As such, the scenes on the streets of Dundee on Monday 27 January 1997, the day of his funeral, perhaps befitted the city's most famous son in recent history, with the pavement outside St Andrew's Cathedral littered with weeping mourners, many of them strangers even to the singer's friends and family. Originally the plan had been for there to be a brief ceremony held at J & J Gray funeral directors, although in the days that followed the news of Billy's death, it soon became clear from the subsequent flood of calls to the family – many of them from the singer's friends in Europe and America planning to travel to Scotland – that the fifty-six-seat parlour was ill-equipped to cope with the hundreds now expected, and so hasty arrangements were made for the cavernous cathedral to become the venue.

During the service, Father Joe O'Farrell spoke of the trauma that Billy had suffered following the death of his mother and paid tribute to his vocal talents and even the promise he'd shown as an athlete in his younger life, before the congregated mourners sang 'Amazing Grace', just as many of them had done only months before at the funeral of Lily MacKenzie. Later, as the coffin was being lowered into the ground in the leafy calm of Balgay Cemetery at the MacKenzie plot where his mother had also been laid to rest, Billy's uncle played a bagpipe lament. Following that, even the buoyant will of the family could not raise the atmosphere of the wake held at the nearby Bonar Hall to the celebration of life that had followed the funeral of Billy's mother. Despite Jimmy MacKenzie's efforts in setting up a sound system and playing a selection of Associates records from down the years, those gathered there were either too acutely distressed or coldly numb to fully appreciate the tribute.

Just over two weeks later, on Tuesday 11 February, a memorial was held in London for music-industry colleagues at St Francis of Assisi church in Notting Hill and attended by many of Billy's former musical collaborators and contemporaries including Roddy Frame, Boris Blank and Martyn Ware, all of whom sang from a hymn card quoting the opening lines of 'Skipping', which in this context seemed to hold a sense of otherworldly peace: 'Doors lead to other doors/Roads lead to other roads.' One of the speakers was a visibly emotional Chris Parry, who talked of how the industry should use the lesson of Billy's death to be more sensitive to the pressures that many artists are forced to absorb. 'I think the thing I tried to touch on,' the Fiction boss explains, 'is that artists are always on the edge in terms of how they work. The hurdles over which they have to jump are quite high and as sharp as razor blades . . . they can cut themselves badly. All I questioned is why do they have to deal with it, and why is there so much of it?'

Alongside the many printed eulogies and obituaries that appeared in both the music papers and the broadsheets, more letters from fans appeared in the press than might possibly have been expected in response to the death of an artist whose work had appeared to have lost much of its relevance over recent years. In particular, nearly two columns of the letters page of the 15 February edition of *Melody Maker* were filled with tributes, a selection reading: 'I'll still be wanting to listen to these [songs] in 30 years' time, for the sheer beauty of that voice . . . I'm truly sorry that it has gone' (Andrew Miller, Warwickshire); 'If I could have done anything to bring even a fraction of the joy he brought to me, then I would have' (Steven Biram, Rochdale); 'I felt I knew Billy through his records. I wish I could have been there to talk to him' (Anon).

In the weeks and months that followed, the burning question as to what should be done with Billy's last recordings was to add a significant charge to the relationship between Nude Records and his family and colleagues. In death, it seems, as in life, the singer's output was fated to become the focus of turbulent interactivity between the concerned parties, even if what followed by no means paralleled MacKenzie's business struggles while alive. The dilemma, of course, was a delicate one, as the decision whether to release or respectively shelve – for fear of being seen to be capitalizing on – the final work of an artist in the light of their sudden death inevitably proves to be.

In this case the two parties approached the situation from opposing starting points. As the singer's last major collaborator, Steve Aungle was in agreement with the MacKenzie family that the album he had planned to make with Billy should be released as faithfully as the existing master tapes allowed. Since there had been no contact between the musician and Nude in the days following Billy's death, he first raised the question with Saul Galpern at the wake in Dundee, where the label boss stated that he'd already decided not to attempt to issue any of the unreleased material. Galpern remembers that when he had first learned of the singer's suicide: 'I was stunned . . . I made the conscious decision that we shouldn't put out anything because it would be in bad taste. His family encouraged us . . . then obviously conversations took place for quite some time as to how it would be done.'

Having sifted through the many tapes that remained in one form or another, Aungle compiled a running order of twelve basic tracks that he felt could be used as a blueprint for the album. Three songs in particular – 'The Soul That Sighs', 'MacArthur's Son' and 'Liberty Lounge' – had to be omitted since the masters had been lost, the ultimate result of Billy's habit of borrowing tapes from Aungle's room at Holland Road and then subsequently leaving them in a cab or just simply misplacing them while on his travels. Galpern and Laurie at Nude, still far keener on the piano ballads than the electronic tracks, didn't agree with two of the inclusions in the suggested running order, particularly one dance track from the sessions with John Vick in Edinburgh called 'Falling Out With The Future'.

'They immediately said we couldn't use that because of the title, even though it had been written two years before,' Aungle explains, further arguing, 'but they could've said the same about "Give Me Time" or "Beyond The Sun".' David Laurie admits that the label was still less favourably disposed to the electronic material: 'I'd have loved for us to have had a Winter Academy-styled album, with just songs like that. But there wasn't enough.'

The twelve-track blueprint was whittled down to ten songs and then further trimmed to eight. Following that, Galpern made an announcement at a conference for Nude Records' distributors 3MV that the forthcoming album, now entitled *Beyond The Sun*, would be a combination of these new tracks and a twelve-song retrospective from the back catalogue of the Associates. Word of this leaked to the music press and was duly reported. Galpern explains the label's reasoning behind this at the time: 'Our thinking was, Let's do it properly. If we're now going to do it, let's do a fantastic fitting tribute. He's not around any more, we don't have anyone to promote it, so why don't we try and bring in the people that remembered him and get them turned on again to a fantastic collection of songs? At the same time, they get the new songs. We thought it would be a great double album.'

Shortly afterwards the scheme began to collapse when the MacKenzie estate voiced their extreme disapproval of the idea. Keith Bourton, in his diplomatic managerial role, insists that he never really expected the plan to be fully realized: 'In my experience of dealing with record companies, they come up with ideas like that when they're not sure what they're getting. My view on it always was that once we'd delivered what would have been a twelve-track finished album, they would've been quite happy to put that out. To be fair, they weren't exactly banging a drum about it, they just thought it would be a nice idea. I know that Jimmy and Steve tied themselves in knots about it, but I was never really that worried about it happening . . . I didn't think they were going to do it.'

By this stage there had been another important development. The process of picking through the legalities that followed Billy's death revealed that the bulk of the Associates' recordings were not, in fact, owned by Warners Brothers, but had merely been licensed to the company in Beggars Banquet's complicated sale of the duo's contract in 1981. As a result, the initial ten-year period of the licensing agreements had now lapsed, with the ownership of the masters reverting back to MacKenzie's estate and, in the case of their work together, Alan Rankine. Jimmy MacKenzie – who stepped forward as the spokesman for the family since, through his past work as an A&R scout for ZTT, he had the most experience in dealing with the industry – informed Nude that the estate were refusing to allow the tracks to be used. 'It was like they were saying that the new tracks couldn't hold their weight on their own,' he feels.

Despite these conflicting opinions over what form the resulting album should eventually take, both parties wholly agreed that the new tracks that had been selected all required either additional production or fresh mixes before release. Producer Pascal Gabriel, who had mixed part of *Outernational* five years before and had been offering his services free of charge as early as the funeral, was allotted two tracks, 'Give Me Time' and 'Sour Jewel'. The six others – comprising mainly the Scott Walker-echoing piano ballads – were entrusted to Simon Raymonde, the Cocteau Twins' bassist, whose father Ivor Raymonde, perhaps coincidentally, had been the arranger on many of the revered 60s singer's best-known hits. Everyone present at the recording of the fifteen-piece string section added to both 'Winter Academy' and 'Nocturne VII' at the Cocteau Twins' studio September Sound in June remembers a palpable sadness lingering in the air, the melancholic nature of the music now revealing a painful depth in the light of the recent tragedy.

In the midst of this, the negotiations between the label and the estate were continuing, if now steering over even rockier terrain. At a meeting held in August, John and Jimmy MacKenzie, together with Aungle, sat down with Galpern and Laurie to thrash out the details of the release. By this stage, the musician admits, 'We were pissed off with the whole thing, so it was hard to be diplomatic. We felt hard-line about things and there was a tense atmosphere. They'd brought their lawyer in, which made us a bit uneasy.' At the top of the agenda was the matter of Nude's decision to donate their share of the profits to the Samaritans and

Macmillan Cancer Relief and to still try to come to a compromise with the estate over the possible inclusion of some of the older Associates tracks.

Saul Galpern says: 'The reason we wanted a double album was because it would maybe sell more and then more would go to charity. We had to be sensitive about it, but we were just trying to be realistic about the whole thing. At the end of the day, we knew the level he was at and we had a prediction of how many records we were going to sell. But Jimmy in particular was quite stubborn.' From their perspective, MacKenzie and Aungle felt that the idea that *Beyond The Sun* was mutating into a charity project denigrated the album in certain ways, the latter arguing, 'We just thought it should be put out as if Billy was alive, like any other album.'

Still, in the meeting, the MacKenzie brothers showed that they were prepared to bend in Nude's direction on the possibility of inclusions from the back catalogue. The company suggested that the eight new songs might be supplemented by a similar quantity of older tracks. Swiftly convening outside the meeting room, the brothers made the decision to agree to the approval of four songs from the archives, with Aungle further stipulating that with this position of bargaining power they should insist that at least one of the electronic tracks, '3 Gypsies In A Restaurant', appear on the album, and Nude reluctantly agreed to this. In the weeks that followed, Aungle took it upon himself, in an illicit manoeuvre, to reconstruct a new track, '14 Mirrors', from the vocal recorded by Billy four months before his death for a piano song with the working title of 'I'd Rather Lose You As A Lover Than Keep You As A Friend'. When he played the result to Laurie and Galpern, they expressed their approval and agreed to its inclusion. Now there were ten new tracks.

Knowing this, the estate shrewdly began to retreat in their compliance regarding the inclusion of the older material, with Jim MacKenzie using his authority to insist that *Beyond The Sun* should comprise the ten tracks that Nude had now agreed to release and no others. Aungle, for one, was concerned that this tense stand-off would more than likely result in the album's release being aborted. This prospect took one step closer to becoming a reality when both parties, issuing threats to shelve the album, reached stalemate. Galpern says: 'The problem was that there was a lack of communication. At the eleventh hour, there was this whole new plan.'

Following the breakdown in communications, Nude were the first to relent, by seeming to be giving in to the MacKenzies' demands. As a result, Aungle and Jimmy MacKenzie were invited to the label's offices to view the proposed cover artwork. When he arrived, Aungle says, Galpern informed him that he had changed his mind once again, having decided that the album was too difficult to market without any of the older material and that it was perhaps best if the project was put on ice.

When Jimmy MacKenzie walked in minutes later and learned of this sudden development, he immediately rose from his seat and motioned to walk out of the office: 'I knew that if I stood up and said, "See you later then", and they pulled me back, then they still wanted to put the album out. If they were gonna shelve it, then shelve the fucking thing. But they pulled me back and it was obvious that it was a total bluff.' When he is questioned about whether this was indeed a last-ditch attempt to get his own way, Galpern's face lights up with the type of cheeky, knowing grin that – like that of Billy MacKenzie himself – is never best conveyed in print. In the end, there is the nagging feeling that, had the singer lived, the creative and corporate tug-of-war that would have doubtless continued between MacKenzie and Nude Records was set to have been no less colourful than any in the singer's illustrious history.

As a footnote, by the time of the album's release on 6 October 1997, both of the quarrelling parties were reported in the press as being delighted with the results. From his overview of the proceedings, Keith Bourton wryly notes of the troubled realization of *Beyond The Sun*: 'It wasn't really World War Three, it was just sort of . . . handbags at five paces.'

The most cutting irony is that the posthumous *Beyond The Sun* was undoubtedly the best album accredited to Billy MacKenzie since *Sulk*, even if the two could not have been more stylistically extreme in their differences. While *Sulk* was kaleidoscopic in both its sound and sleeve imagery, the noir musical overtones of *Beyond The Sun* were reflected in the moody, pensive black and white shot of the singer featured on the cover.

While there is an introspective atmosphere prevalent even within the electronic or band-based material, there is also a sense of positivity and even certain transcendental qualities to parts of *Beyond The Sun*. The rhythm underpinning 'Give Me Time', co-written with Paul Haig in 1995, drags Kraftwerk into the hip-hop age, with spy-thriller guitar shadowing the controlled bitterness of MacKenzie's vocal, seemingly crying out for breathing space in a suffocating and dangerous relationship. 'At The Edge Of The World' is remixed from the original Pink Floyd-like demo from the reunion sessions with Alan Rankine and transformed by the programming of the Cocteau Twins' guitarist Mituso Tate into something approximating the warm, sub bass-driven trip hop of Massive Attack, Billy detailing a strange, lyrical landscape: 'It's a place where you know you've been before/In another time, through another door.'

In '3 Gypsies In A Restaurant', MacKenzie and Aungle's vision of a cross-pollination of the Prodigy with the early Associates is fully accomplished, as 'Firestarter' collides headlong into 'Kitchen Person', spirit-summoning Moorish chants battling with dark, apocalyptic imagery. 'Sour Jewel', a paean to the over-the-top glam rock of Roxy Music, is propelled by a Motown groove and given top-spin by MacKenzie's oblique, almost delirious outbursts ('Let all our senses play truant') and was possibly – above even the unreleased 'MacArthur's Son' – the most likely Top Ten hit he'd written or co-written for many years.

It is in the piano ballads that dominate, however, that the true beauty of *Beyond The Sun* is revealed. Rooted in the part Euro soundtrack, part orchestral Scott Walker-fashioned stylisms of 'Breakfast' and the Ronnie Scott's set in 1984, MacKenzie's voice is revealed in its every expressive detail in these last recordings, from powerful vibrato to fragile whisper. 'Blue It Is' echoes both the smoky inflections of Billie Holiday and Julie London's 'Cry Me A River' in its reflective, languid tone, with MacKenzie turning in possibly the most gently delivered performance he ever committed to tape. The similarly delicate 'And This She Knows' paints a tranquil, hashish-clouded depiction of a quiet, peaceful existence, while the bare verses of 'Winter Academy' find the singer in the throes of some reminiscence, most consciously with the lines, 'All around town as young pretenders/So jagged the crown, breakfast remembered', before the strings sweep in a chorus where Billy's emotional delivery of the climaxing ' . . .before the autumn came' revives and rivals Jacques Brel's own racked reading of 'If You Go Away'.

The centrepiece of *Beyond The Sun* is its title track, originally entitled 'The Pill', as if to unsettlingly underline how the lyric is perhaps the writer's imagined conception of an afterlife where 'a new eclipse' darkens the sky above 'oceans of crystal ships'. In retrospect, with the acquired knowledge of the precarious emotional state MacKenzie was in when he wrote and performed the song, lines such as 'What are we going through?/What are we going to do?' carry an almost unbearable weight. In 'Nocturne VII', the brooding conclusion of *Beyond The Sun*, the singer appears to be ready for his journey: 'I read it in the sand/You come for me and take me by the hand.'

In the largely effusive praise of *Beyond The Sun* in the press, the perceptions of the critics were seemingly uncoloured by the tragedy, in their united agreement that the album was Billy MacKenzie's finest work in years. The *Daily Telegraph* noted: 'Pop history has shown that tragic death too often results in tragic music, but "Beyond The Sun" stands on its own merits as one of the year's essential albums.' *Melody Maker* described it as 'a desperately sad affair, a collection of supremely heart-breaking, yet perfectly beautiful songs.' *Time Out* poignantly asked: 'The only thing wrong with "Beyond The Sun"? Do you really have to ask?'

The sad reality is that at the time of his death, all of Billy MacKenzie's recorded work remained long deleted, his increasingly rare albums only to be found in the dusty racks of second-hand record shops. With his passing, as the estate attempts to locate and collect the many master tapes, there are growing plans for a reissue programme to rightfully restore the availability of his work.

In the end, it is his voice and his music, not his life story, that is Billy MacKenzie's lasting legacy. Once he said: 'If I'd written the love songs John Lennon had written . . . well, I wouldn't mind if Billy MacKenzie wasn't here any more.'

No one can deny that, in his own maverick way, he did just that.

EPILOGUE

In relating or reading the story of Billy MacKenzie's life, the plot draws inexorably – through the stranger-than-fiction detail of his youth, the helium highs of his success and strangely childlike innocence and wonder of his maturity – to its desolate conclusion. At points, as a writer sharing in the exhilaration of his being until those last few weeks, it was tempting to change the ending of this book, to one where the subject reached fulfilment and went on to live a long and contented life as a well-dressed, wilfully eccentric pensioner living in a picturesque Scottish cottage, the interior of which is being ritually destroyed by packs of free-spirited whippets. But Billy's eventual fate was in his own hands, and the path he chose to follow has to be respected by everyone.

In my conversations with his friends and family, I often raised the question of what Billy's reaction to having a book devoted to him might have been. Some said he would have feigned horror. Others said that there is no question that he would have been flattered and thrilled, even if the exhaustive research would have inevitably unearthed too many truths and resulted in there ultimately not being enough in the way of disinformation and red herrings for his liking. One even went as far as to wryly suggest that in the months after his death, he was probably sitting twiddling his thumbs in the afterlife, wondering 'Why isn't anyone writing a fucking book about me?' and that with his strange action of cupping his hand on my head at our last meeting, he had perhaps planted psychic information into my subconscious mind: 'Write the book . . . write the book.'

The matter of Billy MacKenzie's premature death has only heightened the paradox that in his life he was forever the man who would be king, but that through his own fear and loathing of fame, he continually threw his hand, thwarting the ascension to international stardom that others believed was his right. In many ways, however, that is to miss the point, since Billy seemed always to be continually struggling to carve out a niche for himself where he wouldn't be forced to dilute his left-field approach, while still achieving enough success to reap the lifestyle benefits and to continue the glamour chase.

In this way, perhaps he was born merely one decade too early, since within the diversity of much of the music that has proved hugely successful in the mid-to-late 1990s, he would surely have found his place. A possible template is the mainstream acceptance and house-hold-name status of Björk: another uncompromising artist and idiosyncratic vocalist with a magnetic personality who operates within the musical field of blending skewed jazz with surreal pop, bubbling electronics with grand orchestral arrangements.

Similarly, the corporate belts of the record industry that threatened to strangle Billy appear to be in the process of loosening, the avarice of the 1980s giving way to the growing cottage-industry approach of subsidiary labels – Nude Records, of course, being a key example – where a respectful distance exists between the creative and financial worlds. In addition – thanks to the costly and bold protestations of Prince and George Michael – there now appears to be a slow revising of the grossly unfair contracts and pitiful standard royalty agreements that have more in common with the exploitative studio system of Hollywood in the 1940s than of a leading export industry in the British and American economies as we near the millennium. It's only a pity that Billy MacKenzie isn't around to witness – and, let's face it, roundly abuse – the future outcome of this quiet revolution.

One of the interviewees for this book pointed out that, if they're being truly honest, everyone who came in contact with Billy fell in love with a part of him. Whether it be his charm, his mysteriously impish and somehow guilty grin, his mercurial nature, his mindless generosity or even his imaginative head games and cutting in-sightfulness, he possessed an electric life-force that others couldn't resist tapping into. Even his enemies kind of liked or at least admired him. Perhaps those who made the mistake of trying to harness his affections or creativity for their own sole attention overlooked the fact that in trying to tame his flirtatious nature, they would lose the vital essence of what made him special in the first place. In that sense, his chosen trading name was perfect, since Billy MacKenzie's life – outside of his devotion to his closest friends, family and dogs – was a chain of associations.

Let's not forget either that he was as wily as a wolverine and no doubt fully aware – even if it need not have taken the tragedy of his passing – that unique talent, overlooked and left to fester in obscurity, can slowly accrue a lasting legendary status for an artist. One acquaintance remembers sharing part of a train journey to Scotland with him in 1988, at the height of the Warners wars. As they parted, Billy revealingly summed up his predicament by saying: 'Ach well, y'know, I'd like to be remembered for what I *might* have achieved, rather than what I did achieve.'

As to how he viewed the prospect of his own middle age and eventual retirement, at one point he expressed a simple desire to be 'really suave and wrinkly'. While he variously talked of relocating to Amsterdam, Paris, Zurich, Berlin or Toronto, he would likely have spent his last natural years wandering the Scottish hills, his spiritual home, with his faithful dogs in tow. Still, he once lightly envisaged a future of 'breeding misfits like myself', spent in 'a ranch in Montana with sixteen whippets, three Arab horses, a peregrine falcon and Ann-Margret'. The fact that his life never made it to a more satisfying conclusion should perhaps not be lamented, since in his nearly forty years he achieved and experienced more than most people do if they make it to ninety. 'I want other people to get as much out of life as I have,' he once stated. 'Unfortunately, they won't.'

Ten years ago, at the close of an interview, I asked him how he pictured his demise. After barely a moment of thought, he flashed that sly grin.

'I'd probably like to die,' he grandly announced, 'by falling off a bar stool in the best nightclub ever.'

Maybe, in his own mind, he made it there in the end.

ACKNOWLEDGEMENTS

Deepest thanks to the MacKenzie family, particularly Jim, John and Jimmy.

For their often limitless time and patience, thanks also to: Steve Aungle, Alan Rankine, Christine Beveridge, Paul Haig, Steve Reid, Chris Parry, Michael Dempsey, Boris Blank, Roberto Soave, Howard Hughes, Flood, Martha Ladly, Chris Carr, Trevor Horn, Martin Rushent, Martyn Ware, Glenn Gregory, Ian Sclater, Bob Johnson, Sunie Fletcher, John Hollingsworth, Keith Bourton, Steve Knight, Max Hole, Noko, Saul Galpern, David Laurie, Ronnie Gurr, Tarquin Gotch, Billy Sloan, Thomas Felhmann, Philipp Erb, Judy Lipsey, Ashley Newton, Bruce Findlay and Barry Adamson.

In addition this book would have probably been impossible without the help and advice of: Bono (for his laptop PopMart Airways action), Steve Phillips (even just for understanding that I understood), Craig Burton (for his unrivalled archives and being the undisputed keeper of the flame), Mark Adams (for the sleepless completion of the discography), Eliz Feeney (for the amazing kitchen interview), Happy the psychoanalyst (for his 'hot and cold' theory), Penny Phillips, Helena Drakakis and Richard Dawes at Bloomsbury, Garry Mulholland, Chris Heath, Regine Moylett, Louise Butterly, Martin Low, Julie Bland, John Aizlewood, Mat Snow, Paulette Constable, Tony Horkins, Lucy O'Brien, Lee Ellen Newman, Barbara Charone, Ian Gittins, Richard Lowe, Arthur Brown, Andrew Perry, Simon Plaskett, Roz Earls, Jim Shelley, Grant McInally, Caragh McKay, John Dingwall, Roddy Isles, Allan Campbell, Ita Martin, Mick Houghton, Kimberly Kriete, Mike Woodcock,

Graeme Melville and Anth Brown (for the dozens of times I couldn't wander down Scabby Road).

Finally, thanks to Dad, Brian and the clan for that week in Dundee – particularly to Heather for rightly telling me I'd be tearing my hair out within a fortnight – and to Karen: for encouraging me to do it in the first place, for the gold and silver stars and for putting up with all the moaning and ranting and swearing and coughing.

Lyrical excerpts to the following songs appear by kind permission of Fiction Songs Ltd: 'A', 'A Matter Of Gender', 'Logan Time', 'Transport To Central', 'Q Quarters', 'White Car In Germany', 'No', 'Skipping', 'Club Country', 'Party Fears Two', 'The Stranger In Your Voice', 'Take Me To The Girl', 'Snowball', 'Country Boy', 'Outernational', 'Stephen, You're Still Really Something', 'International Loner'.

Lyrical excerpts to the following songs by kind permission of Sony/ATV Music Publishing: 'Beyond The Sun', 'At The Edge Of The World', 'Sour Jewel', 'Winter Academy', 'Nocturne VII'.

In the course of my research, information and quotes from the following titles and sources proved invaluable: *Melody Maker, NME, Q, Sounds, Smash Hits, Record Mirror, FHM,* Forth FM, *The Face, Number One, Time Out, Cut, Daily Telegraph, Sunday People, Evening Standard, Sunday Post, Daily Record,* Tyne Tees TV, *Jamming, Blitz, Music Box, Record Collector.*

All Billy MacKenzie/Associates fan correspondence to be directed (with sae) to: Obsession Magnificent, PO Box 4394, Chelmsford CM1 7PQ, UK.

DISCOGRAPHY

Compiled by Craig Burton and Mark Adams

ASSOCIATES SINGLES

(All picture sleeves (p/s) unless otherwise stated)

7-inch Boys Keep Swinging/Mona Property Girl – (no p/s) – Double Hip DHR1 1979

7-inch Boys Keep Swinging/Mona Property Girl – (Remixed reissue, no p/s) – MCA537 1979

7-inch The Affectionate Punch/You Were Young – Fiction FICS 1 1980

7-inch Tell Me Easter's On Friday/Straw Towels – Situation 2 SIT1 1981

12-inch Tell Me Easter's On Friday/Straw Towels – Situation 2 SIT1 1981

7-inch Q Quarters/Kissed – Situation 2 SIT4 1981

12-inch Q Quarters/Kissed/Q Quarters (Original) – Situation 2 SIT4T 1981

7-inch Kitchen Person/An Even Whiter Car – Situation 2 SIT7 1981

12-inch Kitchen Person/An Even Whiter Car – Situation 2 SIT7T 1981

7-inch A/Would I...Bounce Back – Fiction FICS13 1981

12-inch A/Would I...Bounce Back – Fiction FICSX13 1981

7-inch Message Oblique Speech/Blue Soap – Situation 2 SIT10 1981

12-inch Message Oblique Speech/Blue Soap – Situation 2 SIT10T 1981

7-inch White Car in Germany/The Associate – Situation 2 SIT11 1981

12-inch White Car in Germany/The Associate – Situation 2 SIT11T 1981

7-inch Kites/A Girl Named Property – (A-side credited to 39 Lyon

Street: Christine Beveridge lead vocal and Billy MacKenzie backing vocal. B-Side credited to the Associates) RSO RSO78 1981

12-inch Kites/A Girl Named Property – (Details as above) RSO RSOX78 1981

7-inch Party Fears Two/It's Better This Way – WEA ASC1 1982

12-inch Party Fears Two/It's Better This Way – WEA ASC1T 1982

7-inch Club Country/A.G. It's You Again – WEA ASC2 1982

12-inch Club Country/A.G. It's You Again/Ulcragyceptemol – WEA ASC2T 1982

7-inch 18 Carat Love Affair/Love Hangover – WEA ASC3 1982

12-inch 18 Carat Love Affair/Voluntary Wishes, Swapit Productions/ Love Hangover – WEA ASC3T 1982

7-inch A Matter Of Gender/Even Dogs In The Wild (Instrumental) – Fiction FICS16 1982

12-inch A Matter Of Gender/Would I...Bounce Back – Fiction FICSX16 1982

7-inch Those First Impressions/Thirteen Feelings – WEA YZ6 1984

12-inch Those First Impressions (Extended)/Thirteen Feelings – WEA YZ6T 1984

7-inch Waiting For The Loveboat/Schampout – WEA YZ16 1984

12-inch Waiting For The Loveboat (Extended)/Schampout (Extended) – WEA YZ16T 1984

12-inch Waiting For The Loveboat (Extended)/Waiting For The Loveboat (John Peel Session Version)/Schampout (Extended) – WEA YZ16T 1984

7-inch Breakfast/Breakfast Alone – WEA YZ28 1985

7-inch Breakfast/Breakfast Alone (picture disc) – WEA YZ28P 1985

12-inch Breakfast/Breakfast Alone/Kites (Re-recording with Billy on lead vocal: different from 39 Lyon Street recording) – WEA YZ28T 1985

7-inch Take Me To The Girl/Perhaps – WEA YZ47 1985

10-inch Take Me To The Girl/Perhaps/God Bless The Child/Dogs In The Wild/The Boy That Santa Claus Forgot (Last three tracks live at Ronnie Scott's) – WEA YZ47TE 1985

12-inch Take Me To The Girl (12-inch Mix)/The Girl That Took Me/ Perhaps/Take Me To The Girl (Instrumental) – WEA YZ47T 1985

7-inch Heart of Glass/Her Only Wish – WEA YZ310 1988

12-inch Heart Of Glass (Auchterhouse Mix)/Heart of Glass (Auchterhouse Instrumental)/Her Only Wish – WEA YZ310T 1988

12-inch Heart of Glass (The Temperament Mix)/Heart Of Glass/Her Only Wish/Heaven's Blue (3D sleeve with 3D glasses) – WEA YZ310TX 1988

CD Heart Of Glass/Her Only Wish/Breakfast/Those First Impressions – WEA YZ310CD 1988

7-inch Country Boy/Just Can't Say Goodbye (Unissued) – WEA YZ329 1988

12-inch Country Boy/Heart Of Glass (Dub Mix)/Just Can't Say Goodbye (12-inch Mix) (Unissued) – WEA YZ329T 1988

CD Country Boy/Just Can't Say Goodbye (12-inch Mix)/Take Me To The Girl/Heart Of Glass (Dub Mix) (Unissued) – WEA YZ329CD 1988

The Peel Sessions – Strange Fruit SFPS 075 1989

12-inch It's Better This Way/Nude Spoons/Me, Myself And The Tragic Story/A Matter of Gender/Ulcragyceptemol (Also released on CD – SFPSCD 075 and MC – SFPSC 075)

7-inch Fever (Single Version)/Fever in the Shadows (Edit) – Circa YR46 1990

MC Fever (Single Version)/Fever in the Shadows (Edit) – Circa YRC46 1990

12-inch Fever in the Shadows/Fever in the Shadows – Circa YRTPR46 1990

12-inch Fever/Groovin' With Mr. Bloe/Fever in the Shadows – Circa YRT46 1990

12-inch Fever (Album Version)/Green Tambourine/Groovin' With Mr. Bloe – Circa YRTB46 1990

CD Fever (Single Version)/Groovin' With Mr. Bloe/Fever in the Shadows – Circa YRCDT46 1990

7-inch Fire to Ice/Green Tambourine – Circa YR49 1990

MC Fire to Ice/Green Tambourine – Circa YRC49 1990

10-inch Fire to Ice/The Glamour Chase/Green Tambourine/Groovin' With Mr. Bloe – Circa YRX49

12-inch Fire to Ice (Extended)/Green Tambourine/The Glamour Chase – Circa YRT49 1990

CD Fire to Ice (Radio Version)/Green Tambourine/The Glamour Chase/Fire To Ice (Extended) – Circa YRCD49 1990

7-inch *Poperetta* EP: Waiting For the Loveboat/Club Country – WEA YZ534 1990

MC *Poperetta* EP: Waiting For the Loveboat/Club Country – WEA YZ534C 1990

12-inch *Poperetta* EP: Waiting For The Loveboat (Extended Voyage)/
Club Country Club/Club Country Club (Time Unlimited)/Waiting
for the Loveboat (Slight Return) –
WEA YZ534T 1990
CD *Poperetta* EP: Waiting for the Loveboat (Slight Return)/Club
Country Club/Waiting for the Loveboat (Extended Voyage)/Club
Country Club (Time Unlimited) –
WEA YZ534CD 1990
7-inch Just Can't Say Goodbye/One Two Three – Circa YR56 1991
MC Just Can't Say Goodbye/One Two Three – Circa YRC56 1991
12-inch Just Can't Say Goodbye (Time Unlimited Mix)/Just Can't Say
Goodbye (US Version)/Just Can't Say Goodbye (Time Unlimited
Piano Mix) – Circa YRT56 1991
12-inch Just Can't Say Goodbye (Karma Mix)/Just Can't Say Goodbye
(Time Unlimited Instrumental Mix) – (Dye-cut cover, no p/s) –
Circa YRTX56 1991
CD Just Can't Say Goodbye (7-inch Version)/Just Can't Say Goodbye
(Time Unlimited Mix)/Just Can't Say Goodbye (US Version)/I'm
Gonna Run Away From You – Circa
YRCD56 1991

ASSOCIATES ALBUMS

(All with inner sleeves and all released on MC, but not on CD, unless
otherwise stated.)
The Affectionate Punch – Fiction 2382585 1980
The Affectionate Punch/Amused As Always/Logan Time/Paper
House/Transport To Central/A Matter of Gender/Even Dogs In
The Wild/Would I...Bounce Back/Deeply Concerned/A
Fourth Drawer Down – Situation 2 SITU2 1981
White Car In Germany/A Girl Named Property/Kitchen Person/Q
Quarters/Tell Me Easter's On Friday/The Associate/Message
Oblique Speech/An Even Whiter Car – (Gatefold sleeve no inner
sleeve, produced in Germany, imported as UK release)
Also released as:
Fourth Drawer Down – Situation 2 BEGK 58373 (SITU2) 1981 – (No
gatefold sleeve)
Fourth Drawer Down – Beggars Banquet BEGA43 1982 – (Gatefold
sleeve, no inner sleeve, includes poster)

Fourth Drawer Down – WEA BEGK 58373/UK: WX21 (SITU2) 1982
  (No gatefold sleeve, no inner sleeve, budget issue)
Sulk – WEA ASCL1 1982
Arrogance Gave Him Up/No/Bap De La Bap/Gloomy Sunday/Nude
  Spoons/Skipping/It's Better This Way/Party Fears Two/Club
  Country/nothinginsomethingparticular
(This UK version had a limited CD release in 1988.)
Also released as:
Sulk – WEA 240005-1 UK: WX24 1982
It's Better This Way/Party Fears Two/Club Country/Love Hangover/
  18 Carat Love Affair/Arrogance Gave Him Up/No/Skipping/White
  Car In Germany/Gloomy Sunday/The Associate (Budget issue with
  same track listing as US release. This version was also released on
  CD as 240005-2.)
Sulk – WEA 240005-4 UK: WX24C 1982 (MC issue combining both
  the above versions as a double play cassette)
The Affectionate Punch – Fiction FIXD5 1982
Amused as Always/The Affectionate Punch/A Matter of Gender/
  Would I...Bounce Back/A/Logan Time/Paper House/Deeply
  Concerned/Even Dogs In The Wild/Transport To Central (This
  remixed version was issued with a new sleeve.)
Also released as:
The Affectionate Punch LP/MC – Fiction SPELP33 1983
The Affectionate Punch CD – Fiction FIXCD5 537211-2 1997
Perhaps – WEA WX9 1985
Those First Impressions/Waiting For The Loveboat/Perhaps/
  Schampout/Helicopter Helicopter/Breakfast/Thirteen Feelings/
  The Stranger In Your Voice/The Best of You/Don't Give Me That
  I Told You So Look
Also released as:
Perhaps – WEA WX9C 1985
Those First Impressions/Waiting For The Loveboat/Perhaps/
  Schampout/Helicopter Helicopter/Perhaps (Instrumental)/
  Breakfast/Thirteen Feelings/The Stranger In Your Voice/The Best
  Of You/Don't Give Me That I Told You So Look/Breakfast Alone
  (Instrumental)/Thirteen Feelings (Instrumental)/The Stranger in
  Your Voice (Instrumental) (MC issue with instrumentals)
The Glamour Chase – WEA (Unissued) 244619 1988
Reach The Top/Heart Of Glass/Terrorbeat/Set Me Up/Country

Boy/Because You Love/Snowball/You'll Be The One/Empires Of
Your Heart/In Windows All/Heaven's Blue/Because You Love*/
The Rhythm Divine*/Take Me To The Girl* (*Extra tracks
intended for MC/CD release. Limited quantities of review tapes,
white labels and CDRs were distributed for review purposes only.)
Wild And Lonely – Circa CIRC11 1990
Fire To Ice/Fever/People We Meet/Just Can't Say Goodbye/Calling
All Around The World/The Glamour Chase*/Where There's
Love/Something's Got To Give/Strasbourg Square/Ever Since That
Day/Wild And Lonely/Fever In The Shadows* (*Extra tracks on
CD release (CIRCCD11))
Wild And Lonely – Circa BILLY1 1990
Fire To Ice/Fever/Ever Since That Day/Wild And Lonely (Four-track
album sampler released on 12-inch/CD/MC. 12-inch has different
sleeve from album.)
Popera – WEA East West 9031-72414-1 UK: WX363 1990
Party Fears Two/Club Country/18 Carat Love Affair/Love Hangover/
Those First Impressions/Waiting For The Loveboat/Breakfast/Take
Me To The Girl/Heart Of Glass/Country Boy/The Rhythm
Divine*/Waiting for the Loveboat (Slight Return)*/Tell Me
Easter's On Friday*/Q Quarters*/Kitchen Person*/Message
Oblique Speech*/
White Car In Germany* (*Extra tracks on CD/MC release (East West
9031-72414-2))
The Radio 1 Sessions – Nighttracks CDNT 006 1994
Me Myself And The Tragic Story/It's Better this Way/A Severe Bout
Of Career Insecurity/Love Hangover/Waiting For The Loveboat/
Theme From Perhaps/Don't Give Me That I Told You So Look/
God Bless The Child/Breakfast/This Flame/Kites/A Matter Of
Gender/The Affectionate Punch/Obsession Magnificent/Give/The
Girl That Took Me (CD release only)

ASSOCIATES MISCELLANEOUS

MC *Irrationale*. Includes: Even Dogs In The Wild (Alternative Version)
– Rationale RATE8 1979
MC *Pleasantly Surprised* – An Hour Of Eloquent Sounds. Includes:
Helicopter Helicopter (By Billy MacKenzie Sings Orbidöig) – P.
Surprised KLARK002 1981

7-inch Even Dogs In The Wild – flexidisc with Flexipop magazine
issue 20 – LYNTONE LYN11649 1982

7-inch Even Dogs In The Wild – unissued hard vinyl test pressing –
LYNTONE LYN11649 1982

7-inch Tell Me Easters on Friday/Straw Towels – unissued white label
– Beggars Banquet BEG86 1982

MC *NME* compilation: *Mad Mix II.* Includes: Aggressive And Ninety
Pounds – NME 008 1984

7-inch *Sounds* compilation: *Christmas Cracker.* Includes: Breakfast (live)
– CRACKER1 1985

10-inch *Debut* magazine compilation. Includes: Champout – LPMAG10
1985

MC *Record Mirror* compilation: *Spools Gold.* Includes: The Best Of You
– SPOOLS GOLD 1986

CD Strange Fruit *21 Years Of Alternative Radio 1.* Includes: It's Better
This Way – SFRCD200 1988

CD *Stranger Than Fiction.* Includes: Janice – CIFCD 301 1989

CD *Winters Of Discontent – The Peel Sessions.* Includes: A Matter Of
Gender – SFRCD20 1991

CD/MC *Cool Christmas.* Includes: The Little Boy That Santa Claus
Forgot (Live) – WEA 95483224852 1993

BILLY MACKENZIE SOLO SINGLES

(All picture sleeves unless otherwise stated)

7-inch Ice Cream Factory/Excursion Ecosse En Route Koblenz Via
Hawk Hill – WEA MAK1 1982

12-inch Ice Cream Factory/Cream Of Ice Cream Factory – WEA
MAK1T 1982

(Credited to: MacKenzie Sings Orbidöig)

7-inch Baby/Sacrifice And Be Sacrificed (CH8032 Mix Edit) – Circa
YR86 1992

12-inch Baby/Colours Will Come (Larry Heard Remix)/Opal Krusch/
Colours Will Come (Raw Stylus Remix) – Circa YRT86 1992

CD Baby/Sacrifice And Be Sacrificed (CH8032 Mix)/Grooveature (D1000
Mix)/Colours Will Come (US60659 Mix) – Circa YRCD86 1992

7-inch Colours Will Come/Opal Krusch – Circa YR91 1992

12-inch Colours Will Come/Opal Krusch/Look What You've Done/
Feels Like The Richtergroove – Circa YRT91 1992

CD Colours Will Come/Opal Krusch/Look What You've Done/Feels
Like The Richtergroove – Circa YRCD91 1992
CD Pastime Paradise/Outernational II/Ever Since That Day (US
Mix)/Because You Love (unreleased promo-only CD) – Circa
YRCDJ102 1992

BILLY MACKENZIE SOLO ALBUMS

Outernational – Circa CIRCD 22 1992
Outernational/Feels Like The Richtergroove/Opal Krusch/Colours
Will Come/Pastime Paradise/Grooveature/Sacrifice And Be
Sacrificed/Baby/What Made Me Turn On The Lights/In Windows
All (Also released on MC)
Beyond The Sun – Nude NUDE8CD 1997
Give Me Time/Winter Academy/Blue It Is/14 Mirrors/At The Edge
Of The World/Beyond The Sun/And This She Knows/Sour Jewel/
3 Gypsies In A Restaurant/Nocturne VII (CD only release)

ALAN RANKINE SOLO SINGLES

(All picture sleeves unless otherwise stated)
7-inch The Sandman/Rumours of War – Crépuscule 7TWI598 1986
12-inch The Sandman/Rumours of War/Rue Traversière/Sunny Lee
– Crépuscule TWI598 1986
7-inch Last Bullet/Your Very Last Day – Crépuscule 7TWI762 1986
7-inch The World Begins To Look Her Age/Can You Believe
Everything I See (Part 2) – Virgin VS971 1987
12-inch The World Begins To Look Her Age/Can You Believe
Everything I See (Parts 1 and 2)/The World Begins To Look Her
Age (7-inch version) – Virgin VS971-12 1987
7-inch The Sandman (Remix)/Can You Believe Everything I See (Part
3) – Virgin VS1003 1987
12-inch The Sandman (Remix)/Can You Believe Everything I See
(Part 3)/The Sandman (7-inch version) – Virgin VS1003-12 1987

ALAN RANKINE SOLO ALBUMS

The World Begins To Look Her Age – Crépuscule TWI672 1986
Elephants Walk In Morning Glory/Mission For The Don/Your Very

Last Day/The Best In Me/The World Begins To Look Her Age/
The Sandman/Last Bullet/Love And Adversity (LP)
She Loves Me Not – Virgin V2450 1987
Beat Fit/Days And Days/Loaded/Last Bullet/Your Very Last Day/The
Sandman/Lose Control/Break For Me/The World Begins To Look
Her Age (LP/CD)
The Big Picture Sucks – Crépuscule TWI8692 1989
Shambok/Pop Off/Once In A Blue One/Glory To The Take And
The Killing/Happens Every Minute/Lies (CD)

ALAN RANKINE MISCELLANEOUS

From Brussels With Love – Crépuscule TWI007 1986
2 x LP: Various artists. Includes: Can You Believe Everything I See
Operation Twilight – Crépuscule Instrumentals – Crépuscule Interior
IM005 1988
LP: Various artists. Includes: Love And Adversity/Rumours Of War
Medley

ASSOCIATES/ BILLY MACKENZIE – ASSOCIATED

(All picture sleeves unless otherwise stated. *= Billy MacKenzie lead
vocal, **= Billy MacKenzie backing vocal.)

With BEF (British Electric Foundation)

LP BEF Presents *Music Of Quality And Distinction Volume 1* – Virgin
V2219 1982
Various artists. Includes: Secret Life of Arabia*/It's Over*
Also released as:
5 x 7-inch Box Set BEF Presents *Music Of Quality And Distinction
Volume 1* – Virgin VV2219 1982
CD BEF Presents *Music Of Quality And Distinction Volume 1* – Virgin
CDBEF1 1991
7-inch BEF Featuring Billy MacKenzie It's Over*/Secret Life of
Arabia* – VIRGIN VS498 1982
LP BEF Presents *Music Of Quality And Distinction Volume 2* – Ten
DIX108 1991
Various artists. Includes: Free*

Also released as:

CD BEF Presents *Music Of Quality And Distinction Volume 2* – Ten
   DIXCXD108 1991

7-inch BEF Featuring Billy MacKenzie – Free (Edit)*/Secret Life of
   Arabia* (Unissued) – Ten TEN386 1991

MC BEF Featuring Billy MacKenzie – Free (Edit)*/Secret Life of
   Arabia* (Unissued) – Ten TENC386 1991

12-inch BEF Featuring Billy MacKenzie – Free*/Secret
Life of Arabia* (Unissued) – Ten TENX386 1991

CD BEF Featuring Billy MacKenzie – Free*/Secret
Life of Arabia* (Unissued) – Ten CDTEN386 1991

With Yello

(Apart from the releases mentioned below, multi-format single
   releases were made of most of the songs that Billy recorded with
   Yello.)

LP *One Second* – Mercury MERH100 1987

includes: Moon On Ice*/Call it Love**/The Rhythm Divine**/
   Goldrush**

Also released as:

CD *One Second* – Mercury 830956-2 1987

LP *Flag* – Mercury 836426-1 1988

includes: Of Course I'm Lying**/Otto Di Catania**

Also released as:

CD *Flag* – Mercury 836426-2 1988

MC *Flag* – Mercury 836426-3 1988

LP *Baby* – Mercury 8487911 1991

includes: Rubberbandman**/Capri Calling*/Drive-Driven**

Also released as:

CD *Flag* – Mercury 8487912 1991

DCC *Flag* – Mercury 8487913 1991

CD *Essential Yello* – Mercury 512390 1992

Includes: Drive-Driven**/Rubberbandman**/Of Course I'm Lying**/
   Call it Love**/Goldrush**/The Rhythm Divine**

12-inch Yello Featuring Billy MacKenzie – The Rhythm Divine
   (Version Two)*/Dr Van Steiner (Instrumental)/The Rhythm
   Divine (Original 7-inch Version)** – Mercury

MERX253 1987

Other Guest Appearances

Skids

7-inch Fields**/Brave Man – Virgin VS401 1981
12-inch Fields**/Brave Man – Virgin VS401-12 1981
LP *Joy*. Includes: Fields** – Virgin V2217 1981
CD *Dunfermline*. Includes: Fields** – Virgin COMCD10 1987

Orbidöig

7-inch Nocturnal Operations/Down Pericomoscopes (Features Billy on
   tubular bells) – Situation 2 SIT15 1981

Stephen Emmer

LP *Vogue Estate* (Features Billy MacKenzie and Martha Ladly) –
   Includes: Wish On* – German WEA Idiot 28407 1982

The Sensational Creed

7-inch Nocturnal Operations/Down Pericomoscopes (Reissue of
   Orbidöig single) – Beggars Banquet BEG125 1984
12-inch Nocturnal Operations/Down Pericomoscopes/Voyage Of The
   Titanic (Reissue of Orbidöig single) – Beggars Banquet BEG125T
   1984

Holger Hiller

LP *Oben Im Eck* – Includes: We Don't Write Anything On Paper Or
   So*/Whippets*/Oben Im Eck*/Oben Im Eck (Version)* – Mute
   STUMM38CD 1986
12-inch Whippets*/Waltz – Mute MUTE55 1987

Uno

12-inch Cinemas Of The World Extended Version*/7-inch Version*/
   Moodswing – Barclay 885734 1987
LP *Uno* – Includes: Cinemas Of The World* – Barclay 831938 (CD)
   1987

Jih

12-inch Take Me To The Girl**/Come Summer Come Winter**/
   Wake Up** – Jungle JUNG32T 1988

Loom

CD Anacostia Bay (At The Edge Of The World) Original Version*/
Berlioz Mix*/Radio Edit*/Instrumental Version – Millenium MILL
022CD 1996

12-inch Anacostia Bay (At The Edge Of The World) Original
Version*/Berlioz Mix – Millennium MILL 022T 1996

Barry Adamson

CD *Oedipus Schmoedipus. Includes: Achieved In The Valley Of Dolls** – *Mute
STUMM 134 1996*

Apollo Four Forty

CD *Electro Glide In Blue.* Includes: Pain In Any Language* – Sony
SSX2440 1997

Paul Haig

7-inch Listen To Me**/Looking/Irresponsible – Syntactic NICE49
1997

(Listen To Me is dedicated to the memory of Billy MacKenzie 1957–
1997.)

A NOTE ON THE AUTHOR

Tom Doyle has written for *Q*, *Mojo*, *Elle* and *Melody Maker*. He
was born in Dundee and lives in London.